DIVIDING THE STATE

What could fill the absence of the desaparecidos*? The only answer I could find was justice.*

Dividing the State

Legitimacy, Secession and the Doctrine of Oppression

PAUL GROARKE
St. Thomas University

Routledge
Taylor & Francis Group
LONDON AND NEW YORK

First published 2004 by Ashgate Publishing

Reissued 2018 by Routledge
2 Park Square, Milton Park, Abingdon, Oxon, OX14 4RN
711 Third Avenue, New York, NY 10017, USA

Routledge is an imprint of the Taylor & Francis Group, an informa business

Typeset in Times Roman by N^{2}productions

A Library of Congress record exists under LC control number: 2004046265

ISBN 13: 978-0-815-38861-6 (hbk)
ISBN 13: 978-1-351-15972-2 (ebk)

Contents

Acknowledgements

The following book began with a question about revolution, which is usually described in law as a legal discontinuity. Is it possible, I wondered, to bring revolution within the rule of law? And what would that mean? The question changed over the course of my research, and many people contributed to the book over the years. It was Margaret Moore who introduced me to the concept of legitimacy. I still remember the conversation that turned my attention to the role of such a concept in any legal theory of secession. Joseph Novak lent me a copy of Otto Gierke's treatise. Jason West mentioned Vitoria. I cannot remember who introduced me to Max Weber. My brothers also provided many practical suggestions.

There were other contributions. The Social Sciences and Humanities Research Council of Canada and the Atlantic Human Rights Centre at St Thomas University provided me with fellowships during the course of the research that led to the present book. I think the largest contribution, however, came from my colleagues and students at St Thomas, who forced me to explain my views.

Series Preface

The principal objective of this series is to encourage the publication of books which adopt a theoretical approach to the study of particular areas or aspects of law, or deal with general theories of law in a way which is directed at issues of practical, moral and political concern in specific legal contexts. The general approach is both analytical and critical and relates to the socio-political background of law reform issues.

The series includes studies of all the main areas of law, presented in a manner which relates to the concerns of specialist legal academics and practitioners. Each book makes an original contribution to an area of legal study while being comprehensible to those engaged in a wide variety of disciplines. Their legal content is principally Anglo-American, but a wide-ranging comparative approach is encouraged and authors are drawn from a variety of jurisdictions.

Tom D. Campbell
Series Editor
Centre for Applied Philosophy and Public Ethics,
Charles Sturt University, Canberra

Introduction

Many ethnic and linguistic minorities have claimed the right to secede. This requires some means of transferring the sovereign power. The claim may be for independence, but independence is not possible without dissolving the existing compact and divesting the state of its authority to govern. This has prompted enormous resistence and has led to intolerance, war and brutality on all sides.

There have been movements calling for secession in Quebec, in Greenland and the Faroe Islands, in Corsica and Savoy, in the Basque region of Spain, in the former Yugoslavia and in Kosovo. There was, in the words of one commentator, 'an outburst of self-determination' as the Soviet Union collapsed.[1] The established order of states has been challenged again and again. There are 'splittists' in Tibet and independence movements across the subcontinent, in Sri Lanka, Kashmir and lesser known areas like Assam and the territory of the Hmong.

These are only a few of the contemporary conflicts. There have also been violent clashes in Aceh, Moluku and across the Indonesian archipelago, inside Turkey, Iraq and throughout the area claimed as Kurdistan. There are struggles in the north of Africa, the Western Sahara and further south, in Angola and Namibia. Although it has been relatively immune from such contests, even the USA has independence movements in Hawaii and Puerto Rico. Everywhere it seems, the integrity of the state has been questioned.

Minorities claiming the right to secede have suffered injustices ranging all the way from discrimination in the provision of public services and schooling, to genocide and forced migrations. Governments that resist secession have been responsible for all manner of human rights abuses. Their opponents commonly resort to terrorism. Although I have left it for others to document the social and political aspects of secession, it is apparent that we need a way of resolving such conflicts without the suffering, dislocation and economic adversity that comes with them.

There are three ways of dealing with secession: one is by politics, another is by violence and another is by law. The dynamics of secession run against the possibility of a political solution, however, since it usually serves the interests of political actors on both sides to foster such divisions. The product of politics is often violence, which is not a viable solution. This book deals with the third alternative: the law.

The book has two goals. The first is to set out a theory that brings secession firmly within the rule of law. The second is to develop a conceptual framework for a legal resolution of the claim that a minority has a right to secede. The purpose of the book is theoretical and occupies itself with questions of philosophy and legal theory. It does not provide case studies or study the practical mechanics of the devolution of power. That is a task that is better left to political science or the study of the existing international law.[2]

This comes with an important reservation. The present endeavour is pragmatic in the philosophical sense and adopts an instrumental view of theory. This is seminal. I believe that the major role of philosophy in the area is to provide a theoretical framework that can be applied to the circumstances that arise in the world. This allows us to formulate the intellectual machinery that is needed to resolve contested claims. As a result, the legal theory of secession that I have set out is subject to a higher standard of utility than most academic and philosophical work.

The theoretical question that arises in developing a legal theory of secession is whether the state's title to the right to govern is legally defeasible. History says no. Whether a minority has a right to secede is decided by political forces that are not amenable to regulation by the courts. The courts have refused to rule on such an issue and the common law still holds that a unilateral act of secession, like an act of revolution, creates an interregnum in which there is no legal order. There is a narrow sense in which the 'legality' of secession might be determined by the provisions of a domestic constitution or the conventions regarding the international recognition of independent states. This is an impoverished notion of legality, however, which only recognizes political events like revolution and secession as *fait accompli*, after they have occurred.

The traditional view is accordingly that secession is a political event that takes place entirely outside the law. It is essentially a form of revolution, which creates a hiatus in the continuity of the legal order. The idea is that a revolution overthrows the sovereign. This ruptures the continuity of the legal order, which has its source in the sovereign power, and extinguishes the authority in which it vests. The result is anarchy, since this at least theoretically removes the legal and conceptual basis of legal claims, rights and obligations. There are additional difficulties in explaining how the legal order is reconstituted and what parts of the existing law have survived.

The reality is that much of the ordinary legal order continues. But the conceptual issue still presents a problem. The solution is to recognize that there is a supervening legal standard, which determines the legality of the actions taken in the interval between the dissolution of the original state and the inception of a resulting state.[3] This would maintain the integrity of the legal order, in spite of the transfer of the sovereign power from one political authority to another. It would also allow a court to formulate the criteria needed to determine the legality of any actions undertaken by a seceding government.

The difficulty is that the historical authority of the law derives from its genealogy, which can be traced to the sovereign power. As a result, it is impossible for a court to rule on the ownership of the sovereign power without ruling on the validity of the legal order from which it derives its authority. This is logically incoherent. There is another view, however. It is that the authority of the legal order derives from a body of moral principle, which gives a court the authority to regulate but not intervene in political decisions. There is nothing on this view to prevent the law from extending beyond the ordinary sphere of the domestic law, into the extra-constitutional realm in which the state and the sovereign power exist.

The effects of the historical view are evident in the intensity of the conflicts regarding secession. States frequently resist the campaign for independence with violence and impunity. There may be sociological reasons for this, but the legal reality is that the domestic law is within the keeping of the state and does not provide a meaningful check on its actions. The responses on the other side are equally drastic. Those who seek secession are engaged in a 'political' struggle that places them above the law. The striking feature of secession is accordingly that it justifies unilateral action on both sides, without regard to moral or legal principles that ensure the larger good.

It follows that the question of secession is in dire need of moral regulation. The problem is that the political forces that come to the fore in the context of the question lend themselves to abuses. They are not self-regulating. The necessary moral regulation is not available in the political process. It accordingly requires some form of legal intervention, which can only be supplied by a court. This is not possible, however, without a binding law of states. Any other view fails to recognize the stubbornness with which states resist secession.

The practical reality is that any law designed to regulate an issue as contentious as secession can only do so if it is compulsory. The first step in establishing such a system is simply to recognize that there is a binding extra-constitutional law, which applies within the state. This is in keeping with the practice of domestic courts, which operate on the assumption that we are required to obey the law. The means of enforcing such a law requires its own discussion, after the first and essential premise has been established. It would be naive, however, to think that such a system can operate without some means of coercion.

The primary obstacle to the development of the legal right to secede lies in the historical doctrine of sovereignty, which gives the state a free hand in its internal affairs. The only way of dealing with such a formidable obstacle is to remove it, with a simple rebuttal. The idea that states are legally sovereign in some unconditional sense is conceptually wrong. Sovereignty has legal limits. The historical idea of the state as an authority unto itself is simply fallacious, a product of the success of the state and a good measure of political expedience. The sovereign power and the principle of territorial integrity are subject to legal constraints, and a state that fails to respect these constraints is illegitimate in law.

The central issue is simple enough. Under the Westphalian system, a state is entitled to pursue its internal affairs without interference from other states. This is complimented by the positivist view that the law has its source in the state. This 'municipal law', to use the quaint phraseology of the international law, does not extend into the international arena. The so-called international law does not apply in the internal sphere and merely governs the external relations between states. Most of this law has its source in treaties and other forms of agreements, and cannot be considered law in the strict sense.

The founders of the international law recognized that such a system of law fails to capture the nature of many of the state's obligations. There is, accordingly, another side to the international law, which can be found in the customary international law and the *jus cogens* (literally, 'compulsory law'), which is included in the *Vienna Convention on the Law of Treaties*. It is essentially assumed that states have accepted these parts of the law, which are theoretically binding.

Under the *jus cogens*, it is usually said that a treaty that conflicts with a 'peremptory norm' of general international law is void. The word 'norm' is revealing however, since normative injunctions set expectations rather than rules. They reflect common standards of behaviour and cannot be described as 'compulsory' in the ordinary sense of the word. The idea is still that these standards derive from the implicit agreement of states, rather than moral principle. They do not contemplate the imposition of an external standard of conduct, which derives its authority from a moral source outside the conventions of states.

The reality is that these are political norms, which do not possess the force of law. The plain truth is that states regularly flout these norms. Powerful states are relatively immune from the minimal sanctions that are available in the international context. The frequent assertion that states are not permitted to derogate from a norm of the *jus cogens* only demonstrates the emptiness of these words. The rights of individuals and minorities within the state cannot be guaranteed in the Westphalian system. It is impossible to regulate the internal affairs of the state with an external law based on the acquiescence of states that remain sovereign in their internal affairs.

This expresses the theoretical problem. The situation is more complex in practice, since the international law has begun to encroach on the domestic sphere. It is now recognized that the *jus cogens* contains obligations *erga omnes*, towards all, which extend beyond the borders of the state.[4] The idea is that certain violations of the norms of international law are so significant that they harm the international community as a whole. As a result, states are legally obliged to redress them. These obligations extend as far as racial discrimination, a vague right to development and a safe environment.

The concept of obligations *erga omnes* is momentous because it recognizes that these moral obligations are paramount. They accordingly take priority over the doctrine of sovereignty. The concept also recognizes that states have legal obligations towards individuals in other states. This includes an obligation to protect the fundamental rights of the person. This is in keeping with the domestic law, at least in the West, where the concept of human rights already provide a constitutional check on the powers of government.

The most significant development in the international law is the development of a fundamental law. This is a body of supervening law. It is logically prior to the provisions of the domestic law and constitutional enactments however and takes precedence over them. As the term suggests, it contains the most elemental aspects of the law, which provide the foundation of any system or body of law. This provides an extra-constitutional source of binding legal principle.

The significant observation in the present context is that the rights of the person have a place in this fundamental law. It is generally recognized that the provisions in human rights instruments are universal in scope and inherently compulsory. The binding nature of these rights derives from their moral and legal force, rather than the imagined views of states. It is humanity at large that provides the affirmative source of such guarantees.

This reflects a change in the conceptual framework of the international law, which can be seen in the evolution of the political standards for the recognition of independent states. These are all incremental developments, however, which do not address the essential theoretical problem. That problem has its origins in the historical doctrine of sovereignty, which traces the origins of the legal order to the state. The corollary is that the state and the sovereign power exist outside such an order, in some inchoate area where exclusively political decisions are made.

The broader argument of the book is that this is a theoretical error. The notion of legality extends into the lawless region where political events like secession are said to occur. This is where power is exercised most freely. The purpose of extending the law into such an area is to place moral constraints on the exercise of political power. This does not mean that morality and law coincide in such a context: in point of fact the book adopts a limited notion of legality, which leaves political and policy decisions firmly within the hands of political actors.

It is impossible to deal satisfactorily with the issues that arise in the context of secession without reconsidering the relationship between legal and political authority. There is nevertheless a sense in which secession is a political event, and exclusively so. The courts can only exercise a supervisory role in the matter. This would give them the authority to determine when the decision to secede has been fairly and properly made, when it is morally permissible, and when it can be enforced. The actual decision to secede remains entirely within the political realm.

There is therefore a political right to secede, which may arise independently of any legal right. A court with jurisdiction over secession would nevertheless have the authority to rule on the legal disputes that arise in the course of any attempt to exercise such a right. These disputes range from the legality of voting procedures to the validity of the question used in a plebiscite, to the many questions that would arise in determining the terms of departure. There will be a point moreover where a state's refusal to accept the results of the democratic process throws its legitimacy into doubt and gives rise to a legal right to secede.

The details of the legal right to secede have not been canvassed in the literature. It has nonetheless been suggested that such a right might be implemented by constitutional amendments, the use of Security Council resolutions, the appointment of *ad hoc* international tribunals or the use of a formal process before a permanent legal body like the International Court of Justice. The latter solution offers the only cogent legal solution. It cannot be implemented, however, without fundamental changes in the system of international law and a binding law of states.

This inevitably calls for the development of a global system of law, based on a domestic model of compulsory law. This would place some legal restrictions on the exercise of the authority of the state, albeit in a manner that preserves the ordinary powers of government. Under such a system, an oppressed minority would have the right to apply to an international tribunal for an order recognizing its right to secede. This would give rise to subsidiary forms of relief. It is important to appreciate that a legitimate state would have a legal right to continue under such a law.

Allen Buchanan has already argued that the privileges and prerogatives of sovereignty should not be accorded to illegitimate states, which contravene fundamental human rights. This is a normative argument, however, which does not address the need for a binding legal regime in the international arena. This book accordingly goes further and postulates a compulsory body of extra-constitutional law that governs any actions taken in the political realm. This is not convention. The book takes the position that states are obliged to respect the fundamental rights of persons within the state. There is no room for choice in such a requirement.

The general literature already recognizes the need to place legal and ethical constraints on the doctrine of state sovereignty. The matter has been discussed in the General Assembly of the United Nations.[5] There are many developments, like the evolution of a European law and the inauguration of an International Criminal Tribunal, which have made the idea of a legal system emanating from an authority above the state more realistic than it was in the past. The use of electronic forms of communication, the impact of international economic agreements and a global media have all contributed to a common sense of human community. This naturally extends our emotional, ethical and legal obligations beyond the borders of the state.

The Legal and Political Processes

The first part of the book introduces a notion of legitimacy, which holds that states and other international actors are subject to extra-constitutional legal restraints. A state that fails to respect these restraints is illegitimate and loses the legal right to govern. The book then sets out a standard of legitimacy that can be used to identify the kinds of situations in which a minority might be legally entitled to secede from a larger state. The second part of the book sets out a legal theory, which sketches the outlines of a cause of action and introduces the possibility of lawful and unlawful acts of secession.

The extra-constitutional notion of legality goes against the formulations of legal positivism and the common law, which locates the source of the law in the political power of a sovereign state. The legal order owes its existence entirely to the metaphysical state, in which civil authority originates, and cannot exist outside it. From a historical perspective, this kind of conception has been offset by the development of independent courts, which regularly overturn the actions of the legislative and executive branches of government. This does not deal with the philosophical problem, however, and these courts theoretically enjoy a domestic jurisdiction, which derives from the authority of the state.

The other side of the historical formulation holds that secession is a domestic matter, which occurs entirely within an existing state. This might seem to be changing, with events in Kosovo and elsewhere, but the use of Security Council resolutions to police internal conflicts is a political rather than a legal development. The idea that states are sovereign has not been affected by such events. Although states have accepted that they have obligations to the individuals living in other states, they have not accepted that international courts and tribunals have the authority to regulate such matters.[6]

The theory of secession developed in the following book relies on the fundamental distinction between the legal and the political process. The legal process is designed to deal with situations in which disagreement is paramount. This explains the formality of a trial and the concern with a fair process. The legal process is presided over by a neutral party, who exercises an independent moral authority in deciding cases. This is significantly different from a process of arbitration or mediation, which proceeds on the agreement of the parties.

The book subscribes to the view that the political order is based upon some measure of consent. This is not restricted to democratic states, though the argument may be more compelling in that instance. The political process is governed by social forces and resolves the issues of state through some process of agreement. This is problematic where there is an ongoing history of conflict, mistrust or enmity between the parties, since the level of goodwill needed to reach a satisfactory agreement will often be unavailable. The legal process is governed by principle and derives its legitimacy from its moral pedigree.

The existing literature already distinguishes between those situations that call for a legal and a political resolution of a minority's claim that it has the right to secede. The first exists when a minority has been oppressed, in a manner that raises serious concerns with respect to human rights. The second exists when a minority seeks to exercise a political right to self-determination.[7]

It is the former situations that call for legal resolution, and only in those cases where the parties are unable to reach agreement on the question. As long as there is a reasonable prospect of settlement, there is no reason to take the matter out of the political arena.

The application for a legal right to secede generally rests on the claim that the jurisdiction of the original state over a particular minority and territory has been morally compromised.[8] The legal question is whether the state's treatment of the minority is oppressive. The technical issue is discontinuity. The enjoyment of status, rights and obligations all extend over time. Since secession creates a new legal and constitutional order, the conceptual trick is to move from one order into the next, with the equities behind these claims and obligations intact.

The simplest solution is to postulate an extra-constitutional legal order that provides the source of both constitutional orders. This would also provide the obvious source of authority for a court facing a question like secession. The present book accordingly postulates a fundamental extra-constitutional law, above the domestic legal and political orders, which governs the exercise of state authority. This body of law requires that the sovereign power be exercised in accordance with fundamental principles of justice. These principles include substantive guarantees of individual rights and provide a general body of rules and principles that determine the legitimacy of any legal system.

This brings in the legal concept of legitimacy, which would place limits on the institution of sovereignty and extend the full notion of legality into the sphere now reserved for convention. This would give the courts moral authority over actors in the political realm. This does not extend to policy matters. The judiciary has no authority to decide political issues, which are beyond the capacity of the courts. This is fundamental. It is the separation of the two processes that puts the courts in a position to decide whether political actors have exceeded their moral authority.

This theory is not sufficient in itself and must be supplemented with some account of the legal scope of the state's authority. If the legal right to secede arises when a state acts illegitimately, outside the moral norms that govern the conduct of states, we need some positive account of the obligations of the state. The actions of the state are legally legitimate when they meet the requirements of justice. This is a legal rather than a political conception of justice, which determines whether the state has a legal title to the right to govern. It is a minimal standard and cannot be precisely defined. The requirements of such a conception of justice are intentionally vague and can only be established by jurisprudence in the area.

The essential framework of this theory of secession seems relatively simple. It is the moral conduct of the state that determines whether it is legally entitled to exercise the prerogatives of government. The question of political legitimacy does not exhaust the issue. The animating principle is equality. It is when the state treats a minority unfairly and contravenes its substantive rights that it acquires the legal right to secede. This distinguishes the right of secession from a general right of revolution, which arises in cases of general abuse.

The principle of equality gives rise to a general proscription against discrimination, which holds that individuals and groups with similar characteristics should be treated in a similar manner. Those actions that disregard the rights and interests of a minority will not serve the aims of justice. This means that they do not serve the interests of the majority, which has a cardinal interest in living within a just, peaceful and well-ordered community. The same principle applies globally and engages the interests of the international community and humanity as a whole.

The legal principle of equality is an integral part of the common good. The legal common good provides a methodological as well as a substantive basis for adjudicating disputes. A judge cannot decide between competing parties on a neutral basis without a common standard, which has received the endorsement of both sides. This is in keeping with the practice of constitutional courts, which operate on the basis of those broad moral principles that are generally accepted in society. The law in the extra-constitutional realm rests on the philosophical assumption that individual rights, group rights and the prerogatives of government can be reconciled in some larger good that recognizes the legitimacy of each set of interests.

The adjudicative common good includes substantive moral propositions. These propositions belong to the general body of moral and legal principles, widely accepted in human society, that provide the basis of the major legal and religious traditions. The pivotal feature of the common good in a judicial setting is that it requires the use of moral principles that are held in common by people with differing moral views. As a result, it resembles the conception of procedural justice in the contemporary ethical, political and philosophical literature.

The legal principle of legitimacy set out in the following chapters vests the legal order in overarching moral principles that take priority over the interests and even the integrity of the state. The book accordingly argues that the jurisdiction of a court to make rulings with respect to secession derives from a moral rather than a political source. This is an independent source of authority, which invests the courts with moral rather than political responsibilities. These responsibilities include the legal and moral supervision of political actors. This gives a court with jurisdiction over secession inherent powers that go beyond those that it acquires by virtue of any statutory instruments.

The rights of the person and the concept of human rights provides the most significant substantive criteria in identifying the circumstances in which the actions of a state can be characterized as oppressive. It is the breach of such rights that gives a court and the international community the warrant to suspend the Westphalian contract and intervene in the domestic affairs of other states. It is significant in the legal context that these rights are usually seen as individual rights, which together provide the foundation for the collective rights of minorities. There are evidentiary reasons why the state's treatment of individuals will always be the primary consideration in a legal forum.

The question whether a minority has a legal right to secede cannot be decided in the abstract. The issue of discrimination in particular cases may be open to dispute. The scope and substance of legal decisions is inevitably determined by the evidence that comes before a legal body. It is the effect of the state's action on a specific group, however, rather than the precise nature of the discrimination, that is essential in deciding the matter. The right to secede will only arise when the discrimination interferes substantially with the fundamental rights of a particular group. The standard is oppression.

Notes

1 Starovoitova, 'Sovereignty', Intro.
2 For a study of the legal and political dynamics of secession, see Hurst Hannum, *Autonomy, Sovereignty, and Self-Determination*, which contains a number of case studies and examines the larger question of autonomy among peoples. Hannum also provides a brief history of the rights of minorities in the international arena. He does not deal with the theoretical issues raised in the present work. There is also an extensive literature on nationalism, which comments on the question of secession but is not the subject of the present book. For an introduction to some of the authors who have contributed to the area, see Robert McKim and Jell McMahan, *The Morality of Nationalism*.
3 This would provide a rudimentary legal framework, for example, in which to evaluate the culpability of those on either side who resort to violence in the course of the events leading up to secession.
4 See Ragazzi. *The Concept of International Obligations Erga Omnes*.
5 See the 'Verbatim Records of the Plenary Meetings of the 54th Session of the General Assembly', which were held from 14 September to 19 November 1999 and can be found on the United Nations website, at http://www.un.org/ga/54/pv54e.htm, accessed 29 October 2003.
6 There is no reason for example to believe that Yugoslavia's application to the International Court of Justice for an injunction to stop the bombing campaign by the NATO forces was a significant factor in the events that took place in Kosovo. The case merely attests to the ineffectiveness of the international legal system. See *Legality of Use of Force (Yugoslavia* v. *Belgium et al.)*.
7 These situations may naturally coalesce.
8 One can imagine more contractual cases, where a state fails to relinquish its authority pursuant to a political agreement. This raises a different kind of issue.

Chapter 1

Legitimacy

This chapter reviews the etymology of the word 'legitimacy' and discusses the political principle of legitimacy, which is predominant in the literature. This principle holds that the legitimacy of the state derives from the consent of the governed, which can usually be found in the agreement of the majority of individuals within the state.

It is worth noting at the outset that the literature speaks of 'illegitimate' rather than 'illegal' states.The explanation seems to be that states are political rather than legal entities. Although they have a legal personality, they derive their existence from other sources. The historical example is instructive here: a bastard son may have been illegitimate; he nonetheless existed. There was nothing illegal or unlawful in such a fact.

The word 'illegal' seems to be reserved for facts and circumstances that are not recognized in law. A corporation formed for a prohibited purpose might be called an 'illegal corporation', but this is because corporations are legal entities. As a result, there is a sense in which prohibited corporations do not actually exist. The same cannot be said of illegitimate states. Although a court might strip an illegitimate state of its legal prerogatives, it continues to exist, whatever its legal status.[1]

Allen Buchanan has written that it is possible to speak of illegitimate governments or illegitimate states. The question of secession nevertheless presents itself in the context of states.

> The international legal system recognizes states, not governments, as having certain powers, immunities, liberties, and rights. Governments are recognized only so far as they are regarded as the agents of legitimate states, not as entities possessing these juridical characteristics in their own right.[2]

It is true that a state will naturally take on the character of specific governments and there is probably a point where a government can be identified with a state, if its policies actually permeate the constitutional structure of the state. The Third Reich is an obvious example of such a development. In spite of this, it is equally true that movements for secession normally arise in the context of historical policies that extend beyond the duration of particular governments.

There is a distinction in this context between the state and the institutions that have the authority to perform its legal and political functions. There will be situations where courts and legislatures lose their legitimacy in much the same way that a state might lose its political authority. This calls for a different kind of relief, however. The military may seize the political apparatus of the state, in Nigeria, Pakistan or Fiji, but there is no reason why that needs to call the legitimacy of the state and its territorial boundaries into question. If a court or government is illegitimate, the appropriate remedy is to dissolve the government or court and replace it. This does not require the division of the state or the termination of the existing political order. It is the legitimacy of the state that accordingly concerns us in the instance of secession.

General Usage

Although the prevailing concept of legitimacy is primarily political, it has its origins in the law. The *Oxford English Dictionary* (*OED*) traces our use of the word 'legitimacy' to the notion of a legitimate child, which was 'lawfully begotten' and 'entitled to full filial rights'. Thus, David Hume wrote that it 'had been formerly usual for the civil courts to issue writs to the spiritual, directing them to inquire into the legitimacy of the person' *History of England: Henry III*, II (p. 54). This was naturally applied to those in a sovereign position, since the title of the monarch and nobles rested on hereditary principles.

The historical question of legitimacy isolates the adjudicative role of the courts, since it is the courts that have the authority to decide questions like paternity. This was significant because our natural obligations to other people were believed to come from our membership in the family. The moral implication was that the identity of the sovereign was determined by the ordinary laws of succession, in spite of the fact that the sovereign was above the legal order. It is the law that accordingly determines whether the political order is in keeping with the natural moral order.

The *OED* states that the term 'legitimate' originally referred to 'the action or process of rendering or authoritatively declaring (a person) legitimate', and by extension, to the act that renders something lawful or legal. *Webster's* goes so far as to list the word 'lawful' as a synonym of 'legitimate'. It notes that the root of the word lies in the Latin *lex*, or law, and characterizes 'a *legitimate* government' as one which is 'accordant with law or with established legal forms and requirements'.[3] The word was also used, by analogy, to indicate that a proposition follows logically from a given set of premises. It is from this usage, apparently, that the term came to express the notion that an assertion is in 'conformity to rule or principle'.

It is from here that the word 'legitimacy' made its way into popular speech, occasionally in a debased form. Benjamin Disraeli wrote sardonically in 1847 that 'in these days a great capitalist has deeper roots than a sovereign prince, unless he is very legitimate' *Tancred, III* (p. iv). 'It is not in irony', we find the *Saturday Review* stating on 14 April 1860, 'but in sober earnest, that we express our belief, that any throne is, in practice, called legitimate which has not had the consent of the nation ... to its existence.'[4] The latter example is interesting because the use of the term in the academic literature is predicated almost entirely on consent.

The general usage of the term 'legitimacy' reflects two different currents in the history of the concept. The rule of a medieval king was legitimate if it was in keeping with the moral order established by the natural law. The medieval conception was eventually pushed to the side by the concept of natural or inalienable rights, however, which rejects the idea that we derive our individual rights from our membership in society.

This inevitably shifts the focus of any inquiry into the legitimacy of the state. The question is no longer whether the political order is in keeping with the moral order established by divine authority. It is now the implicitly democratic one, whether the individuals within a state have consented to be governed. The division between these two uses of the term is not as clean as it might be, and the word still confers the speaker's moral approval on the use of power or authority. Martha Crenshaw, for example, writes that the 'legitimacy of the Red Brigade', however limited, derives from the failures of the Italian government.[5]

Although the term 'legitimacy' is used in a wide variety of contexts, the moral sense of the term is still evident in its general usage. Rudolph Barnes, for example, has written about 'military legitimacy', in suggesting that something more than the chances of military success are necessary to justify the use of force in peacetime conflicts. This is apparently an official American view, which is endorsed in military documents. 'Legitimacy derives from the perception that [military] authority is genuine, effective and uses proper agencies for reasonable purposes.'[6] The indiscriminate use of force, without regard to human rights and the rule of law, may compromise the moral effectiveness of military intervention in a conflict.

The moral and political questions of legitimacy are commonly combined, however. Barnes refers to a related military document, 'Military operations in low intensity conflict', which states that the

> ... legitimacy of the actions of an armed force, or even individual members of the force can have far-reaching effects on the legitimacy of the political system that the force supports. (p. 62)

And the same issue arises, domestically, for a military that intervenes in a foreign conflict.

> Public support has proved to be both a requirement and a measure of military legitimacy from the jungles of Vietnam to the deserts of the Persian Gulf, even to the killing fields of Somalia. These contrasting conflicts had one strategic common denominator: the legitimacy of the US military in each conflict depended upon public support back home. (p. 133)

The passage is revealing because it implies that an expression of democratic approval is sufficient to establish the moral legitimacy of military action.

This illustrates the difficulty of the current concept, which lies in the assumption that political criteria are sufficient to establish the moral legitimacy of the political order. In a similar manner, Conor Cruise O'Brien, in 'Terrorism under democratic conditions' argues that it is the question of legitimacy that determines whether violence can be described as 'terrorism'. 'The success or failure of political violence depends very largely on the extent to which it is perceived as legitimate. The use of the designation "terrorism" constitutes a declaration of the illegitimacy of the political violence referred to' (p. 94). O'Brien essentially argues that the violence used by a minority is illegitimate if there are other means of seeking changes in the social order. This is a political judgement, as well as a moral evaluation, and rests primarily upon the agreement of the populace.

On the other hand, Paul Gilbert writes that those who describe terrorism as a 'political crime' are commenting on its moral character.

> Such characterizations, more common among political theorists than philosophers, identify terrorist acts as breaches of the criminal law, rather than of the rules of war. These breaches are committed for political ends which ought to be pursued in accordance with the procedures permitted under a legitimate governmental authority. What makes terrorism wrong on this view is not only that it involves violence against citizens, but also that it by-passes constitutional procedures and thereby threatens the legitimate authority responsible for protecting citizens.[7]

What makes the existing government legitimate is that it follows moral standards in pursuing political ends, which exclude random violence against citizens. This is not a political standard.[8]

Most of the contemporary discussion of legitimacy refers specifically to the question of political legitimacy. The general use of such a concept often assumes that the moral and political standards of legitimacy come together in the question of consent. This is reflected in the general political literature, which tends to collapse the two uses. In *King and Congress*, for example, Jerrilyn Marston studies the 'transfer' of political legitimacy from the British monarchy to the American Continental Congress of 1776. There is a sociological tone in her discussion of the concept, which she uses to describe the perception that a government is entitled to the authority that it enjoys.[9]

Marston readily observes that a wide variety of principles have served as legitimating principles:

> ... as another student has observed, 'in some time and place, almost every conceivable political arrangement – feudalism, monarchy, oligarchy, hereditary aristocracy, plutocracy, representative government, direct democracy – has acquired so much legitimacy that men have volunteered their lives in its defense'. (p. 3f)[10]

This is easily misconstrued. There is a sense in which historical principles like heredity were sufficient to establish whether a ruler governed with the consent of society at large. The issue is primarily ethical in each case however, and whatever the modern view, these principles are significant because they established that a ruler had a moral right to govern.

In spite of this, Marston's understanding of the term 'political legitimacy' is implicitly democratic:

> Political legitimacy, as the term is used here, refers to the belief of the governed that their government rightfully exercises authority over them. It is, as [Carl J.] Friedrich notes, the belief of the ruled in the 'just title of the rulers to rule'. Thus for Friedrich, the basic question of legitimacy 'is a factual one, whether a given rulership is believed to be based on good title by most men subject to it or not'.[11] (p. 4)

Marston takes the position that the shift in the allegiance of the American public was based on the perception that the King's right to govern came from a social contract, which the people were entitled to revoke. This leaves no room for disputing the popular will, and the conception that Marston is using fails to recognize that the political and moral standards of legitimacy may diverge.

In *The War Against Authority*, Nicholas Kittrie adopts a similar conception of legitimacy. 'A complex term,' he writes,

> ... *legitimacy* encapsulates the citizens' feelings, attitudes, and trust toward their rulers and political institutions. In new as well as in older nations, political, religious, and cultural traditions help determine the populace's sociopsychological commitment to authority and to the person who hold the reins of power. (p. 75)

Like many contemporary authors, Kittrie expresses a concern that contemporary society is too pluralistic to sustain a single standard of legitimacy.

There is a practical side to Kittrie's concerns, which seem to have manifested themselves in a wide range of social and political crises.

> The recent and unprecedented growth of political turmoil and disorder worldwide, coupled with familial, religious, and other institutional declines, compels us to face the continuously haunting questions: Is the current global unravelling of authority indeed a manifestation of the chronic and long-predicted crisis of legitimacy, or is it the product of passing ... factors? In either case, what, if anything, can be done to help restore the legitimacy of authority and begin the reconstruction of public order? (p. 228)

Kittrie offers no solution to the substantive problem at the root of the instability, however, other than to argue for the 'practice' of procedural justice.[12] This would require some vesting of legitimacy in a principle like fairness, but this is a weak suggestion, which seems unlikely to reconcile the diversity of views that he considers.

It will be evident that this use of the term 'legitimacy' begs the question of morality, since it assumes that the views of the majority will decide the issue.

A state is legitimate, on such an analysis, if the general public believes that its actions are legitimate. This leaves the question of minorities out of the analysis. The matter is crucial, in the instance of secession, since a minority's claim to the right to secede usually arises out of those situations where the majority of the populace support the actions of an existing state.

Sociology

The shift in the academic use of the word 'legitimacy' seems to have its origins in the work of Max Weber, who gave it currency in sociology. Rather than adopt the historical use of the term, Weber argued that the legitimacy of a state derived from the successful exercise of force:

> ... we have to say that a state is a human community that (successfully) claims the monopoly of the legitimate use of force within a given territory ... Specifically, at the present time, the right to use physical force is ascribed to other institutions or to individuals only to the extent to which the state permits it. The state is considered the sole source of the 'right' to use violence.[13]

Weber argued that the legitimacy of the state derived from three sources: from mores that have acquired authority as a result of ancient usage, from the charisma of a leader, or from the statutory warrant of 'rationally created rules' (p. 33f). These criteria are entirely descriptive, however, and it is a mistake to think that they provide any substantive criteria that establishes the moral right to govern.

Weber's concept has been refined by other social scientists, who have generally seen legitimacy as a measure of the capacity of the state to justify itself. Seymour Martin Lipset, for example, has written:

> The stability of any given democracy depends not only on economic development but also upon the effectiveness and the legitimacy of its political system. Effectiveness means actual performance, the extent to which the system satisfies the basic functions of government as most of the population and such powerful groups within it as big business or the armed forces see them. Legitimacy involves the capacity of the system to engender and maintain the belief that the existing political institutions are the most appropriate ones for the society.[14]

This is a clinical view, which has many limitations. Nonetheless, it is this aspect of the contemporary concept that has led to the 'legitimation crisis' in the academic literature.[15] This crisis has been progressively generalized, to the point where the legitimacy of the state, as a political institution, seems in doubt.

This was probably inevitable. As John Scharr has written, the older definitions of legitimacy 'all revolve around the element of law or right, and rest the force of a claim ... upon foundations external to and independent of the mere assertion or opinion of the claimant'.[16] The newer definitions, in contrast, 'all dissolve legitimacy into belief or opinion. If a people holds the belief that existing institutions are "appropriate" or "morally proper", then those institutions are legitimate'. This dissolution of the original concept has eroded our ability to determine whether a particular state is morally entitled to enforce the law.

There are criticisms of Weber's concept of legitimacy in the academic literature. William Connolly has suggested that a theory of legitimacy which accepts that 'belief in the legitimacy of the order is equivalent to the order's legitimacy' misconstrues the way in which social relations are constituted. The limits imposed by the political order are tolerable to most of us, he suggests, 'because they are thought to be necessary to the common good it fosters'.[17] The impetus behind such a criticism is readily apparent: a notion like the common good would at least provide us with an independent basis on which to judge the legitimacy of political authority. It is the capacity for moral evaluation that provides us with a means of judging political institutions, whether they enjoy the consent of the majority of the populace or not.

David Beetham also criticizes the sociological concept in *The Legitimation of Power*, where he writes that Weber's influence on the use of the concept of legitimacy in the social sciences 'has been an almost unqualified disaster'.

> For a social scientist to say that a given power relation is legitimate, Weber argues, is not to make a moral judgement in the manner of the philosopher; it is rather to make a report (which may be empirically true or false) about other people's *beliefs*. Power is legitimate where those involved in it believe it to be so; legitimacy derives from people's belief in legitimacy.[18] (p. 8)

Beetham distinguishes between the philosophical and sociological concepts of legitimacy. The philosophical view, on his account, falls back on 'independent, external standards or criteria', in assessing a relationship based on power. It is this approach to the question that characterizes the legal notion of legitimacy.

Beetham argues that Weber's views are inadequate, even in the context of the social sciences.

> What such an account leaves out is obvious to all but the most hardened exponents of the theory: that people are also moral agents, who recognize the validity of rules, have some notion of a common interest, and acknowledge the binding force of promises they have made – all elements involved in legitimate power. (p. 27)

On the other hand,

> ... normative grounds or reasons are not the only reasons people have for obedience ... power relations are almost always constituted by a framework of incentives and sanctions, implicit if not always explicit, which align the behaviour of the subordinate with the wishes of those in power. (p. 26f)

The problem is that this has led to the 'fashionable' view that our obedience to social and political norms are determined by nothing more than the 'rational choice' of individuals, who merely consult their self-interest in deciding whether to accept the rules of power.

Beetham argues that the two views should be amalgamated in a more sophisticated concept, which would take us outside the 'self-confirming cycle of legitimation' expressed in the sociological standard (p. 246). Although Beetham tries to base this concept on consent, he does not set out any mechanism which can be used to provide the kind of independent standard which he is seeking.[19] Still, he seems to be right in arguing that there is no means of evaluating the specific concept of legitimacy employed by a particular society, unless we adopt a perspective outside the norms and beliefs of that society.[20] Historically, this was found in a moral order like the natural law, which existed independently of the political order and the wishes of any of the participants.

Philosophy

The question of legitimacy is less prominent in the philosophical literature, which seems to have lost itself in the debates concerning the nature and extent of our obligation to obey political authority. This is a different issue. Nonetheless, the sociological concept seems to have found its way into the philosophical literature, which has focused principally on consent. Sergio Cotta, for example, writes that the term 'legitimacy' originally suggested that a de facto political power is 'in conformity to the law' and has become a *de jure* power. Nonetheless, the modern term, in 'accredited political language', has lost something of its original meaning and now refers to a principle or criterion which justifies the existence of power.[21] This justification is necessary because power can only be maintained if it is accepted by those who are required to obey it.

It is possible to distinguish at least three major theories in the philosophical literature. There are a number of authors who take the view that legitimacy is based on the personal consent of the individual and trace the legitimacy of the state to natural rights. The most prominent difficulty with the view of these 'individualists' is that it does not distinguish satisfactorily between the political and legal conceptions of legitimacy. This is discussed in greater detail in the following chapter.

The second theory is more overtly political. It premises the legitimacy of the state on a notion of individual and collective consent, where the real strength of the contractual thesis appears to lie. This is a social concept, which retains the need for some degree of individual consent but recognizes the authority of the social order. This provides a convincing basis for a theory of political legitimacy, since any state will have difficulty maintaining its existence without the agreement of the larger community. There is, in this sense, a democratic rider on every state, a *consensus ad idem*, which places moral and practical limits on the prerogatives of the state.

There has been little scrutiny of other theories of legitimacy in the philosophical literature. Nonetheless, it is possible to discern a third theory, which holds that political legitimacy derives from some form of moral authority, akin to the authority exercised by courts in the constitutional arena. This moral authority has some of the attributes of a legal concept of legitimacy, but has not been explored at any length in the existing literature.

Individualism

In an article entitled 'Individualism and the problem of political authority', Tibor Machan writes that the question of political legitimacy is crucial for individualists. 'The question is whether even the best of human communities, with their myriad of official elements, possess moral underpinnings so that what they require of their members may be enforced by some of their members' (p. 500).[22] Machan sets out a theory of natural rights, which derives the authority of the state from 'an individualist moral framework' (p. 501). This holds that 'objective' self-interest is an inherent part of moral decision-making and significantly restricts the authority of the state.

Machan's theory of political authority rests on the view that the state derives its legitimacy from the personal consent of the governed. This neglects the fact that the sources of the law seem to be found in the conservative belief that people require some form of moral regulation, in the interests of the common good.[23] This kind of assumption is essential in justifying the legal order, which is necessary to maintain peace, justice and stability in society. This may reflect the political discourse in the USA, which often seems to be preoccupied with a narrow conception of individual rights and overstates the significance of the individual to the detriment of group rights and the larger public good.[24]

In any event, Machan's mistrust of political authority is evident in the work of other authors. In the same issue of *The Monist*, Craig Carr offers a limited justification of the authority of state. He seems unwilling to go any further than a statement 'that political authority cannot be dismissed as inherently illegitimate because it compromises the autonomy of the individual'.[25] This defence of political authority is very weak and Carr ultimately adopts the argument that the state cannot legitimately pass laws on 'hard moral questions' (p. 483). This forces him to adopt the rather strained view that states routinely act outside the proper scope of their authority.

The notion of personal consent runs into many difficulties. Machan takes the position, for example, that we cannot consent 'to institutions which are in violation of basic rights', '[n]or can one consent to the authority of enforcing principles of community organization which are in violation of the rights to life, liberty, and property, for that would mean consenting for others without the authority to do so' (p. 511). At the same time, he argues that 'the consent to be governed need not be made explicitly but can be implied, even in ignorance of the consenting party' (p. 511). This undermines the whole notion of individual consent and introduces a hypothetical individual, who may or may not share the attributes of real individuals.

The question of consent seems less important in this context than the parameters in which the individual can exercise his autonomy. As a result, the decisive issue for Machan and others in his camp is whether the political limits on personal freedom can be justified. This raises the need for constitutional restraints on political power and forces us to turn to neutral actors, outside the political realm, to determine the extent of those rights. This is the kind of approach taken by Ellen Frankel Paul in an article 'On three "inherent" powers of government', where she argues that a natural rights approach offers 'the best hope' of resolving the issue of political legitimacy (p. 530).

The problem is that Frankel Paul's concept of individual rights is entirely out of keeping with the American jurisprudence to which she is referring. As a result, she is left to argue that the power of eminent domain, the 'police power' and the power of taxation – 'three supposedly inherent attributes of political power' – 'vitiate the legitimacy of any government which exercises them' (p. 542). This is problematic, since it is out of step with the ordinary practices of government and places important areas of legislation beyond the reach of the political process. It also contradicts the legal view, since the American courts have recognized that all three powers are fundamental attributes of sovereignty.

Frankel Paul complains that the courts have often taken the position 'that government is the original grantor of all rights, and that individuals enjoy these rights only at the instigation, sufferance, and on the conditions attached to it by government' (p. 538). This confuses moral rights and legal rights, however, and it remains something of a truism to say that the law derives from society rather than the individual. The problem here is not with the courts: on the contrary, the problem lies in setting out a theory which attempts to derive the powers of government from individuals rather than society at large.

This is apparent in Frankel Paul's discussion of the police power, which she describes as the power of the state to regulate private property 'to protect and promote the "health, safety, morals", and, since the turn of the century, the "general welfare" of its citizens'.[26] Frankel Paul argues rather stridently that this power: 'has been stretched leagues beyond its legitimate boundaries to justify such governmental tampering with the market as minimum wage and maximum hour laws, workmen's compensation acts, zoning, usury laws, etc.' (p. 539).[27] This merely illustrates the inadequacy of her formulation of legitimacy, which cannot account for the accepted powers of government.

The Majoritarian View

The attempt to base the legitimacy of the legal order on a broader, more democratic notion of consent is more convincing. In 'What is the basis of political authority?', Harry Beran argues that the legitimacy of political authority lies in the consent of a group to that authority. Thus, 'rules for conferring authority cannot confer authority if they are not accepted by the group to which they are supposed to apply. On the other hand, it is clear that authority can be bestowed by a group following rules for bestowing authority which they have undertaken to follow' (p. 492). Unless we take the apparently impossible position that the state must have the consent of all of its members, this gives rise to a concept of legitimacy which is based on the rule of a majority.[28] In Beran's view, this accordingly requires the consent of the majority – in point of fact, the 'vast majority – of residents' – to the political authority of the state (p. 495).

Beran's position reflects the practical reality that, in some sense at least, the right to secede is a group right.[29] Allen Buchanan puts it in the following manner:

> If an individual right is one that ... can be exercised independently by an individual, then the right to secede ... is not an individual right. Its exercise requires collective action, even though we can speak of the individual rights that members of the group have to participate in that collective action. The same holds true for collective property rights and robust minority language rights. All of these are group rights in the sense specified above: they are ascribed to groups and must be exercised collectively, through political mechanisms, on behalf of the group.[30]

Beran's notion of political legitimacy upholds the contractual thesis, but contemplates a contract between the state and the group of individuals, collectively, who come under its jurisdiction.

Beran's argument rests on the agreement of the individuals within the relevant group, rather than a strict notion of consent. The political legitimacy of the state is guaranteed by democratic criteria, which contain a certain degree of moral force and deserve to be respected. This is not sufficient to deal with the problem of secession, however, which generally arises when a majority within a state oppresses a minority. And the fact that the moral problem lies in the wishes of the majority, who feel that it is in their interests to act in an oppressive manner, deprives the democratic process of any broader claim to legitimacy.

It is true that a plebiscite may be necessary to ascertain the wishes of a minority, if the majority permits it, and there may be ways of correcting the problem of majority rule by democratic means. Even if a minority is consulted, however, there is a question as to who is properly included within the minority. In the more troubling circumstances, moreover, where there is a history of enmity between different groups, it is the moral elements in the question of secession that come to the fore. It is naive to think that these elements can be adequately addressed by consulting the wishes of one side or the other.

James Fishkin considers the discrepancy between moral and democratic standards in *Tyranny and Legitimacy,* where he reviews the political principles that have been used to determine the question of legitimacy.[31] It is enough to mention the principles of consent and equality. Fishkin argues that these principles will justify tyranny – which he defines rather awkwardly in terms of 'severe deprivations' – if they are applied too rigorously.[32] One of the examples that he provides is contemporary:

> In August 1972, President Idi Amin ordered the expulsion, within ninety days, of approximately 50,000 Asians in Uganda. Those who considered staying were threatened with detention in military camps. There were strange disappearances, beatings, robberies, and apparent murders. Tens of thousands of Asians, who had built up a position of hard-won prosperity over several generations, were forced to leave the country virtually penniless. (p. 5)

The important factor is that 'Amin's treatment of the Asians was resoundingly popular among black Ugandans' (p. 5).

The question, then, is whether the agreement of the majority of Ugandans was sufficient to establish the legitimacy of the state's actions? Would the government's policy have been justified, if it won a fair plebiscite on the issue?[33] The answer seems to be that the actions of the Ugandan state were inherently illegitimate, whether or not they passed the practical test for political legitimacy. The problem that Fishkin identifies seems simple enough: while the democratic principle may provide a reasonable basis for political action, it is not sufficient to determine the morality of those actions.

This illuminates the purpose of the more traditional concept of legitimacy, which subjected the political order to some form of moral scrutiny outside the political process. The fact that a resolution of a contentious matter is satisfactory from a political perspective does not demonstrate that it is morally legitimate. This can be applied directly to the problem of secession. The argument for introducing a legal right of secession is that the ultimate legitimacy of the political order rests on a supervening moral order.

This does not mean that there is any reason to reject the basis of a view like Beran's, which emphasizes the importance of agreement in determining the political legitimacy of a particular action by the state. Elsewhere in his book, Fishkin quotes Joseph Schumpeter, who writes that 'there are ultimate ideals and interests which the most ardent democrat will put above democracy' (p. 66f). Democracy is merely a political 'method', a means of determining the policy, which is 'incapable of being an end in itself, irrespective of what decisions it will produce under given historical conditions'.[34] The problem is not so much with the notion of consent, broadly construed, as with the fact that political criteria are insufficient to capture the full meaning of the concept of legitimacy.

Moral Theories

There is another argument in the literature, which may make up for the deficiencies in the majoritarian view. Norman Barry sets out two kinds of theories of legitimacy, for example, one which is based on consent and one which is based on authority.[35] The latter view, which borrows from the thought of G.W.F. Hegel, provides a counterpoint to the views of the individualists. It rests on the ascendancy of the state and the community over the individual. Barry argues that a cogent theory of authority 'must be rooted in specific historical experience and in [the] traditional structures of rules: and these must precede the notion of individuality' (p. 200).[36]

The problem with this kind of theory is that it collapses the state, the law, and the normative obligations of the state. 'Since no real distinction is made between state and law', Barry writes, 'there can be no theoretical limits' on the actions of the state (p. 202). This reveals the real problem, which lies in the notion of state sovereignty. Barry solves this difficulty in much the same way as the present book, by arguing for the development of an independent legal tradition, such as we find in the common law, which cannot be seen as 'a function of the state's coercive authority' (p. 203). This leads him to argue in favour of 'the constitutional state', which is governed by the neutral provisions of a procedural constitution and does not favour any 'substantive political and economic creed' over any others (p. 204).

Barry's arguments are convincing, though his argument that a constitution must be exclusively procedural seems to ignore the reality of constitutional litigation. He also fails to consider the need for a court with the authority to rule on the validity of the domestic political order. This is necessary because a state that is politically and constitutionally legitimate may still be legally illegitimate. Nonetheless, the standard of legitimacy that Barry sets out recognizes that the courts provide a separate source of moral authority, which might be sufficient to regulate the political order.

There is a related argument in the philosophical literature, which calls for a substantive concept of legitimacy. This would hold that the legitimacy of political authority ultimately derives from moral values and principles. Jeffrey Paul takes the position that a theory of consent must trace the legitimacy of political authority to moral principles 'that have no contractual origins'.[37] This is essential to any contract: the point of an agreement is that it binds the parties, even if they change their minds, and cannot be revoked unless the other party has repudiated it.[38] It follows that any political consent must rest on moral principles that take precedence over the mere acquiescence of an individual.

If we accept this reasoning, the answer to the question whether the political contract is legitimate will depend upon whether it is morally defensible. This means that it must be justified on the basis of moral principles and sentiments. As Patrick Riley writes, in the context of Jean-Jacques Rousseau:

> Perhaps a species of moral *à priorism* is essential to genuine and full contractarianism: after all, if society must be legitimized at its outset, the source of that legitimacy – the wills of individuals – must in some sense be prior to society. But this is exactly the point on which Rousseau had his doubts, sometimes treating the capacity to make moral judgments and decisions as something all but innate, sometimes treating it as a learned ability that comes from the political education afforded by great legislators.[39]

The truth is probably that our capacity for moral judgements can be traced to both sources, but the important observation is that there is some divergence between our moral and political sensibilities.

Riley's book, published in 1982, complains that the contemporary contractual tradition fails to address the issue of 'voluntarism' in the contractual tradition. Although the work of Michael Walzer, John Rawls, John Tussman and A.J. Simmons have all addressed the issue of consent at length, and occasionally in a critical vein, they have not investigated the nature of 'willing'.[40] Riley suggests that Rawls and other authors have not investigated the full source of our contractual obligations, and argues that 'a metaphysic of morals' is needed to 'shore up social contract theory' and take us to the limits of moral inquiry (p. 214). But the more interesting aspect of his argument, in the context of legitimacy, is that it recognizes the conceptual priority of our moral faculties.

This comes to the fore in considering a question like secession, since it suggests that a standard like consent is only significant if it has a moral footing, and is not decisive when it diverges from a moral standard. It is significant, in this regard, that the more recent debate in the academic literature has passed on, beyond the question of consent. Christopher Wellman, for example, argues that a state's right of coercion is legitimate because we have 'samaritan duties' to each other.[41] This reasoning is convoluted: because we have samaritan duties, the state somehow has the authority to coerce us, in order to secure stability for other people in society (p. 219). We are morally obliged to accept legal and political constraints, in order to provide for others.[42]

The significance of Wellman's argument, in the immediate instance is that it recognizes the moral origins of the state's political authority. If our samaritan duties are augmented by our membership in an ethnic or national group, his argument begins to take on the properties of the communitarian thesis. Wellman's account is more universal, however, and takes the morally appealing view that our political duties

> ... are due to all *humans*, not just fellow *citizens*. This is in stark contrast to most theories which view a citizen as having political duties to only her own state and/or compatriots (since only *it* has benefited her or because only *they* partake in the

> same political association as she, for instance). Because samaritan duties can be owed to anyone, however, the samaritan model of political legitimacy can ground a duty to imperiled foreigners just as it generates a justification for one's own country. (p. 233)

This is of crucial importance, in setting out a legal theory of secession, because such a theory needs to derive its authority from a source that exists above the level of individual groups.

Wellman's argument only goes so far, however. It essentially sets out the reason why individuals must accept the authority of the state and does not investigate the possibility of other sources of authority. Nor does it address the source of legal authority, other than to suggest that it is a necessary part of human life. Still, Wellman's view is significant because it ultimately traces the political authority of the state to its moral sources. The most cogent reason to accept the authority of the state can be found in the moral intuition that we have an obligation to help others. This is not decided by consent, in the usual sense: it is premised on the moral feeling that we should help other people, in the absence of reasons to do otherwise.

Allen Buchanan falls back on a similar mode of reasoning when he argues that we have a 'natural' duty to promote justice for other people. This is a 'simple, intuitive idea': 'the same basic moral considerations that require us to respect a person's basic rights also require us to help bring about a situation in which their rights will be respected'.[43] The notable feature of these kind of arguments is that they rest the nature and extent of political authority on a moral rather than a contractual foundation.[44] The question of legitimacy aside, this envisages a moral order that might provide the foundation of a legal order that extends beyond the state.

The interesting issue is whether the argument from moral authority might be sufficient to make up for the deficiencies in the contractual thesis. This offers the possibility of a remedial jurisdiction, which would provide some form of relief in those situations where the normal political process results in serious unfairness to a minority. As a practical matter, a majoritarian process cannot correct itself, and a political system needs another source of authority to deal with its excesses, which does not deprive the political actors of the right to determine the course of public policy. The question posed by the present book is whether the courts can correct the weaknesses in the political process and protect the rights of minorities.

This requires some delicacy, if the different branches of government are to respect each other's roles. The political process provides us with one means of determining the morality and efficacy of the state's actions in a given set of circumstances. The legal process provides a means of assessing moral issues, complete with its own strengths and weaknesses. The difficulty, in the instance of secession, is that this may require the dissolution of the existing political order, which is usually thought to be the source of the legal order. The following chapter accordingly examines the legal conception of legitimacy, which is based on the moralistic thesis, in order to determine whether it would provide the necessary corrective to the political process.

Notes

1 It is nevertheless possible to think of circumstances in which the term 'illegal state' might be appropriate. A breakaway province might conceivably be called an illegal state.
2 Buchanan, 'Recognitional Legitimacy', p. 62.
3 *Merriam Webster Online*. And see the *Random House Dictionary of the English Language*, which defines 'legitimate' as 'according to law; lawful: *the property's legitimate owner*'.
4 In his essay on Milton, in 1880, Thomas Macaulay speaks of the 'doctrine of Divine Right, which has now come back to us, like a thief from transportation, under the *alias* of Legitimacy' (*OED*).
5 Crenshaw, 'Introduction' to *Terrorism, Legitimacy and Power*, p. 32f: 'what legitimacy the Red Brigade possesses (undoubtedly small, but a quality which is impossible to measure) is surely attributable to the Italian government's corruption, general inefficiency, and inability to solve persistent social and economic problems'.
6 Barnes, *Military Legitimacy*, p. 62.
7 Gilbert, 'Community and civil strife', p. 6.
8 If a government acts in a manner that is immoral and oppressive, it can at least be argued that the use of random violence to achieve political ends might be morally justified, and therefore legitimate. Gilbert distinguishes between the view that terrorism is 'political crime' and the view that it is 'politically motivated crime', as Michael Walzer suggests in *Just and Unjust Wars* (New York: Basic, 1973), at p. 199f.
9 See Marston, *King and Congress*, p. 3: 'Barring the extremes of anarchy and totalitarianism, government cannot exist unless the ruled voluntarily submit to the rules of their society and to the authority of their rulers. For the ruled to do this, they must believe implicitly that their rulers have the right to ask that they obey, that is, that they believe that their government possesses "political legitimacy".'
10 The quotation is from R.A. Dahl, *Modern Political Analysis*, 3rd edn (Englewood Cliffs, NJ: Prentice-Hall, 1976), p. 61.
11 In footnote 2, at p. 321, Marston traces the derivation of modern theories of legitimacy to Max Weber's *Theory of Social and Economic Organization* (New York: Free Press, 1947; orig. pub. 1922). The reference to Carl J. Friedrich is to *Man and His Government: An Empirical Theory of Politics* (New York: McGraw-Hill, 1963), at pp. 233–4.
12 In *The War Against Authority*, Kittrie also argues for a decentralized state in which the smallest unit of government that can perform a given function is given the authority to do so. See p. 256: 'Denominated *subsidiarity* and described as "the ghastly Euro-word", the doctrine promises to supply one of the supporting pillars for the building of legitimacy amidst diverse and potentially conflicting populations and interests. Having emerged in conjunction with the planning for a unified Europe (a continent to be united by an overriding parliament, executive, and judiciary), subsidiarity was advanced as a counterforce by the national groups fearing domination and oppression from above. The principle of *subsidiarity* means that the smallest unit of society which can properly perform a given function, should be allowed to do so. A larger organization should not take over a task which can be adequately accomplished at a lower level ... .' The definition of 'subsidiarity' is taken from Joseph Dunner (ed.), *Dictionary of Political Science* (New York: Philosophical Library, 1964). And ghastly it is.
13 Weber, 'Legitimacy', p. 33.
14 See Seymour Lipset, 'Social conflict', at p. 88. Cf. Scharr, 'Legitimacy', at p. 108, where he offers three 'professional definitions' of the term 'legitimacy': '(1) Legitimacy involves the capacity of the system to engender and maintain the belief that the existing political

institutions are the most appropriate ones for the society. (2) In the tradition of Weber, legitimacy has been defined as "the degree to which institutions are valued for themselves and considered right and proper". (3) We may define political legitimacy as the quality of "oughtness" that is perceived by the public to inhere in a political regime. That government is legitimate which is viewed as morally proper for a society.' For a convenient book of readings in the area, see Connolly, *Legitimacy and the State.*

15 See Jürgen Habermas, *Legitimation Crisis* (Boston, MA: Beacon Press, 1973) and the literature commenting on his work.

16 Scharr, 'Legitimacy', p. 108.

17 Connolly, 'The Dilemma of Legitimacy', p. 224.

18 Beetham cites Scharr, Hannah Pitkin and Robert Grafstein, who have all criticized the reigning view. See *Legitimation*, p. 8ff.

19 Beetham argues that the 'normative structure' of legitimacy has three different aspects: it includes a notion of 'validity according to rules, the justifiability of rules in terms of shared beliefs, and expressed consent on the part of those qualified to give it' (p. 97).

20 See Beetham, at p. 245f: 'Just as social scientists cannot explain [changes to established norms of legitimacy] if they remain confined within the terms of a particular set of society-specific norms or beliefs, so neither can philosophers evaluate them, except from a standpoint which is outside the given tradition, and from which they might prioritise particular elements within it. For this reason I do not see how it is possible to avoid some external or transcendent position altogether in political philosophy, even if it remains implicit and unconscious.'

21 Cotta, 'Legitimacy: a mirage?', p. 96.

22 This debate has an American flavour. See the comment by Machan, 'Individualism', at p. 502: 'When the Black Panthers fought the police in the late 1960s, they or their leaders often argued on TV talk shows that they wholeheartedly disputed the moral authority of the officers of "white America's law", regardless of the wisdom or lack thereof of the particular matter at hand during some confrontation. It is when these sorts of challenges or protests are leveled that we are faced with what comes closest to a genuine questioning of political authority.'

23 It is notable that Machan goes no further in speaking of the need for government, than to assert that people 'possess' the capacity to be evil (p. 505).

24 See Mary Ann Glendon, *Rights Talk: The Impoverishment of Political Discourse*, at p. 14: 'The most distinctive features of our American rights dialect are the very ones that are most conspicuously in tension with what we require in order to give a reasonably full and coherent account of what kind of society we are and what kind of polity we are trying to create: its penchant for absolute, extravagant formulations, its near-aphasia concerning responsibility, its excessive homage to individual independence and self-sufficiency, its habitual concentration on the individual and the state at the expense of the intermediate groups of civil society, and its unapologetic insularity. Not only does each of these traits make it difficult to give voice to common sense or moral intuitions, they also impede development of the sort of rational political discourse that is appropriate to the needs of a mature, complex, liberal, pluralistic republic.'

25 Carr, 'The problem of political authority', p. 484.

26 See Frankel Paul, 'On three "inherent" powers', at p. 537: 'In an early case, *Gibbons v. Ogden*, Chief Justice Marshall wrote about the police power, giving it broad sweep, and simply assuming that such a power naturally inhered in the states ... Chief Justice Taney, too, considered the police power as tantamount to sovereignty itself.' There seems no reason to dispute such legal assumptions. The references are to *Gibbons* v. *Ogden*, 9 Wheat. 1, 202 (U.S., 1824) and *License Cases*, 5 How. 504, 582 (U.S., 1847).

27 This seems to require more faith in the 'free market' system than most of us can muster. See Frankel Paul, ibid.: 'Free market remedies could, most likely, replace the overweening regulatory framework our states now enforce. Building codes and fire codes could presumably be replaced quite easily by privately enforced codes drafted by insurance

companies. Few developers would construct hazardous firetraps if they knew beforehand that they could not acquire insurance for their buildings. And as Bernard Siegan brilliantly demonstrated in his "Non-zoning in Houston", egregious, incompatible property uses will not often cohabit if land use regulations were summarily abolished. Restrictive covenants that run with the land, renewable at intervals of several decades, could very expeditiously insure that a slaughterhouse will not locate in the middle of Shaker Heights, Beverly Hills, or Boca Raton.'

28 There may well have been societies where the consent to political authority was virtually unanimous, if only because the idea that it could be questioned was absent.

29 Other authors, like Christopher Wellman, speak of an individual right to secede. See 'Liberalism, samaritanism and political legitimacy', at p. 219: 'To emphasize: the reason that *I* have no moral right to be free from political coercion (to secede) is because, even if *I* would rather forego the benefits of political society, *I* have a moral duty to others ...'

30 Buchanan, *Secession: The Morality of Political Divorce*, p. 76f.

31 See Fishkin, *Tyranny and Legitimacy*, at p. 4f, where he sets out three kinds of criteria. These criteria include procedural principles 'such as majority rule, unanimity, and theories of consent'; structural principles 'such as equality, utilitarianism, and Rawl's theory of justice'; and principles which hold that rights are absolute, 'such as the famous recent theory of Robert Nozick'.

32 See Fishkin, at p. 18: '*A policy choice by the government is an instance of simple tyranny when that policy imposes severe deprivations even though an alternative policy would have imposed no severe deprivations on anyone.*' And see the additional propositions at pp. 42f, 44 and 52.

33 Cf. Richard Taylor, 'The Basis of Political Authority', p. 470, where he uses the same example: 'And if there happens to be a prosperous and easily identifiable minority, such as the Asians in Kenya, then it is but a matter of time before they are virtually driven from the country and their property and business expropriated – by the official threats of a legislature which correctly claims to "represent" the people, and thus express the dreadful will of the majority. We view outrages like this as corruption. We fail to see that it is simply democracy ...'

34 The reference, at page 142, footnote 2, is to Joseph Schumpeter, *Capitalism, Socialism and Democracy*, 3rd edn (New York: Harper and Row, 1950), pp. 240 and 242.

35 In 'The state and legitimacy', Barry refers to these as 'agency' and 'organic' theories. See p. 194 for example: 'The agency theory takes a purely subjectivist view of the state: it is a device or contrivance for transmitting individual choices into collective outcomes.' And p. 200: 'The organic theory of the state seeks to establish legitimacy by reference to authority rather than individual choice.'

36 But see ibid., at p. 201, where Barry writes that this does not make it 'conservative in a *substantive sense*', and argues that it 'can easily be made consistent with the features of a classical liberal order, private property, market exchange, the rule of law and so on' (p. 201).

37 Paul, 'Substantive social contracts', p. 528. And see page 527: 'Any contractual process, whether hypothetical or actual, which aims at deriving legitimate principles regulating the liberties of its members cannot do so, by itself. Such a process already presupposes the legitimacy of a pre-contractual normative principle proscribing [*sic*] the self-ownership and autonomy of every contractor.'

38 And of course the same logic applies to any government with a term that continues into the future, whatever the views of the electorate. Or to a referendum on secession, which presumably prevents a government from calling a second referendum for some unspecified period of time thereafter. The American notion of recall may have eroded such a principle.

39 Riley, *Will and Political Legitimacy*, p. 124.

40 See the discussion in Riley, at pp. 206–209.

41 See Wellman, 'Liberalism, samaritanism and political legitimacy', at p. 216. See Wellman's comment at p. 212: 'Unfortunately, only wishful thinking supports the belief

that existing states have garnered the morally valid consent of all of their citizens.' And at p. 220: 'Although the consent theory of political legitimacy historically has enjoyed a great deal of support, it has more recently been thoroughly discredited. This approach is doubly flawed since (1) citizens almost never consent to their governments, and (2) any act even resembling that which implies consent (like voting) is a moral nullity because it is performed under coercion (the voter in a political election will be – and has been – subject to the state's laws no matter how, or even whether, she votes).'

42 See ibid., at p. 216: 'The state's right to coerce its citizens correlates to the latter's lack of rights to be free from political coercion, and this absence of rights stems from their samaritan duties to others. In short, our samaritan duties to others curtail our own political liberty.' The assumption, as in most of the literature, is that the matter needs to be discussed from the perspective of personal rights, even where those rights do not exist!

43 Buchanan, 'Recognitional legitimacy', p. 71.

44 Buchanan endorses the view of A. John Simmons (1979), in *Moral Theory and Political Obligation* (Princeton, NJ: Princeton University Press), ibid., at p. 56: 'a political entity,' he writes, 'is legitimate if and only if it has the authority to enforce legal rules within its territory where this authority carries with it an obligation to obey that entity on the part of the citizens.' This is rather oblique.

Chapter 2

The Legal Concept of Legitimacy

This chapter reviews the legal principle of legitimacy, which has not received significant attention in the literature. Although the legal principle of legitimacy also derives from the consent of the governed, it does so indirectly. A state is legally legitimate when it governs in accordance with generally accepted moral principles, which have been accepted by society at large. These principles find expression in the constitutional law, which expresses a legal consensus between the members of society. This includes the members of minorities.

A minority that claims the right to secede is claiming the right to free itself from its obligation to obey the existing legal order. This is a difficult issue, philosophically, because the legal order is inherently compulsory. The question of secession accordingly raises a question as to our moral and legal obligation to accept the authority of the state. This is usually seen as an issue that goes to the legitimacy of political authority and calls for an explanation of the source of political power.

John Locke canvasses the question in *The Second Treatise on Civil Government*, where he argues that man is 'naturally free' and can only be subjected to the power of government by his own consent. This is a problem, since it runs against the empirical fact that we are obliged to obey the law, whether or not we have consented to it. In one of the more famous passages in the *Treatise*, Locke retreats to the position that 'tacit consent' is sufficient. He nevertheless seems willing to acknowledge that this is not entirely satisfactory: 'The difficulty is, what ought to be looked upon as a tacit consent, and how far it binds – i.e., how far anyone shall be looked on to have consented, and thereby submitted to any government, where he has made no expressions of it at all.'[1] Although this is a political question, it is pressing in a legal context, since there is very little in the law to support the contention that our obligation to obey the law rests upon personal consent.

In spite of the position that Locke adopts, he applies a compulsory rather than a consensual standard in a legal context.

> And to this I say, that every man that hath any possession or enjoyment of any part of the dominions of any government doeth hereby give his tacit consent, and is as far forth obliged to give obedience to the laws of that government, during such enjoyment as anyone under it, whether this his possession be of land to him and his heirs forever, or a lodging only for a week; or whether it be barely traveling freely on the highway; and, in effect, it reaches as far as the very being of anyone within the territories of that government. (§119)

This position is in keeping with the common law, which holds that the legal jurisdiction of the state extends to whatever happens in its territory. It nevertheless seems to stretch the notion of consent beyond its breaking point. If the individual is bound by the mere fact that he finds himself within the state, it is evident that his consent to the legal order is irrelevant for any legal or practical purposes.

As Jerrilyn Marston writes, it was accepted in the eighteenth century that the social contract had a compulsory character.

> The idea of an uncomplicated, mutually binding contract was so essential to Whig theory that the terms of the contract became an eighteenth-century political cliché reiterated by Whigs on both sides of the Atlantic. Thus 'Cato' laid down as a political maxim 'that Protection and Allegiance are reciprocal'. 'A true Whig is of the Opinion', [Robert Viscount] Molesworth asserted, 'that the *Executive* Power has as just a Title to the Allegiance and Obedience of the Subject ... as the Subject has to *Protection*.'[2]

This became an integral part of the discussion that led up to the American revolution: the argument in support of the revolution was that the King had failed to honour his obligation, thus freeing his subjects. This does not deny the binding nature of the citizen's obligation to obey the laws of a duly constituted government.

The contemporary inquiry into our obligation to obey legal and political authority seems to have obscured the compulsory nature of our legal obligations. This is regrettable, and has inevitably brought the legitimacy of the authority exercised by government into question. In a collection entitled *On Political Obligation*, for example, Tom Campbell follows the lead of Joseph Raz in arguing that 'law as such has no moral authority' and it is only 'good legal systems' that can claim our obedience.[3] Paul Harris sets out three conditions, 'under which there is a general prima facie moral obligation to obey the law'.[4]

In much the same vein, Rex Martin argues that 'some laws may establish ways of acting or ways of being treated that are not in the interest of each and all, and the citizen might use such a contention to justify his or her refusal to conform to such a law'. This, he writes, 'might even license, conceivably, some cases of civil disobedience – where, for example, the citizen regarded an alleged law as ... specifying a way of acting (or of being treated) that he or she could not endorse'.[5] Martin argues for a notion of civil responsibility and general 'allegiance' that neglects the reality of our obligation to obey the law.

These kinds of views implicitly suggest that the legitimacy of the legal order derives from the individual's approval of the law. There is a collectivist response, which is in keeping with the majoritarian view discussed in the previous chapter. Leslie Green, for example, identifies 'two faults' in the theory of consent. The first is that it fails to recognize the fact that political life is essentially public and not private. The second is that the individualists fail to recognize the role of 'communal traditions' in establishing moral relations in the state.

If we accept this argument, the question of consent raises a collective rather than a personal issue, and the signatories to the political contract are the state and the majority of individuals living in the state. This is an important argument and rests the legitimacy of the state on the existence of an agreement, rather than consent, narrowly construed. The interesting feature of this line of argument is the suggestion that our obligation to obey the law flows from the agreement of other people to the social contract. Nor is there any reason to reject such a view, within reasonable limits.

More importantly, Green writes it is evident that 'these two faults in consent theory are not merely incidental; they are intimately connected with its main feature, the analogy between life in a state and a voluntary association'.[6] This is a fundamental error: 'Descriptively, states are not like that, for the scope of their authority is maximal and their jurisdiction compulsory' (p. 102). It seems fair to say that the compulsory nature of the jurisdiction enjoyed by the state finds its primary expression in our obligation to obey the law.

The same descriptive error has made its way into the commentary on the derivation of the law. In *The Ethics of Legal Coercion*, for example, John Hodson provides a theoretical framework for an analysis of legislation (p. xi). His theory starts with the principle '*of respect for persons*': 'all action must be consistent with recognition of the supreme moral importance of each person's having control over his or her own life in accordance with his or her own unencumbered choices' (p. 129). He then sets out a '*primary exclusionary principle*', which states that the state can only use coercion if it is authorized by this initial principle.

There are many reasons to dispute such a statement. The idea that the function of the law is to let individuals make 'unencumbered choices' is dubious at best. This is an empirical rather than a theoretical observation, but it has deep philosophical implications. Although the legal regimes under which we live are increasingly complex and cannot be reduced to a simple set of imperatives, the ordinary law is only incidentally consensual. It is readily apparent that the judicial inquiry rests on the assumption that the authority of the courts over individuals is inherently legitimate.

David Hume provides a better explanation of the origins of law in an essay on the origins of government, where he takes the position that 'all men are sensible of the necessity of peace and order for the maintenance of society'. Faced with the 'incurable' weakness of human nature, and the inevitable conflict between self-interest and justice, society

> ... must institute some persons, under the appellation of magistrates, whose peculiar office it is, to point out the decrees of equality, to punish transgressors, to correct fraud and violence, and to oblige men, however reluctant, to consult their own real and permanent interests. In a word, OBEDIENCE is a new duty which must be invented to support that of JUSTICE ...[7]

The existential premise of the law is accordingly that the citizen is obliged to obey it: there may be exceptions to such a principle, and restrictions on the authority of the state, but the legal order is compulsory.

Hume entrenches our obligation to obey the law in its moral authority. The law exists as an ethical necessity: it secures justice and preserves the social order, which is necessary to enjoy the benefits of human society. This is probably sufficient to provide a moral justification of the state, and justify its legal jurisdiction over a particular territory. It follows that there is a moral presumption that we should, as a general rule, obey the legal and political authorities within society.

From a legal perspective, there is little reason to decry the compulsory nature of political and legal authority, which is a necessary facet of any social order.[8] It is contrived to suggest that our obligation to obey the law derives from our consent. The courts have no interest in whether individuals have consented to the legislative schemes that they are asked to interpret and apply. The authority of the law derives from its moral and therefore obligatory character rather than some personal species of contract. The dichotomy between the attitudes that prevail in the legal arena and some areas of academic inquiry could hardly be more stark.

There will inevitably be situations where our *prima facie* obligation to obey the law is superseded by moral considerations, but that raises other issues. Although the courts strike down laws that infringe individual rights and freedoms, these rights and freedoms are more accurately seen as concessions carved out of the existing legal order. They do not provide the foundation of the law. Whether we are speaking about the substantive law or regulatory regimes, the ordinary law encapsulates a particular view of the good, which cannot be divorced from the moral views of society. Laws derive their political authority from the fact that the majority has agreed that we are obliged to obey them, whatever our personal views.

This requires some degree of qualification. The notion that the law is inherently compulsory does not negate its contractual aspect. In an essay on the 'original contract', David Hume writes that there is a sense in which the source of all political authority is consensual. 'When we consider how nearly equal all men are in their bodily force, and even in their mental powers and faculties ... we must necessarily allow, that nothing but their own consent could, at first, associate them together, and subject them to any authority.'[9] There is something right about the contractual position, since it is probably impossible to govern a country without a substantial degree of consent from the populace.

On the other hand, it is a mistake to suppose that the individual members of society have consented to the rule of government. Hume argues that we could not enjoy the benefits of society:

> ... without laws and magistrates and judges, to prevent the encroachments of the strong upon the weak, of the violent upon the just and equitable ...

> If the reason be asked of that obedience, which we are bound to pay government, I readily answer, *because society could not otherwise subsist*: And this answer is clear and intelligible to all mankind.[10] (p. 456)

If we rest our obligation to obey the law upon a promise, that only raises the question: 'why are we bound to observe our promise?' The answer, which turns the idea of a promise inside out, is that we have no choice but to promise to obey the law, since the social order could not persist without it.

Hume ridicules the suggestion that an individual consents to government by living within a particular territory:

> Can we seriously say, that a poor peasant or artizan has a free choice to leave his country, when he knows no foreign language or manners, and lives from day to day, by the small wages which he acquires? We may as well assert, that a man by remaining in a vessel, freely consents to the domination of the master; though he was carried on board while asleep, and must leap into the ocean and perish the moment he leaves her. (p. 451)

This might be compared to the situation of a minority that finds itself within a state dominated by another group, since the same logic appears to apply in either case. But of course people may continue to live within a particular state, for any number of reasons, without accepting the legitimacy of the state in which they live.[11]

This is not entirely fair to Locke, since there is no real disagreement between the two philosophers on the fundamental issue. While the fact of consent creates moral obligations, it is on the legal basis that we are not entitled to enjoy the benefits of a political society without accepting its authority. Locke essentially sees the 'tacit consent' of the populace as a condition precedent, in legal terms, which interposes itself between a person's decision to make use of a public benefit and his subsequent act in doing so.

The word 'consent' is troubling here, since the legitimacy of the legal and political orders appears to rest on our mere acceptance of the fact that it is compulsory. This is not the same as the statement that we have consented to it. It is nevertheless in keeping with the normal rules of social intercourse: in using a public highway, we have agreed to observe the speed limit and it is irrelevant whether we have addressed our mind to the specific limit.[12] Many circumstances in our lives are similar: when we rent a car, or take a ferry, or open a bank account, the law assumes that we are bound by a multitude of restrictions, whether we have considered them or not.

The essential argument in Hume and Locke is that we are bound by the social contract, merely by virtue of living in a particular society. This is a common theme in philosophy. Emmanuel Kant argues, for example, that we are obliged to enter into the civil contract and accept the legal order. This does not compromise our autonomy because we cannot exist independently of society and can only exercise our autonomy in a meaningful way within the social contract.[13]

There is a legal and political question of legitimacy that raises itself in this context. Although the right of a government to pass specific laws derives from its political mandate, it is not the fact that we consent to a law that creates our legal obligation to obey it. On the contrary, the legal force of the law has its origins in the moral provenance of the principle of justice. This is the source of the law's legal legitimacy, which ultimately derives from the right of government to act in the common good, rather than in the particular good of individuals and groups. Properly construed however, the common good includes these goods.

Laws generally derive their political legitimacy from the fact that they reflect the views of the majority. They derive their legal legitimacy however from the fact that they are in keeping with the basic principles of justice. These principles include procedural standards, which govern the fairness of the process. This brings a moral component into legal analysis: the validity of legal restrictions is only indirectly determined by consent, and depends more directly on the application of broad meta-ethical principles. It is these principles that determine whether the political and legal orders are in keeping with the moral order.

This is a legal rather than a moral standard. Although the moral issues that arise in the courts are attenuated, the legal and moral standards naturally coincide. It is plainly erroneous to think that it is our failure to consent to unconstitutional provisions that deprives them of their legal force. On the contrary, it is the fact that the state has imposed terms and conditions upon us that are manifestly unreasonable or morally untenable. It is moral concerns that are uppermost in the legal inquiry and statutory requirements that cannot be justified on a general principled basis are open to challenge, however popular they may be.

The major issue with respect to secession is whether the members of a minority are legally entitled to reject the political authority of the state. This cannot be decided judicially unless the legal order exists outside the political order and derives its authority from principles that take priority over the usual presumption that we should obey the directives of the state. It follows that we need to trace the authority of the legal order to substantive principles rather than the existence of political power.

This kind of reasoning goes against the positivist reduction, which has raised considerable doubt as to the moral legitimacy of the legal order. Kai Nielsen is borrowing from Max Weber, when he argues that the legitimate *de jure* authority of the state may simply derive from its successful claim to a monopoly on 'the *de facto* legitimate use of violence'.[14] This is only true if the courts abandon their moral jurisdiction and adopt the position that their authority derives entirely from the political order. This is an impossible position in the instance of secession, since it leaves the judiciary with no power to free the members of a minority from their obligation to obey the laws promulgated by the existing state.

The Legitimacy of the Legal and Political Systems

The authority of the legal system rests on its legitimacy. This has a moral and a political element. The legal system derives its political legitimacy from the consent of the governed, who accept the authority of the courts. This consent rests on a moderated positivism that leaves the fundamental law-making power in the hands of political actors, who are directly accountable to the governed. The courts have a general duty to apply the laws enacted by the legislative branch of government.

The legitimacy of the law and the legal system rests more prominently on its moral aspects, however. The problem with legal positivism is precisely that it substitutes a political for a legal or moral standard of legitimacy. This is reflected in the Austinian view that the law is merely the command of the sovereign.[15] It follows that judges should leave their moral views at the doorstep of the courthouse and apply the law in accordance with the wishes of the sovereign. David Dyzenhaus discusses the poverty of such a view in an article dealing with the provenance of the 'plain fact' school of adjudication in apartheid South Africa.

Dyzenhaus argues that the source of this tradition can be found in Thomas Hobbes, who was wary of the common law.

> Hobbes ... says that the sovereign should not be subject to any power in the social order and that his commands as to that order should be in the form of positive law, so that they can be understood without courting the dangers of moral argument. It is this last consideration that explains Hobbe's contempt for the common law. He regards the common law as a bog of moral values which gives a license to lawyers and judges to impose their views about right and wrong on the social order.[16]

Although there are real concerns with a wilful judiciary, this reflects a certain *naïveté* as to the nature and discipline of the common law, which has never given judges the freedom to impose their moral views on the rest of society.

It may be ironic that this kind of view had a profound effect on the development of the English common law, which severely restricted the role of the judiciary and left the courts with the task of 'interpreting' the intentions of Parliament. There were notable exceptions to such a tradition, however, and the criminal law, the most overt of all moral jurisdictions, was left in the keeping of the courts. In spite of this, it seems fair to say that the recent historical tradition traces the authority of the courts to the political order, as it manifests itself in the statutory powers of an elected Parliament.

There is no difficulty in saying that a statute derives its political legitimacy from the political order under which it came into being. This only captures one aspect of the judicial role, however. The difficulty with the positivist tradition in Dyzenhaus's view is that it fails to recognize the moral independence of the judicial decision to apply and enforce the law. It is the moral question of legitimacy that arises in the context of South Africa, where the Appellate Division of the Supreme Court upheld legislation delegating wide powers to executive officials. This allowed the South African executive to carry out the racial policies of the government outside the scrutiny of the courts.

Dyzenhaus argues that we can draw three conclusions from the failure of the South African judiciary to intervene in such a development:

> These are, first, that the process of adjudication is a central element of legality, a central element, as it were, of the (read 'our Western') idea of law. Secondly, in order to make sense of that central place, we have also to see that such adjudication is not merely formal – it is adjudication in terms of some substantive moral values that are also legal values. Finally, there is, therefore, an intimate connection between legality and legitimacy. (p. 93)

The thrust of this argument is that the courts are obliged to inquire into the morality of legislation and lose their legitimacy when they fail to do so. Even if the laws in apartheid South Africa were politically legitimate, there is a question as to whether the courts could legitimately apply them.

The positivist view is unworkable in the instance of secession, since it does not permit a court to rule on the legitimacy of the political order. This is because a positivist court cannot question the sheer existence of political power without questioning the source of its own authority. It follows that a court with the jurisdiction to decide a question like secession must have a superior source of authority, which gives it the jurisdiction to determine the legal legitimacy of the political order. This can be found in the moral jurisdiction of the courts, which supplies the moral corrective needed to supplement the political principle of legitimacy.[17]

Dyzenhaus does not explore the nature of a judge's obligation to apply the law, which is impersonal, approximate and procedural, even when it finds its source in substantive principles. That is a different issue, however, and it is the moral question of legitimacy that explains the inherent jurisdiction of the courts. There is an element of moral discretion in the judiciary's exercise of its obligation to interpret and enforce the law, which secures the independence of the courts from political institutions.

The significance of the legal concept of legitimacy is borne out by the existing jurisprudence, which recognizes the moral source of the courts' authority. In *Planned Parenthood* v. *Casey*, 505 U.S. 833 (1992), for example, the United States Supreme Court was asked to overturn *Roe* v. *Wade*, 410 U.S. 113 (1973), where an earlier bench of the same court had found that a law against abortion was unconstitutional.[18] The majority in *Casey* refused to overturn the earlier decision on the basis that it contravened the principle of *stare decisis* and would imperil the court's legitimacy.

The majority in *Casey* relied upon the political and legal aspects of the concept of legitimacy in its reasoning: 'The Court's power lies ... in its legitimacy, a product of substance and perception that shows itself in the people's acceptance of the Judiciary as fit to determine what the Nation's law means and to declare what it demands.' 'The underlying substance of this legitimacy', it continues,

> is of course the warrant for the Court's decisions in the Constitution and the lesser sources of legal principle on which the Court draws. That substance is expressed in the Court's opinions, and our contemporary understanding is such that a decision without principled justification would be no judicial act at all. (p. 865)

In the view of the *Casey* court, then, judicial decisions derive their legitimacy from the use of principle and the process of rational justification.

The argument is that the political authority of the court rests on the legal legitimacy of its decisions. 'The Court', the majority wrote,

> ... must take care to speak and act in ways that allow people to accept its decisions on the terms the Court claims for them, as grounded truly in principle, not as compromises with social and political pressures having, as such, no bearing on the principled choices that the Court is obliged to make. (p. 865f)

Although Chief Justice Rehnquist and three other judges dissented, they took the position that the legitimacy of the court does not derive from 'following public opinion', but from deciding 'by its best lights' whether the legislative actions of the popular branches of government 'comport with the Constitution'.[19]

There are two different tasks here: the normative issue in the political realm is whether a government should implement a particular policy. This is often a matter of consent rather than strict approval, though the language of politics is muddy and the ultimate issue is whether the actions of the government are politically legitimate. This issue usually arises on specific issues: the government should reduce income tax, increase its spending on the military or provide assistance to those in need. Political reasoning is results oriented: in a democracy at least, a government is in the business of justifying its policies to the people.

The criterion of validity is different in the legal realm. Legal reasoning proceeds by inference and primarily demonstrates that a certain conclusion follows from a specific set of legal principles. Both sides in *Casey* recognized that a court derives its legitimacy in many instances from the fact that it refuses to conform to a democratic standard. It is accepted within the profession that a judge who is motivated by the need to arrive at a particular result is not acting in a judicial manner. A legal decision that does not follow logically from its premises is fallacious, even if it attracts popular support.[20]

This still leaves a question as to the source of those principles from which the courts derive their moral legitimacy. The answer appears to lie in the substantive consensus on which society is premised. As the Supreme Court of Canada recognizes in *Reference re Secession of Québec*, [1998] 2 S.C.R.

217, these fundamental principles are not restricted to the provisions of a written constitution.[21] 'Underlying constitutional principles may in certain circumstances give rise to substantive legal obligations ... which constitute substantive limitations upon government action. These principles may give rise to very abstract and general obligations, or they may be more specific and precise in nature' (p. 249).

It is significant that the Supreme Court saw these principles as an integral aspect of any valid legal or political process. 'The principles are not merely descriptive, but are also invested with a powerful normative force, and are binding upon both courts and governments' (p. 249). A valid political system, the court held, must

> ... possess legitimacy, and in our political culture, that requires an interaction between the rule of law and the democratic principle. The system must be capable of reflecting the aspirations of the people. But there is more. Our law's claim to legitimacy also rests on an appeal to moral values, many of which are imbedded in our constitutional structure. (p. 255)

It follows that there are underlying constitutional principles that place substantive limitations on the actions undertaken by political actors.

The political conception of legitimacy is inadequate in a legal forum. 'The consent of the governed is a value that is basic to our understanding of a free and democratic society. Yet democracy in any real sense of the word cannot exist without the rule of law ... To be accorded legitimacy, democratic institutions must rest, ultimately, on a legal foundation' (p. 256). This is predominantly moral. 'Our law's claim to legitimacy also rests on an appeal to moral values, many of which are imbedded in our constitutional structure. It would be a grave mistake to equate legitimacy with the "sovereign will" or majority rule alone, to the exclusion of other constitutional values' (p. 256).

It follows that a valid political system must be legally legitimate. This conception of legitimacy has a moral and substantive character, that goes well beyond the bare requirement that the parties follow certain rules or procedures. It is the courts that have the particular duty to ensure that the state adheres to fundamental legal and moral principles, There is nothing in the political process that logically guarantees that it complies with such principles. This requires the moral approval of the courts, which have the inherent authority to subject the conduct of the state to legal scrutiny.

The court in the *Secession Reference* essentially reserved its right to rule on the legal legitimacy of the actions of the political actors in any controversy over secession.[22] This raises a question of justice and must be decided on moral grounds. The legality of any agreement between Canada and Quebec is accordingly open to question, even if the two governments followed recognized political practice and the majority on both sides of the question consented to the agreement. The legal question is whether the agreement deals so unjustly with a third party that the courts are obliged to intervene.

The Substantive Nature of the Legal Process

It follows that the legal question of legitimacy is substantive. This runs against the view in much of the contemporary philosophical literature, where there has been a determined attempt to substitute procedural for substantive criteria in law, political theory and, even, ethics. The attitudes in the courts are more in keeping with the popular view that the law rests on substantive moral values. This is a common-sense issue: the idea that the law of negligence or contracts or human rights has a procedural foundation is rather fanciful.

The matter is more complicated than this might suggest however. Legal reasoning does not address the precise morality of narrow ethical issues. The scepticism of a jurist like Oliver Wendell Holmes illustrates how much room there is to question the veracity of substantive legal principles, inside and outside the law. This is a product of the general nature of the legal inquiry however, which is more approximate and indefinite than the inquiry in other areas.

The older comparisons between mathematics and legal reasoning are more accurate than the contemporary literature acknowledges. The substantive nature of the legal process derives from the fact that legal axioms have a moral component and include substantive moral values. The examples are innumerable. These include the prohibition against cruel and unusual punishment, the principle that the courts should respect our bodily integrity and the principle that natural parents have certain prerogatives with regard to their children.

The law is nevertheless a body of general rules and principles. The nature of a claim that a given exercise of authority is legally legitimate is moral but jurisdictional. This gives it a procedural character. The issue in constitutional cases is whether the relevant political actors have acted within the scope of their moral authority, rather than whether they have chosen the right policy or followed the best course of action.

Many of the concerns in philosophy of law derive from the separation of law and morality in the positivist tradition. There is a sense in which the character of the law is essentially moral and another sense in which it separates itself from moral judgements. This is apparent in the methodology of the courts, which is more impersonal and tentative than ordinary ethical decision-making. This goes more to the nature of the judicial act, however, than the nature of legal principles.

The legal process stands in contrast to the political process. Although the concerns that inform decision-making in the political arena are substantive, the democratic process is essentially a procedural process. The opposite can be said of the legal process. The courts are driven by pragmatic concerns and legal reasoning is governed by the facts of specific cases. If it is not possible to do justice without employing substantive principles, a court will feel compelled to make use of such principles. It is probably impossible to draw a firm distinction between substantive and procedural principles in the law.[23]

There are many cases in which judges are tempted to rely upon their private moral views. This runs many risks, however, and undermines the integrity of the system if it takes the law beyond the consensus on which it is premised. This consensus varies in different societies and evolves over time. It is also evident that the consensus within the state may differ from the consensus in the extra-constitutional realm. This provides the natural basis for distinguishing between those principles that belong in a binding extra-constitutional law and those that come more properly within the ambit of a constitution.[24]

Moral and Legal Legitimacy

There is a discussion of the concept of 'moral legitimacy' in the philosophical literature. Although this has taken place outside the legal context, it is helpful in explaining the concept of legal legitimacy, which has different origins than the political concept. In an article in *Philosophy and Public Affairs*, for example, Arthur Applbaum examines the question whether public officials can legitimately depart from government policy, even when it has received the consent of their superiors, the legislature and the public. This raises the same kind of issue that faces the courts: how should an official respond, when the actions of government are politically legitimate but morally suspect?

Applbaum's discussion is helpful because it makes a clear distinction between the concept of legitimacy and the ethical correctness of particular decisions. 'A finding by a dissenter that a political mandate has not been decided in the legitimate jurisdiction or on legitimate reasons is, of course, still a judgement. But it is a judgement about legitimacy, not a judgment about the good or the just' (p. 257).[25] These questions come together in some instances, since it seems impossible to justify some decisions, no matter how sincere or well intentioned they may be. But the important point is that the question of legitimacy raises a second kind of moral issue, which asks us to consider the parameters in which a legislature exercises its prerogatives, rather than the simple ethics of his decision.

This takes us into legal terrain: when assessing the conduct of an entity like a state, it is not the moral accuracy of the decisions taken by the state that come under scrutiny. It is the process by which such decisions were made and the substantive parameters in which they exist that forms the proper subject of legal review.[26] Some decisions stand outside the moral pale: nothing can justify genocide and there are substantive limits on the decisions that a state is morally and legally entitled to make.[27] On the other hand, there are decisions that are illegitimate because they have been taken without any regard for the minimal standards of consultation and fair process.

As Applbaum writes, the question of legitimacy takes us beyond ordinary ethical considerations. A public official has more to consider than his own views, in deciding whether to act in a manner that is contrary to the spirit of a legislative scheme. There is an analogy here with the judiciary, who have no mandate to impose their moral views on the rest of society. It is necessary to distinguish between ordinary moral evaluation in this context and the question whether the government is morally entitled to adopt such a policy. It is the second kind of analysis that provides the basis of any inquiry into the moral legitimacy of a particular policy.

The problem of secession raises larger issues. These issues have a contractual character. The essential question is whether a minority has the right to revoke the existing political contract, which is expressed legally in the constitution. There are at least two questions here. The first is whether the majority has repudiated its moral obligations under the constitution. The second, more substantive however, is whether the contract itself is morally legitimate. This brings into question the moral legitimacy of the domestic legal and political order in its entirety.

The second question raises general public policy issues. There are moral limits on the power of the state to enforce the social contract, just as there are limits on the capacity of the state to pass binding legislation. This raises a legal question of legitimacy, which brings the moral discretion of a court into play. This discretion is primarily substantive. The question that it raises is different than the question of legitimacy that raises itself in the political arena, which is whether the different parties have consented to the contract.

There is some recognition in the literature that these are separate issues. In 'Moral conflict and political legitimacy' for example, Thomas Nagel argues that the conduct of political actors needs to be justified on moral grounds. This calls for a different process of ethical evaluation. It requires 'something' like the position taken by John Rawls, who argues that there is a fundamental distinction 'between what justifies individual belief and what justifies appealing to that belief in support of the exercise of political power'.

Nagel argues that we need to distinguish between appeals to our own beliefs and appeals to those 'truths' that are open to the kind of 'impersonal justification' that is needed to justify public policy (p. 230). This calls for a more general process of validation, which distinguishes between the legitimacy of legislative acts and whether they are in keeping with our personal beliefs. 'Though it has to do with epistemology, it is not skepticism but a kind of epistemological restraint: the distinction between what is needed to justify belief and what is needed to justify the employment of political power depends on a higher standard of objectivity, which is ethically based' (p. 229).

The fundamental premise seems to be that the jurisdiction of the legislature has ethical limits. The question of moral legitimacy raises issues with respect to the nature and extent of this jurisdiction. These issues are meta-ethical rather than ethical, and do not call upon us to determine the precise moral correctness of particular policy decisions. This may raise psychological questions as to whether we can put aside our personal opinions in deciding such issues. This is a matter of degree however. It does not detract from the essential argument, which is that people with different views may nevertheless agree that they need to justify their opinions on 'a common ground of justification'.

Nagel shies away from the idea that we can find agreement on the content of our moral opinions. Instead, he speculates that there might be a set of objective beliefs, which exists outside the normal categories of personal opinion.

> The real difficulty is to make sense of this idea, the idea of something which is neither an appeal to my own beliefs nor an appeal to beliefs that we all share. It cannot be to the latter because it is intended precisely to justify the forcible imposition in some cases of measures that are not universally accepted. (p. 231)

But the idea that there is some third category of beliefs is metaphysically dubious.

Nagel nevertheless postulates some universal but subjectively uncommitted perspective, which allows us to judge policy issues from a vantage point outside our personal opinions. It is the concept of impartiality that provides the 'universal standpoint' that is needed to decide contested cases (p. 231). Although there are substantive elements in this concept, it operates on broad procedural principles. In the end, there is not enough room for agreement on matters like 'abortion, sexual conduct, and the killing of animals for food' to subject them to moral restrictions.[28] This seems to defeat the purpose of the exercise, since these are exactly the kind of pressing moral issues that call for regulation.

Nagel seems to miss the relevant issue. It is a mistake to try and articulate a set of ethical opinions that we all can share, whatever perspective we adopt. The question that arises in the context of legitimacy is merely whether there is an identifiable set of opinions and policies that can be justified on the basis of the moral consensus in society. This is a wide-ranging set of opinions, which includes many conflicting views. The active principle lies in the converse of such a proposition: there are certain policies that cannot be justified under the body of moral and legal principles that we hold in common. It is these policies that are morally and legally illegitimate.

There is a sense in which it can be said that the legal principle of legitimacy is based on the general consent of the members of society. Jürgen Habermas expresses this when he writes that 'laws count as legitimate only if their *addressees* can jointly regard themselves as their *authors*'.[29] Properly understood, this means that the legal inquiry is based on a unanimous body of principle. This gives legal principles a more authoritative moral pedigree than democratic decisions, which merely rest on the support of the majority. The significance of this in the context of secession lies in the fact that it includes minorities.

This explains a great deal of the constitutional process. The central feature of legal and constitutional reasoning is that it rests on beliefs and principles to which we have consented. It is universally accepted, for example, that individuals are equal in some inherent sense. Nor is there any debate whether individuals are entitled to freedom of expression, security of the person or a host of similar rights and freedoms. The political legitimacy of a particular measure is not sufficient to establish its legal or constitutional legitimacy, that violates these rights and freedoms which is rooted in general principles rather than the outcome of a particular case.

It is the formal and deductive nature of the legal process that gives the judiciary the moral independence to determine the legal legitimacy of the actions of political actors. This is primarily because it leaves room for the courts to develop moral inferences that are out of keeping with popular views. As a result, the courts are not merely entitled to disagree with the public; they are often obliged to do so.

It is only the most fundamental moral principles that will serve as legitimating principles. The court in *Casey* acknowledges this in holding that the principles that justify a legal decision must, in the court's words, be 'beyond dispute'. They accordingly provide a neutral means of deciding legal questions, in spite of their substantive character. It is not particularly relevant whether underlying legal principles are thought to be morally valid because of their substantive content, because they meet with general agreement or because they meet some other criteria.

The authority of the legal process comes from its moral sources. Much of the mandate of the courts in constitutional cases derives from this moral jurisdiction, which places practical, procedural and substantive limits on the actions taken in the political realm. A court that decides a constitutional issue is determining whether the legislature has acted within the legitimate confines of its jurisdiction. This calls for a process of reasoning that determines whether private and public actors have acted within the parameters in which they are morally and legally entitled to act.

The reasoning of the courts is general and tentative, and differs from the kind of reasoning that is employed in determining whether ordinary ethical decisions are correct. The applicable legal standard can be found in the notion of reasonableness. This is a familiar judicial concept and informs the concept of proportionality, which finds its way into any constitutional analysis. This requires an analysis of the relative importance of the purpose of legislation, the extent of its effect on individual rights, and its logical success in meeting such a purpose.[30] The constitutional task is purposive and contextual.

The standard of reasonableness is flexible and is not open to precise determination. The relevant test must be something like implausibility: it is only when the decisions of the state lose their moral plausibility that they fail to meet the standard of reasonableness and lose their legitimacy. This test is permissive and the implausibility must be stark. It is those in political power who retain the fundamental responsibility for making policy decisions.

The tension between the political and legal standards of legitimacy has a number of consequences. For one thing, it opens up the possibility of ideological struggles between the legal and political branches of government.

This may consist of rearguard skirmishes by a conservative judiciary, or progressive forays into the moral debates of the day. These forays come at a price, however, and a court that enters too far into the political arena will undermine its own legitimacy. It is notable that this legitimacy has a fundamental political element, since a judicial system cannot function meaningfully without popular support.

Notes

1 Locke, *Second Treatise of Government*, §119.

2 Marston, *King and Congress*, p. 18. Marston continues: 'By midcentury, Blackstone had incorporated the concept into his lectures and ultimately into his *Commentaries*, giving semilegal status to the idea that "allegiance is the tie or *ligamen*, which binds the subject to the King, in return for that protection which the King affords the subject".'

3 Campbell, 'Obligation: social, political and legal', p. 148.

4 Harris, 'The moral obligation to obey the law', p. 178f. And see the passage at p. 178: 'The three conditions under which there is a general prima facie obligation to obey the law in a particular society (the institution of law is necessary to help secure the social conditions for a moral life for any moral person in that society, the law fulfills that function, and does so in accordance with the requirements of reasoned discourse and the respect due to moral persons) may be thought to constitute such a stiff test that it is unlikely that they could be satisfied by the way law operates in any large modern society, even a liberal democracy.'

5 Martin, 'The character of political allegiance in a system of rights', p. 212.

6 Green, 'Consent and community', p. 101f.

7 Hume, 'Of the origin of government', p. 114.

8 See Christopher Wellman in 'Liberalism, samaritanism, and political legitimacy', at p. 217: 'Put plainly, there will always be people unwilling to honour the moral rights of others if there were no legal repercussions of violating them. Moral rights will be respected and peace will be ensured only if police effectively protect individuals and recognized judges impartially adjudicate conflicts according to established rules.'

9 Hume, 'Of the original contract', p. 445.

10 'What necessity', Hume writes, '... is there to found the duty of *allegiance* or obedience to magistrates on that of *fidelity* or a regard to promises, and to suppose, that it is the consent of each individual, which subjects him to government; when it appears, that both allegiance and fidelity stand precisely on the same foundation, and are both submitted to by mankind, on account of the apparent interests and necessities of human society?' (p. 455).

11 The members of a minority might remain in a country precisely because they wish to dispute the legitimacy of the state.

12 This goes into moral territory. As a matter of common sense, we agree that a theatre will be darkened when the a film is shown. And we cannot complain if we stumble, merely because the lights are out. This goes beyond our personal knowledge of theatres. In a very real sense, we have consented to such a circumstance, in purchasing a ticket, and accepted that the owners of the theatre are entitled to act in the manner of reasonable theatre owners. The law of contract and negligence constantly addresses these kinds of issues.

13 For a discussion of Kant's position as it pertains to private property, see Kevin Dodson's article, 'Autonomy and authority in Kant's *Rechtslehre*'. And see the laconic comment at p. 109, where Dodson concludes: 'Outside of civil society, there can be no juridical legislation compatible with the autonomy of moral agents.'

14 Nielsen, 'State authority and legitimation', p. 219. Nielsen moves away from such an argument in the rest of the paper however, postulating 'ideal speech conditions' in which

an 'undistorted discourse' might reveal the conditions under which we can 'impute' the 'rational consent' necessary to determine when the state has a legitimate *de jure* authority (p. 230). This is a highly conjectural argument, which ultimately holds that the possibility of democratic forms of socialism deprives the capitalist state of its *de jure* legitimate authority.

15 This view comes down to us from John Austin. Henry Sidgwick summarizes it as well as anyone in the Appendix to *The Elements of Politics*, at p. 651: 'Austin's view may be briefly stated thus: Every Positive Law of any State is a general command to do or abstain from certain acts, which is issued directly or indirectly by the Sovereign of the State to a person or persons subject to his authority, the Sovereign being that determinate person, or body of persons combined in a certain manner, that the bulk of the members of the State habitually obey ...'. The important factor for Austin is that the power of the King 'cannot be legally limited', since it is the unlimited nature of the sovereign power that gives him the authority to make and enforce the law.

See Beran, 'What is the basis of political authority?', at p. 489, where he distinguishes between 'the fact of being obeyed' and the 'right to be obeyed'. But this kind of distinction dissolves in the traditional positivist analysis. It is the fact that the King is obeyed that establishes his right to be obeyed.

16 Dyzenhaus, 'The Legitimacy of Law', p. 84

17 This jurisdiction could be derived from a political order, over and above the state. But the idea that we could premise the legitimacy of the relevant legal order in some form of world government does not address the fact that many aspects of the legal process cannot be explained by reference to a political standard.

18 The judgements in *Casey* are available at: http://supct.law.cornell.edu/supct/html/91-744.ZO.html.

19 See *Casey*, at p. 963: 'The Judicial Branch derives its legitimacy, not from following public opinion, but from deciding by its best lights whether legislative enactments of the popular branches of Government comport with the Constitution. The doctrine of *stare decisis* is an adjunct of this duty, and should be no more subject to the vagaries of public opinion than is the basic judicial task' (p. 10).

20 The authority of such a process has been diminished by the prevailing skepticism with regard to the practice of giving reasons. See Margaret Moore, for example, 'On reasonableness'.

21 The judgement in *Reference Re Secession* is available at: http://www.droit.umontreal.ca/doc/csc-scc/.

22 See the comment of Friedman, in 'Is there a modern legal culture?', at p. 129: 'Legitimacy is a procedural concept; and there is some evidence that people do value fair procedure for its own sake (Tyler 1990). But they may value *substance* more; and the courts, when they deliver the goods, can rank high indeed in public esteem. The elective or majoritarian principle is after all not totally beyond criticism or discussion (Offe 1984). Indeed, the whole concept of rights is a denial of the majoritarian principle.'

23 One might ask whether the principle of natural justice that gives a party affected by a decision the right to know the substantive reasons for the decision is a procedural or a substantive principle?

24 The moral standards within states are converging and by the same reasoning could eventually provide the constitutional basis for some form of world government.

25 Applbaum, 'Democratic legitimacy and official discretion'.

26 See the passage from Applbaum, at p. 251: 'A purely procedural view of justice, in which justice is nothing other than the outcome of a specified procedure, may collapse into a view of legitimacy, where the justice question of "what to decide" – given substantive conflict of interests, beliefs, or values – cannot be separated from the legitimacy question of "how to decide" or "who is to decide". But the procedural view will always raise an issue of legitimacy, and the significant question, in such a context, is whether it is sufficient to decide substantive issues.'

27 See Applbaum, at p. 256, footnote 37, where he refers to an article by Amy Gutmann and Dennis F. Thompson entitled 'Moral conflict and political consensus', *Ethics* **101** (1990): 64–88, and comments: 'Gutmann and Thompson emphasize principles of public deliberation – consistency and mutual respect, for example – but substantive principles might govern legislative reasons as well: protect minorities, benefit the least advantaged, strengthen democratic institutions, and so on.'

28 There is more room for agreement on these matters than Nagel acknowledges. Few people would object to regulating abortion in the final trimester of a pregnancy. And few people would accept that the killing of animals for food is justified, if it is accompanied by cruelty. Many forms of sexual conduct – paedophilia, bestiality, sadism, necrophilia – come within the normal range of legislative action.

29 Habermas, 'Human rights and sovereignty', p. 10.

30 See the early case of *Dudgeon* v. *United Kingdom* (1981) 4 European Human Rights Reports 149 (Eur.Ct.H.R.), at 165–8, where the court ruled that laws prohibiting homosexual acts failed the proportionality test and therefore violated the petitioner's right 'to respect for his private life' under Article 8 of the *European Convention on Human Rights*. And see *R.* v. *Oakes* [1986] 1 S.C.R. 103, which sets out the Canadian methodology for determining whether legislation is a 'reasonable limit' under the *Canadian Charter of Rights and Freedoms*. One of the basic questions that arises in this context is whether the purpose and effect of the legislation are proportional.

Chapter 3

The Historical Problem of Sovereignty

This chapter discusses the historical problem of secession. The problem lies in the concept of sovereignty, which provides the major obstacle to any theory that requires the transfer of the title to the sovereign power. The traditional view vests this title in the political legitimacy of the state. On such a view, any questions regarding the validity of the state's title to the sovereign power can only be decided politically. It is only the people who have the right to determine, outside the constitutional order, whether the political authority of the state is valid.

This leaves no room for a legal solution to the problem of secession. The chapter accordingly argues that the principle of legality must be extended into the realm in which states exist. This principle must takes some measure of priority over the political will. This is a departure from the Westphalian system, under which states were entitled to pursue their domestic policies without interference. As a result, states have essentially existed outside the legal order.

It has become customary to remark that the term 'sovereignty' has its difficulties. Daniel Philpott, for example, observes: 'Lassa Oppenheim wrote in 1905 that it is "doubtful whether any single word has caused so much intellectual confusion", and Richard Falk has more recently suggested jettisoning the concept altogether.'[1] The historical sense of the term can be seen in F.H. Hinsley's definition of sovereignty as 'the idea that there is a final and absolute political authority in the political community' and that '*no final and absolute authority exists elsewhere*'.[2]

The older conception of sovereignty has lost ground to a more qualified concept, which seems more in keeping with the current state of international affairs. Philpott, for example, argues that the concept of authority lies under all of the different meanings that have attached themselves to the notion of sovereignty. He then quotes R.P. Wolff, who writes that 'authority' is 'the right to command and correlatively, the right to be obeyed'.[3] This leads him to describe sovereignty as '*supreme legitimate authority within a territory*' (p. 357).

It might seem that territory is the decisive issue in secession, since a legal decision on the issue will have to address the state's claim to territory. It is the state's jurisdiction over persons that matters, however, and the territorial question merely reflects the fact that the legal jurisdiction of a state is usually measured by the land under its control. The state has a title to the legal, moral and physical government of the territory, rather than the land itself.

This deserves a legal gloss: it might be said that the state has the underlying title to the land, but this is not a title in the proper sense of the word. It is the residual concretion in which any other title vests. The point of title is that it is severable; whereas the state's interest in land cannot be severed or relinquished.

Philpott writes that authority in a general sense 'is legitimate when it is rooted in law, tradition, consent or divine command, and when those living under it generally endorse this notion' (p. 355). This opens up a variety of possibilities, but the argument that sovereignty is only 'legitimate' if it is assented to, or 'regarded as part of the normal, proper state of affairs' rests the authority of the state on its political legitimacy.[4] This neglects the legal aspects of the concept.

The law-making power of the state was historically traced to its political legitimacy. In the international arena at least, this was measured by the fact of its rule. The essential issue is whether the state has effective control of the population and territory inside its borders. This is important because the legal order cannot function satisfactorily without the certainty provided by a sovereign government, which guarantees the stability of the legal order. The state is a guarantor, which cannot maintain its guarantee without the power to determine, finally and without contest, the contents of the positive law. The danger lies in the unqualified nature of such an assertion, which leaves out the role played by the courts in managing the process.

The state has historically been seen as the source of positive law. In the view of the sixteenth-century Jesuit, Francisco de Vitoria, for example, the state protected and preserved the common good. As John Doyle writes, this justifies the existence of a 'public power', much like the legal prerogative that David Hume describes in his essay on the original contract. 'For if the good condition (*incolumitas*) of men requires their association and gathering together, it is also a fact that no society can persist without some force (*vis*) and power (*potestas*) governing it and providing for it ...'[5] It is the sovereign power that contains the coercive authority of the state and thereby generates the legal order. The possession of this power provides a state with the resources to require that the people obey the law. Since the legal power is unlimited, it guarantees the independence of the state.

There is an extensive literature that vests the 'sovereignty' of the state in its claim to the legal jurisdiction over a particular territory. Thomas Biersteker and Cynthia Weber write that Hans Morgenthau, among more recent authors, 'defined sovereignty in legal terms as "the appearance of a centralized power that exercised its lawmaking and law-enforcing authority within a certain territory"'.[6] This again reflects the fact that the law has its source outside itself, in a political power that invests the legal order with the certainty that gives it the compulsory character of law.

As Daniel Philpott writes, the modern concept of sovereignty is usually said to derive from the Peace of Westphalia in 1648:

> Westphalia set new standards for each of sovereignty's three faces. It made the sovereign state the legitimate political unit. It implied that basic attributes of statehood such as the existence of a government with control of its territory were now, along with Christianity, the criteria for becoming a state. Finally, as it came to be practised, the Treaty removed all legitimate restrictions on a state's activities within its territory.[7] (p. 364)

The Treaty of Westphalia established that foreign powers were obliged to respect the religion of the state, as determined by the ruler. This eventually gave rise to the general principle that states are not entitled to intervene in the affairs of other states.

In *Natural Law and the Theory of Society*, Otto Gierke argues that the evolution of the concept of the state has been determined by two conditions:

> One is the existence of a society (*societas civilis*), directed to the objects which compel men to live together: the other is the existence of a sovereign power (*majestas, summa potestas, summum imperium, supremitas,* etc.), which secures the attainment of a common end. Both of these attributes recur in every definition of the state. (Vol. I, p. 40)

It is the second attribute that is the more significant, historically, and Gierke informs us that the 'philosophical theory of the State ... becomes increasingly, and essentially, a theory of sovereignty' (Vol. I, p. 36).[8]

This gives rise to a question regarding the creation of new states, or political events like the annexation of one state by another. How is the title to the sovereign power transferred from one state to another? This is important because any legal right of secession will place limitations on the ownership of the sovereign power and subject the state to legal restrictions. There are historical precedents for such an explanation in the development of the concept of the state, and Vitoria makes a significant distinction between the sovereign and the state. This permits him to hold that while the sovereign derives his power from God, the warrant to exercise it comes from the people. As a result, the Indians in the new world had the right to transfer their political allegiance to the Spanish King. Such a transfer, endorsed by the consent of the majority, would grant the Spanish King 'lawful title, even by natural law' Doyle, *Vitoria* (p. 54).

Vitoria's successor, Francisco Suárez, provides a more detailed account of the genesis of the state. In becoming a political society, the people of the state become a 'mystical body', from which the power of the state derives.[9] It is the state's possession of this power that brings it into being. As Carlos G. Noreña writes, 'God created human nature in such [a] way that once humans decide to congregate into a political body, they are invested with a sovereign power which they are free to transfer or not to transfer to a king or to an assembly'.[10] This brings in the notion of a contract. Although Suárez argued that this act of will transferred all the power within the state to the King, the people as a whole were entitled to reclaim their liberty 'according to the conditions of the original contract or according to the requirements of natural justice' (p. 266).

This recalls the position taken by Hobbes, who appears to have been familiar with the work of Suárez and gives the people a similar right to defend themselves against an oppressive sovereign. As Richard Tuck writes, however, Hobbes does not believe that the people have the right to take on government themselves.

> In all his political works, Hobbes distanced himself from the republicans by insisting that 'the people' could not withdraw their collective permission from their sovereign to act as their agent and take government into their own hands. His argument here rested on the subtle point that the unity of the people was constituted by the initial agreement to follow the sovereign's judgement and could not be retained if the sovereign was repudiated – the people would become what he termed a 'multitude' rather than 'a people' ...[11]

There is no people without a state, and the sovereign power can be dissolved and re-created. This kind of argument would permit the break-up of one state into a number of states, since the 'multitude' could be refashioned as a number of peoples. It does not, however, provide for the transfer of the sovereign power – and the legal continuity that goes with it – from one state to another.

There may be historical reasons for Hobbes's position, since it would have justified the execution of Charles I. John Locke, on the other hand, was writing under the shadow of the events that culminated in 'the glorious revolution' of 1688. These events called for a theory that explained how the moral and legal features of the system could survive the dissolution and reintegration of the state. Locke deals with this problem by holding that society survives the dissolution of the government. As a result, the people retain a residual authority over the government and the legal order created by the constitution, which preserves the continuity of the state.

This is an important step towards the recognition of an extra-constitutional legal order that determines the validity of the state's title to the sovereign power. Although Locke's position is sufficient to provide a feasible theory of revolution, which takes place outside the legal and political orders, it retains a political character. Locke essentially locates the source of political power in the people, and argues that the sovereign power exists in the popular will, above the constitution and the state. The people constitute something like a political personality, outside the political order, which can transfer the coercive power of the state to another state. This political personality only emerges in the act of revolution, however, and is not subject to any legal regulation.

Locke was arguing against the views of Robert Filmer, who argued that political authority was based on the relationship between a father and his children. People are never free, on such a view, and have no right to choose a government. 'Contrary to Filmer's "great position"', Joshua Cohen writes,

'Locke held that human beings are naturally free *because* such natural human obligations as those of children to parents are not political obligations nor do they imply the existence of political obligations (1.6; 2.6).'[12] The argument is that these 'natural human obligations' are moral rather than political. This is important because it places the question of legitimacy in the political rather than the moral arena, where it can only be decided on a contractual basis.[13]

On the other hand, Locke's position acknowledges that there are moral obligations outside the political realm, which are essential to the maintenance of society. It therefore raises the question whether the political order and the contract on which it rests can be externally justified, on the basis of the natural law. As Patrick Riley writes, this law:

> ... is not instituted by consent, even by a Groatian 'universal' consent, as Locke explains best in his *Essays on the Law of Nature*. Nor does it merely define 'certain privileges in this or that place'. It is rather the law 'which God has set to the actions of men', and it is 'the only true touchstone of moral rectitude'. (p. 64)

It is the existence of this moral jurisdiction that raises the possibility of a legal ruling on the question of legitimacy.

The historical view was that the natural law is a product of the divine order. It accordingly applies whether we agree to it or not. The natural law is available to everyone however, through the exercise of the faculty of reason and there is nothing to prevent us from reaching a consensus as to the body of principles that comprise it. This is significant in dealing with the sovereign power, since it allows us to distinguish between the consent of the people to the political authority of the state and their consent to the moral principles under which this authority must be justified. It is the latter form of consent that provides the possibility of an independent standard of legal legitimacy, outside the political arena.

The significant factor is that the natural law has the force of law, in spite of its extra-constitutional character. This is evident in the *Second Treatise*, where Locke distinguishes between the source of a magistrate's authority to punish a native and an alien offender. As Riley writes,

> ... since the alien offender is in a state of nature with respect to the host state, and since the state of nature has a law of nature to govern it, those magistrates can certainly, as executors of the law of nature, enforce that law against the offender. A native offender, however, would be punished under the civil law to which he had in some way consented, and this law would be merely 'regulated' by the natural law. (p. 68)

It follows that the courts are entitled to fall back on the natural law in the exercise of their judicial functions.

Locke believed the moral legitimacy of civil authority derives from a divine or theocratic order. Riley writes that this emanates from his belief that the divine order contains the moral law:

> A little later in the sixth *Essay* [in the *Essays on the Law of Nature*] contractarianism is left out of the account altogether, and Locke defines legitimate authority simply in terms of a delegation of power by the will of God: 'all that dominion which the rest of law-makers exercise over others ... they borrow from God alone, and we are bound to obey them because God willed thus, and commanded thus, so that by complying with them we also obey God'. (p. 70)

There is a sense in which Locke rests the validity of the state's title to the sovereign power in its legal legitimacy, since it is the natural law that gives the people the right to rebel in an appropriate set of circumstances.

Locke's account of the relationship between the natural law and political authority sets out two important principles. One is that the people have a right of revolution. This gives them the underlying title to the sovereign power, which can be transferred from one sovereign to another. The second is that the natural law extends well beyond the positive law. It would accordingly provide a convenient foundation for any body of law that determines whether a state possesses a valid title to the sovereign power. The contemporary question is whether there is a universal body of substantive principle that could be used in deciding issues regarding the ownership of the sovereign power.

The practical problem with Locke's view is that it does not provide for any adjudication of disputes regarding the title to the sovereign power. There is no independent authority that can determine the justice of a particular cause. There is only God. This does not present a problem in a simple case of revolution, where the interests of the people converge in a common desire to remove themselves from the social contract. It is exactly the problem, however, in the instance of a right to secession, which arises most visibly when a majority oppresses a minority. Locke's theory does not provide for an impartial judge to adjudicate disputes between the majority and a minority and does not address the problem of an immoral majority.

Locke's view is much in keeping with the historical account. In *Natural Law and the Theory of Society*, Otto Gierke writes that the traditional sources of the public law, the *jus naturale*, the *jus gentium* and the *jus positivum*, were simplified in the period leading up to the middle of the seventeenth century.

> ... the category of *jus gentium* inevitably proved itself to be inapplicable to public law. The result was – in the sphere of the philosophy of law and of political theory as well as in the legal treatises of jurists who included public law in their scope – that the tripartite division of law yielded more and more to a simple division between the categories of natural and positive law. (Vol. I, p. 38)

This is a broad concept of the natural law, which needs to be distinguished from the more restricted concept that provided the basis of the contemporary international law.

The irony is that the natural law theoretically continued to take priority over other forms of law, even as the political notion of sovereignty deprived the courts of any means of enforcing it against the state. As the 'theocratic idea' waned, the natural law 'was no longer derived from the divinely ordained harmony of the universal whole ... it was simply explained by itself'.

> The starting-point of speculation ceased to be general humanity: it became the individual and self-sufficing sovereign State; and this individual State was regarded as based on a union of individuals, in obedience to the dictates of Natural Law, to form a society armed with supreme power. (p. 40)[14]

The essential assumption was that the state was formed 'in obedience to the dictates' of the moral order, which ultimately licensed the state, and provided the obvious means of evaluating its legitimacy.

At the same time, however, the separation of the natural and the positive law gave rise to a conception of the state that enjoyed the *potestas legibus soluta*, the absolute plenitude of legal and political power that we associate with later conceptions of the sovereign state. As Gierke writes:

> The original negative conception – the conception of a power which is not externally subject to any *Superior* – is made to assume a positive form by being as it were turned 'outside in', and used to denote the relation of the State to everything which is within itself. From the quality of being the 'supreme' earthly authority [i.e., the quality of being simply the *highest* authority], there is deduced the whole of that absolute omnipotence [i.e. the quality of being the *only* authority, and therefore unlimited and all-powerful] which the modern State demands for itself. (Vol. I, p. 41; Barker's interpolations)

This is presumably explained by historical and economic factors that concentrated secular power within individual states, even as it undermined any competing religious or moral power.

Be that as it may, it was the natural law that provided the basis of any legal justification of the state.

> Positive law being denied any capacity to affect or disturb the foundations of Natural Law, the solution of every fundamental problem in regard to the relation of the community to the individual, or that of the Ruler to the People, was accordingly left to the scope of a Law of Nature which sat high enthroned above the whole of historically established law. (p. 39)

The natural law accordingly has a constitutional character and provides a legal source of authority that regulates the political will. This is where the concept of legal legitimacy can be found historically, outside the system of ordinary positive law.

Gierke's larger argument is that the increasingly unrestricted power of the state ultimately led to the conceptual division of the sovereign power. This placed moral boundaries on the state: political authority 'was by its nature divided', so that the state, the individual and groups all retained some inalienable aspects of the sovereign power.

> The truth is that a contract between king and people is the basis of their relations (§§17–20); and in interpreting this contract we must start neither from Hobbes' view that the people necessarily devolved the whole of its rights, nor from the view of Althusius that the people could not in any way alienate its supreme authority, but rather from the assumption that there is at one and the same time a real alienation of majesty and a reservation of popular rights which limit its exercise.[15] (Vol. I, p. 138)

Gierke suggests that the purpose of the law is to regulate these relationships and rights, in accordance with the moral order.[16] This requires a legal umpire, who has the final say in any resolution of the conflicts between the parties within the state.

This has the features of a constitutional democracy, but does not address the questions that arise with respect to the ownership and transfer of the sovereign power.

> ... the more sovereignty was exalted, the hotter raged the dispute about its 'Subject' or owner. Here again the ultimate decision was sought on the basis of Natural Law. Though there was a general agreement that a variety of constitutional forms had been produced by positive law, the fundamental issue of the ownership of sovereignty was none the less regarded as prior to the historical differentiation of constitutions. (p. 42)

The problem is that matters like secession throw the legitimacy of the entire constitutional order into question. As a result, they must be decided under an external source of authority like the natural law, which exists outside the constitutional order.

Although secession occurs inside rather than outside the state, it accordingly takes place outside the ordinary legal and political orders. This is a product of the principle of political primacy that places the source of political authority above the source of the legal order. The difficulty is that this places it beyond the reach of legal constraints. It follows that the extra-constitutional realm is inchoate: there is no law, in the ordinary and compulsory sense, in the place where the sovereign power originates.

The jurisdiction of the civil and constitutional courts does not extend into this area. As a practical matter, the argument is that the validity of the state's title to the sovereign power can only be decided politically and informally. This means that the extra-constitutional norms that govern the state's title to the sovereign power can only be enforced by the people, in an unrestrained exercise of the popular will. We have only the political will to regulate such matters. There may be moral conventions, or the expectations of a civil people. But there is little else.

It follows that the rights of a minority are at the mercy of the majority in the extra-constitutional realm. This explains the rationale of a legal right to secede. There must be something to deal with the exercise of the political will in the extra-constitutional realm, when it runs against the rights of minorities. This is only possible, however, if there are substantive principles outside the positive law that bind the state. This is a new natural law, which can be found in the moral consensus that exists within the entire community of states. The compulsory character of this body of principles is essential, if it is to be of any use against an unwilling state.

Without such a legal regime, there is nothing to bind the state in the extra-constitutional realm. Gierke struggles with this issue, and is essentially forced to adopt the much weaker position that states are obliged to respect moral conventions:

> ... the fact that a supreme power is needed, in order to realise fully the compulsoriness demanded by the nature of Law, does not prevent Law from still being Law even though, in a particular case, compulsion is lacking, or can only be imperfectly applied, or is altogether impossible for want of a higher power which is capable of using it – provided only that there really is a common conviction that compulsion would be right if it were possible, or if a competent authority were in existence. (Vol. I, p. 225)

This is determined but feeble. Gierke is visibly uncomfortable with the lack of compulsion in such a scheme and his assertions are evasions, which only draw attention to the deficiencies of the modern state system.

The historical development of the political notion of sovereignty may have reached its apogee in the work of Carl Schmitt, who believed that there are aspects of government beyond the reach of any constitution. As Renato Cristi writes, in *Carl Schmitt and Authoritarian Liberalism*:

> According to Schmitt's *Politische Theologie*, the state had 'the monopoly of the ultimate decision' ... This meant that the essence of sovereignty, which he defined 'not as the monopoly of domination or coercion, but as the monopoly of decision' ... was the ability to lift its subject above the legally constituted order.[17] (p. 108)

The importance of Schmitt's concept is that sovereignty is an exclusively political attribute, which has primacy over the legal order.

The sovereign power is found in the *pouvoir constituant*, in Schmitt's view, which sustains the constitutional order and maintains its continuity. This creates a level of government policy or practice that exists outside constitutional restraints. 'Constituent power', Cristi writes:

> ... cannot be destroyed, changed or altered in any way; it perseveres as the extraconstitutional ground of constitutions and constitutional laws. It is not exhausted by its exercise and 'retains the ability to persevere in its existence'. The positive constitution, as an accident supported by constituent power, may be born, suffer alterations and eventually die, but alongside and above it the *pouvoir constituant* continues to exist. (p. 199)

Schmitt held that the National Constituent Assembly formed after the Kaiser's abdication, was, in Cristi's words, 'animated by the constituent power of the

German people'. As a result, it possessed a completely unrestricted authority and could be described as 'a sovereign dictatorship' (p. 197).

The ownership of the constituent power is free of legal and moral regulation, and exists in the unregulated political realm where the original contract between the people and the ruler was formed.[18]

> According to Schmitt, this power, the demiurge or *natura naturans* of a constitution, 'remains always outside the realm of the rule of law' ... The distinction between constitutional liberal and political elements finds here its ultimate foundation. All attempts to situate sovereignty within the constitution itself remained abstractions that missed the reality of the political. (p. 132)

The title to the sovereign power is accordingly found in the popular will, unhindered by any constraints. There is nothing in Schmitt's formulation that requires that the constituent power be exercised in accordance with moral prescriptions. This asserts the primacy and ultimately the supremacy of the political authority.

There are elements of Schmitt's view in other authors. Sergio Cotta suggests that there are four sources of legitimacy in the historical evolution of the term: the first is consent, deriving from the notion of a social contract; the second is hereditary succession; the third is republican, expressing the tradition of a political community; and the fourth is a written constitution. All of these, he suggests, express the political will, and implicitly reverse the classical conception.

> This is of course a radical reversal of the classic relationship between the juridical order and the political order, since it is the latter that from then on would be superior to the first ... We thus arrive at a purely political theory of legitimacy, freed from its dependence on juridical theory.[19]

Cotta goes on to argue that the origins of the political theory of legitimacy can be found in the 'classic idea of the *common good*' and propose a phenomenology of the common good, which expresses the will of the people.

The problem in all these accounts of the title to the sovereign power is the same. There is nothing in the act of willing that keeps it within moral bounds. The historical view is that the manifestation of the collective will that transfers the ownership of the sovereign power to a new state is exclusively political. As a result, there is no legal machinery to regulate the actors in this area and it is impossible for the courts – which stand historically inside the constitutional order – to decide the validity of such a title. This does not in itself mean that the actors in this inchoate political realm are fee of moral obligations. The point is that these moral obligations are not compulsory and cannot be legally regulated.

These statements come with an important reservation, since common law courts have occasionally exercised a provisional authority to determine whether a particular political order is legitimate. The issue has arisen, historically, in the context of revolution. And while Allen Buchanan recognizes the connection between revolution and secession, there is a stronger affinity between the two events than his comments would suggest.[20] That is because the essential facet of a revolution is that it annuls the constitutional order and dissolves the legal personality of the state. The same is true for secession: although movements for secession are geographically restricted, the legal significance of secession derives from the fact that it replaces the sovereign and brings the existing legal order to an end.

The legal problem of secession is therefore one of transition. In the view of the common law, a unilateral act of secession constitutes a revolutionary act, which creates a hiatus in the legal order. As Peter Hogg, Canada's foremost constitutional scholar, writes with regard to the prospect of Quebec's secession:

> In assessing the legality of a regime established by revolution – meaning any break in legal continuity – the issue for the courts is simply whether or not the revolution has been successful. As de Smith says, 'legal theorists have no option but to accommodate their concepts to the facts of political life'.[21]

In the last century, the courts in South Africa, Pakistan, Cyprus, Uganda and what was Rhodesia, have all ruled on the legality of political actions that disrupt the existing constitutional order.

This may be as simple as a ruling as to the legal efficacy of a *coup d'état*, or a more complex decision with respect to the status of Imperial and colonial statutes. In 1952, to cite one example, the South African courts ruled that the ordinary legislation creating the apartheid regime was invalid.[22] The legislation explicitly repealed provisions of the existing constitution and could only be construed as an extra-constitutional measure, which arose outside the ordinary legal and political orders.

It will be apparent that the South African government eventually succeeded in its original aims, through a variety of legal and political strategies. The case is nonetheless significant, since it illustrates that the extraordinary political realm where the title to the sovereign power exists is subject to some degree of judicial scrutiny. S.A. de Smith, to whom Hogg is referring, writes that this kind of decision contains a moral element:

> ... although, for anybody living within that legal order, the attitude of the judges in office must be conclusive for the time being, it does not follow that the judges ought to regard themselves as having an arbitrary discretion in deciding what view to take. Judges are no more exempt from moral obligations than other officers of state in revolutionary situations. Indeed, moral obligation may weigh more heavily on them than on any other group of officers. For on the one hand, if they resign in protest their successors may be of so low a calibre that justice may not be done in the courts; whilst on the other hand, if they continue in office their real or apparent acknowledgement of the authority of the new regime will clothe it with the valued prize of legitimacy. (p. 104f)

This takes us to the doorstep, at least, of the legal question of legitimacy. In spite of this, the instincts of the judiciary seem to lie in the direction of preserving the social order, and courts have used the doctrine of necessity to preserve the continuity of the legal order in revolutionary situations.

Smith argues that doctrines like necessity merely obscure the fact that the courts are making a political rather than a legal decision in such circumstances. The obvious historical example is the American revolution. How, de Smith asks,

> ... did the thirteen colonies achieve sovereign independence as the United States of America? The answer, from the point of view of those judges and magistrates who remained on the bench throughout the War of Independence, was that the colonists, the People, had accomplished a successful revolution which untied the apron strings binding them to Britain. The new legal order, from which the sovereignty of Parliament was eliminated, was grounded on political facts.[23]

The people had accordingly annulled their contract with the state. This occurred outside the reach of the judiciary, in the unregulated political realm outside the legal and political orders, and the courts could only obey.

As de Smith notes, this kind of legal argument has a natural corollary:

> ... the English revolution of 1688 legitimised the Bill of Rights 1689 and all that followed because it was successful and because the judges (actuated in some cases, no doubt, by a keen sense of self-preservation) accepted Bills assented to by the usurper, William of Orange, as authentic Acts of Parliament. The revolution of 1642–49 was accepted by those judges who remained in office after Charles I's execution as legitimising Cromwellian legislation; but with the Restoration of Charles II in 1660 all became null and void. Nothing fails like failure.[24] (p. 102)

These are political rather than legal decisions, which cannot be explained by the ordinary canons of judicial reasoning. They nonetheless recognize that questions regarding the ownership of the sovereign power can only be decided outside the constitutional order, in accordance with the primacy of political authority over the legal order.

This is an extra-constitutional principle that exists outside the ordinary legal and political orders. It therefore takes precedence over the lesser principle of parliamentary supremacy, which would arguably prevent any authority – and that includes Parliament – from annulling the legal order.[25] H.W.R. Wade negotiates a way around this difficulty by arguing that the principle of parliamentary supremacy is merely a political principle that prevents one Parliament from binding its successors. It does not apply in the political realm outside the constitutional order, where the state is dissolved and reconstituted.

The principle of parliamentary supremacy is accordingly subordinate to a unique legal rule, which differs from all other legal rules by virtue of its political character. This is the rule that the courts must enforce the *Acts* of Parliament:

> The rule of judicial obedience is in one sense a rule of common law, but in another sense – which applies to no other rule of common law – it is the ultimate *political* fact upon which the whole system of legislation hangs. Legislation owes its authority to the rule: the rule does not owe its authority to legislation.[26]

Although the principle of parliamentary supremacy is a political principle, it has its origins in this legal rule, rather than the political authority of the state. The authority of Parliament rests on the willingness of the courts to apply and enforce the statutory law.

This is in apparent contravention of the principle that political authority is supreme, since the rule of obedience is a discretionary rule, which gives the judiciary the right to transfer its allegiance to a new political order.

> What [Sir John William] Salmond calls 'the ultimate legal principle' is therefore a rule which is unique in being unchangeable by Parliament ... it lies in the keeping of the courts, and no Act of Parliament can take it from them. This is only another way of saying that it is always for the courts, in the last resort, to say what is a valid Act of Parliament; and that the decision on this question is not determined by any rule of law which can be laid down or altered by any authority outside the courts. It is simply a political fact. (p. 189)

The rule of judicial obedience accordingly recognizes that the courts have the prerogative of determining whether the sovereign power and the legal powers that come with it have been transferred from one source of political authority to another.

This is a confirming power and does not challenge the primacy of political authority in the extra-constitutional realm. It nevertheless gives the courts authority to decide the factual question whether the state is politically legitimate. The revolutionary jurisprudence accordingly gives the courts the ascendant role in determining the efficacy of the new political order. If we accept the position urged by authors like Wade, 'the seat of sovereign power is not to be discovered by looking at Acts of any Parliament but by looking at the courts and discovering to whom they give their obedience' (p. 196).

This is more than a legal technicality. It is one thing to possess the sovereign power; it is another thing to legally possess it. This distinction is important because it implicitly recognizes that the legal order morally and logically supersedes the political order. The courts are obliged to apply the law, in these cases as in other cases. There is nothing here so explicit as the legal question of legitimacy, but it is inevitable that there is a moral element in such constraints. The real problem is that domestic courts are not sufficiently insulated from the political order to determine its moral validity.

The primacy of the political order also explains the historical view that there is an extra-legal realm, in which the exercise of the sovereign power cannot be subjected to legal restraints. Locke, for example, attributes a discretionary 'prerogative' to the King, who has the right to act outside the law in pursuit of the state's interests. Pasquale Pasquino writes that this prerogative 'is deployed predominantly in the domain of foreign affairs', where prudence and wisdom must govern instead of the law.[27] The English common law contains a number of immunities, which apply to a head of state, the private communications of cabinet, and suits against the crown, on the basis that the actions of the crown cannot be subjected to legal restrictions.

Although the prerogative of the sovereign has limits, Pasquino writes that these limits lie outside the formal political and legal processes.

> ... if the discretionary power of the modern prince is not a legal power, since it is a power *extra et contra legem*, it is neither an arbitrary nor irresistible power ... And, in fact, the relationship between the prince and the people is, like that which exists between the people and their legislative representatives, a relationship of *trust* and not one of subordination or slavery. If the king makes use of his power of prerogative against the common good, the people may take up arms, 'to appeal to heaven'.[28] (p. 205)

This raises the same issue as Schmitt's conception of the *pouvoir constituant*, since the appeal to heaven takes place outside the law and the political order, as a naked exercise of force. In both cases, it is the implicit permission of the majority and the political legitimacy of the state that ultimately decides the issue.

The state's ownership of the sovereign power accordingly rests on its political legitimacy. The legal problem lies in the exclusiveness of this analysis, under which the state can only preserve its internal title by maintaining the confidence of the people.[29] This vests the sovereign power in those who obtain the consent of the majority, by whatever means are available to them. The irony may be that this is particularly dangerous in a democratic context. There are many situations where it is in the interest of domestic politicians to promote policies that single out the less powerful in society, who provide a convenient target for the ire of the electorate. This includes minorities.

We are left in an impossible position. The primacy of the political order has made it impossible for domestic courts to determine the legal validity of the title to the sovereign power. This has pushed any internal questions with regard to the ownership of the sovereign power into the extra-constitutional political realm. From the perspective of secession, this is self-defeating. Under the Westphalian doctrine of sovereignty, this is a political realm, which is not subject to compulsory legal regulation. The conspiracy of circumstances could hardly be more complete.

The consequences of the prevailing theory are lamentable. We have no means of deciding legal questions with respect to the ownership of the sovereign power. The necessary compulsion can only be provided by force.

As a result, the historical solution to an oppressive state is simply insurrection. The external solution is war. John Dewey complained that this has created a 'war system' in international relations. 'Recourse to violence is not only *a* legitimate method for settling international disputes at present; under certain circumstances it is the only legitimate method, the ultimate reason of state.'[30]

There is a certain idealism in Dewey's argument for the 'outlawry of war', under which war would be a public crime under international law. His idealism was shared by many of his contemporaries, however, and rests on a simple claim.

> Now to settle disputes *finally*, whether they are between nations or individuals, the experiences and wisdom of the world have found two methods, and only two. One is the way of the law and courts; the other is the way of violence and lawlessness. In private controversies the former way is now established. In disputes among nations the way of violence is equally established. (p. 515)

These comments could easily be applied to the internal conflicts that arise with respect to the validity of the state's title to the sovereign power and the right of a minority to secede.

There is no doubt where this leaves us. David Copp is expressing the views of everyone in the area when he writes that the major argument for a legal right of secession is to prevent secessionist wars and the human suffering that comes with them.[31]

Notes

1 Philpott, 'Sovereignty: An introduction and brief history', p. 354, at note 3. Philpott's sources are L. Oppenheim, *International Law*, vol. 1 (London: Longman, 1905), p. 103, and Richard Falk, 'Sovereignty', in *Oxford Companion to Politics of the World* (Oxford: Oxford University Press, 1993), p. 854.

2 From F.H. Hinsley, *Sovereignty*, 2nd edn (Cambridge: Cambridge University, 1986), at p. 26, as quoted in Biersteker, *infra*, note 6, at p. 8.

3 The quotation is from R.P. Wolff, 'The Conflict between Authority and Autonomy', in Joseph Raz, ed., *Authority* (Oxford: Basil Blackwell, 1990), p. 20.

4 See Philpott, p. 355, at note 5: 'Here, I use legitimate in its descriptive sense not to mean justified or morally defensible, but as Max Weber meant it: Something is legitimate if it is assented to, or at least regarded as part of the normal, proper state of affairs. For Weber, authority attains its legitimacy either because it has tradition behind it, it has emotional power, it is rational or it is legal.' Philpott then cites Max Weber, 'The theory of social and economic organization', in Talcott Parsons (ed.), *Max Weber: The Theory of Social and Economic Organization* (New York: Free Press, 1947), pp. 124–32.

5 Doyle, 'Vitoria on choosing to replace a king', p. 46f. Doyle quotes from Vitoria, in *Relectio de potestate civili*, as found in Teofilo Urdánoz (ed.), *Obras de Francisco de Vitoria: Relecciones teologicas*, ed. crítica (Madrid, 1960), n. 5; p. 157: 'For if all men would be equal and subject to no power, with each one tending by his own choice and opinion in a different direction, without some providence which would have common care and concern for the common good, the republic would necessarily be pulled apart and the state would be destroyed ... .'

6 See Biersteker and Weber, 'The social construction of state sovereignty', at p. 4. The quotation is from Hans J. Morgenthau, *Politics Among Nations* (New York: Knopf, 1967), p. 299.

In 'Rethinking Sovereignty in a shrinking, fragmented world', Joseph Camilleri traces this view to the publication of Jean Bodin's *De la République*, in 1577. 'Bodin's ... main contention was that such power had to be given legal recognition. It had to be endowed with *sovereignty*. Here he uses the words *souveraineté*, *majestas*, and *summa potestas* more or less interchangeably. For Bodin, sovereignty was "supreme power over citizens and subjects unrestrained by law" and therefore unlimited in extension and duration.' The quotation is from Richard Knolles, trans. Jean Bodin, *The Six Bookes of a Commonweale* (London: Impencis G. Bishop, 1606), p. 84.

7 Cf. Barkin, 'The evolution of the constitution of sovereignty', p. 236: 'Although elements of the system had been developing for centuries, and remnants of the old feudal order were to remain in some areas of Europe for some time after, the Peace of Westphalia of 1648 is generally seen as the starting point of the modern state system.' And see Leo Gross, 'The Peace of Wesphalia, 1648–1948', *American Journal of International Law* (1948) **42**,1: 20–41, cited by Barkin.

8 And see Gierke, *Natural Law and the Theory of Society*, vol. I, at p. 137: 'So long as the State was simply treated as *societas perfectissima*, and so long as its theory was simply regarded as an illustration (if the best and completest illustration) of the general conception of *societas* already described in the previous subsection, the ideas which found most vigorous expression in natural-law theories of the State were merely the general ideas about the nature of Groups with which we are already familiar; and these general ideas were freely applied, whether their ingredients were consistent with one another or contradictory. But a new situation arose, and thinkers were confronted by fresh intellectual problems, as soon as they turned to face the conception of Sovereignty (which still continued to be the essential core of the theory of the State), and attempted to bring it into harmony with their conception of *societas*.'

9 As quoted by Noreña, *infra*, note 10, at p. 264.

10 Noreña, 'Francisco Suárez on democracy', p. 265. Noreña continues: 'Against Vitoria, however, Suárez, always bent on highlighting the formative power of human choices, maintained that such sovereign power is not immediately given by nature itself (*a natura profectum*), but through an institutional act of the human will (*mediante voluntate humana et institutione*; DF iii.2.10) ... This will is the will to form a community, which, according to natural law, cannot exist without such a power.'

11 Introduction to Hobbes, *Leviathan*, p. xix.

12 Cohen, 'Structure, choice and legitimacy: Locke's theory of the state', p. 313. The references are to the first and second treatises.

13 The contemporary literature neglects many of the difficulties in envisaging a democracy as a social contract. Who, for example, are the parties to the contract? Logically, it cannot be the people and the government, since the government only comes into existence as a result of the contract. See Gierke, vol. II, at p. 335, note 9, where he considers the idea that there is a contract between the 'popular assembly' and the people.

14 The religious aspects of the concept of the natural law should not be overstated. See Gierke, vol. I, at p. 36: 'It is true that, at first, the State was only incidentally mentioned in the works which dealt with the Law of Nature. But the ecclesiastical writers on Natural law, who generally belong to the Jesuit or the Dominican Order, are already [in the sixteenth century] constructing a system of political theory which is based entirely on the law of Reason' (Barker's interpolation).

15 See Gierke, vol. I, p. 341, note 36.

16 See Gierke, vol. I, pp. 223ff.

17 This gives the sovereign the authority to suspend the constitution in the interests of public safety and security.

18 See Gierke, vol. I, at p. 42: 'In all forms of State indifferently, a distinction was drawn

between the Ruler and the body of the Ruled: the legal basis of the Ruler's authority was regularly ascribed to a previous devolution of its own authority by the body of the Ruled; and in this way it was easy to produce a single formula, equally applicable to monarchies and to aristocratic or democratic republics, which expressed, in terms universally valid, the relations always existing between Ruler and People under the system of Natural Law.'

19 Cotta, 'Legitimacy: a mirage?', p. 100.

20 See Buchanan, 'Theories of Secession', p. 35.

21 Hogg, *Constitutional Law of Canada*, pp. 5–35. The reference to de Smith is to de Smith and Brazier, *Constitutional and Administrative Law* (6th edn, 1989), p. 67.

22 See *Harris* v. *Minister of the Interior* (2) S.A. 428 (1952) and *Minister of the Interior* v. *Harris* (4) S.A. 760 (1952), cited in S.A. de Smith, note 1 and 2, *infra*, note 23.

23 S.A. de Smith, 'Constitutional lawyers in revolutionary situations', 101f.

24 And see Wade, 'The Basis of Legal Sovereignty', at p. 188: 'When Charles I was executed in 1649 the courts continued to enforce the Acts of the Long Parliament, the Rump, Barebones' Parliament, and the other Commonwealth legislatures. For a revolution took place, and the courts (without any authority from the *previous* sovereign legislature) spontaneously transferred their allegiance from the King in Parliament to the kingless Parliaments ... This was a political fact from which legal consequences flowed. But in 1660 there was a counter-revolution: Charles II was restored, and it was suddenly discovered that all Acts passed by the Commonwealth Parliaments were void for want of the royal assent. The courts ... shifted their allegiance back to the King in Parliament, and all the Commonwealth legislation was expunged from the statute book. The "glorious revolution" of 1688 was, in its legal aspect if in no other, much like the revolution of 1649, for the courts, recognising political realities but without any *legal* justification, transferred their obedience from James II to William and Mary.'

25 This may have reached its rhetorical height in the House of Commons in 1886, when James Bryce asserted: 'There is no principle more universally assented to than the absolute omnipotence of Parliament ... .' See Wade, at p. 195. Though the word 'omnipotence' finds its way into Dicey.

26 Wade, p. 188.

27 The idea is that the law only provides general rules or principles, which are unable to account appropriately for unexpected circumstances. See Pasquino, 'Locke on king's prerogative', p. 201. Pasquino's article is written as part of a larger attempt to distinguish between the attributes of the sovereignty and dictatorship, and thereby correct the mistakes in Carl Schmitt's *Die Diktatur*.

28 See section 147 of Locke's *Second Treatise*.

29 There are obviously external factors that raise other concerns.

30 Dewey, 'The security of nations', p. 515. And see Dewey, 'Nationalism and internationalism', at p. 472f, where he makes the same observations about the means for resolving international disputes: 'For disguise it as one may, the doctrine of national sovereignty is simply the denial on the part of a political state of either legal or moral responsibility. It is a direct proclamation of the unlimited and unquestionable right of a political state to do what it wants to do in respect to other nations and to do it as and when it pleases.'

31 Copp, 'International law and morality', p. 244.

Chapter 4

Solving the Historical Problem

The solution to the historical problem of sovereignty seems relatively straightforward. It consists of recognizing the legal limitations of sovereignty. This calls for a legal doctrine of sovereignty, which holds that sovereignty is the exclusive attribute of legitimate states. The reigning principle in the new world order is that an illegitimate state is no longer legally sovereign. This brings in the legal and political concepts of legitimacy.

Any legal discussion of secession opens with the observation that the state has title to the sovereign power. If there is a legal right to secede, it is apparent that this title is defeasible. It follows that the state holds its title to the sovereign power on certain conditions. The most important feature of a legal theory of secession from a political perspective is that these conditions must be minimal. They should not be allowed to encroach on the legitimate role of the state in the provision of peace, order and good government. The conditions on this title nevertheless include an obligation to respect fundamental rights. This has a positive as well as a negative manifestation, since a state that abides by these conditions is legally legitimate. It therefore has a legal right to subsist.

This theory of legitimate sovereignty calls for legal regulation of the title to the sovereign power. This is subject to judicial scrutiny under both heads of legitimacy, though the political question remains in the political realm and cannot be decided by a court. The regulation of the sovereign power is for the purpose of placing moral limits on the powers of government. The reality is that the exercise of such a power is already subject to a significant measure of legal regulation in constitutional democracies.

The Mechanics of Legitimacy

It is necessary to set out the mechanics of a legal theory of secession before addressing the problem of sovereignty. There is no clear distinction between the legal and political concepts of legitimacy in the literature. The two concepts accordingly need to be disentangled from each other.

The role of the legal concept of legitimacy is evident in its historical use. The concept originally provided an independent means of determining whether a medieval ruler had a natural title to the sovereign power. The compulsory origins of the concept lie more in the principle of justice however, which at least theoretically placed moral curbs on the authority of a sovereign.

Henry Bracton wrote in the twelfth century that the King is subject to the body of custom that provides the wider framework of the law. This is essentially an argument that the legal principle of legitimacy takes precedence over the political, even though the King is subordinate to no one, other than God.

The legal principle of justice has its roots in the common good. This includes a substantive principle of equality, which provides some measure of legal protection for the rights of individuals and minorities. The decisions of the actors in the political realm are morally binding when they serve the community as a whole. Thomas Aquinas, for example, argues that laws should be established for the usefulness of all the citizens. 'And on account of this, laws of this kind, *imposing proportionate burdens*, are just, and they bind in the court of conscience, and are legal laws.'[1]

John Finnis writes that Aquinas

> ... draws a distinction between tyrants who abuse an authority which they acquired legitimately and tyrants who are also usurpers. Tyrannical usurpers, at least until they have acquired a legitimacy through their subjects' acceptance [*consensum*] or through ratification by some higher authority, can be resisted and repelled by anyone able to do so effectively. But legitimate rulers who govern tyrannously should rather be suffered patiently, unless and until other officials or citizens who have public authority to do so put an end to the regime, if need be by trying and executing the tyrant.[2]

This distinguishes between a political and a legal concept of legitimacy. A ruler who is politically legitimate is still subject to scrutiny of public officials, who retain the legal authority to determine the moral legitimacy of a particular regime.

Some authors have argued that legitimacy was not a significant issue in the medieval world.[3] Joseph Camilleri suggests that this was still the case in the sixteenth century:

> God, it is true, was above the prince, and the supreme power of the prince over his subjects was subordinate to the 'law of God and Nature'. But apart from this limitation, the practical consequence of which remained unclear, the sovereign was above the people, or, as Jacques Maritain has argued, 'separate from and transcendent over the people'.[4]

It may be true that earlier people believed that government was ordained by God and did not require justification. This did not extend to the identity of the monarch, however, and Camilleri underestimates the significance of the historical concept.

A ruler in the sixteenth century held the sovereign power subject to the natural law, for the benefit of all, and was not entitled to tyrannize his subjects.[5] In point of fact, it is the modern state that has become legally transcendent, since its mere existence is enough to establish its legal validity. The reality is that the institution of state sovereignty has not been legally challenged. There have always been political constraints on the state's exercise of the sovereign power, many of them informal. But there is no judicial means of questioning the legitimacy of existing states, in spite of the consensus that a state which defaults on its fundamental moral obligations no longer possesses a valid claim to power.

The historical solution to the problem of an illegitimate state was simple and brutal. The natural law gives individuals a duty of self-preservation, which takes moral priority over our political obligations. This becomes a collective right of self-defence in the work of Thomas Hobbes and John Locke, where it provides the basis of a right of revolution. If a government puts itself 'into a state of War with the People', they 'are thereupon absolved from any farther Obedience'.[6] The people have the right to divest an oppressive government of its title to the sovereign power.

This is a political rather than a legal right, however. It is of limited assistance to a minority, since it does not deal with the problem of an oppressive majority. This provides the most obvious derivation of a moral right of secession. The legal question of legitimacy cannot be remedied by an appeal to the people, if it is the will of the people that requires regulation and scrutiny. There is no historical solution to the problem, legally or politically, since the legal authority of the courts has historically stopped short of questions regarding the ownership of the sovereign power.

There is some recognition of these issues in the literature. Paul Gilbert argues that the legitimacy of the state 'is not something that can be established by a majority vote of the members of the state' (p. 10). His reasons are procedural. It is necessary for example to decide who should participate in a plebiscite. This cannot be decided democratically. It is not possible, Gilbert writes, for the majority in the existing state to decide 'who shall vote to decide who the members of the state shall be'.[7] This will predetermine the results of any vote, since it will simply choose itself. A court will always be in a better position than a political authority to decide these kinds of questions.

The legal and political process address different issues. The political process ascertains the wishes of a given group of people. This can only be decided by the majority. The problem is that majorities may often endorse the unjust acts of the state towards a minority. It is the legal concept of legitimacy that brings the will of a majority under the scrutiny of accepted moral tenets. The problem of secession is theoretically important because it illustrates the deficiencies in a simple conception of political legitimacy. It is the legal conception of legitimacy that remedies these deficiencies.

The purpose of asking whether the state is legally legitimate is accordingly to determine whether the wishes of the majority are in keeping with the principle of justice. This is a matter of maintaining a just and peaceable society, which is not possible without some means of morally correcting the political will.[8] The legal concept of legitimacy accordingly provides a test of the morality of political decisions. As a result, the legal principle takes precedence over the political principle.

The question of legal legitimacy does not arise in the instance of a state that is politically illegitimate, which is simply invalid. The question of political legitimacy is only incidentally before the court on an application for the legal right to secede. The fundamental question on a legal application is whether the state is legally legitimate. There is a second political question, which arises if the state is legally illegitimate. That is whether the minority wishes to secede. This is a matter of personal and collective autonomy.

There is a sense in which the legal right to secede can only be exercised politically, since it merely gives a minority a legal right to pose the political question. The legal right is compulsory in nature however. The purpose of awarding such a right is to require that a state respect the minority's wishes in the matter. The fundamental issue in any legal forum is justice: the legal right to secede accordingly arises when a state acts unjustly in its dealings with a minority. This does not prevent a minority from exercising its political rights in the absence of injustice, independently of any legal right to secede.

There are many examples. The legal right to secede would only arise in the instance of Quebec if the government of Canada breached the fundamental rights of those within the province. This does not prevent the people of the province from pursuing the matter in a political forum. This raises a different kind of concern. To quote Gilbert:

> Vague as it is, the claim that a form of government is undermining communal identity is a common justification for separatist campaigns. Those in Scotland and Wales provide local examples. Independent government may, to an extent, protect communal identity ... (p. 12)

This is a matter of self-determination, which does not raise the same question of injustice as the legal principle of legitimacy.

A Legal Doctrine of Sovereignty

This sets out the basic mechanics of a legal theory of secession. It is not possible to work out the details of such a theory, however, without rejecting the doctrine that states are sovereign in the traditional sense. It is rather hopeful to think that the kind of political issues that come to the surface of human relations in the instance of secession can be satisfactorily resolved in a legal system based on convention. As long as the state remains immune from legal challenges, there will be no meaningful redress for an embattled minority seeking the right of self-determination within the law.

The problem is a simple one. The Westphalian system and the principle of non-intervention may have brought a new measure of stability into the relations between states. There is another side to the Westphalian bargain, however, which has generally been neglected in political theory. It is difficult to say why this is the case. But the major feature of the Westphalian system from a legal perspective is that the conduct of the state within its affairs is not subject to significant external constraints. This means that the only restrictions on the conduct of the state with regard to minorities are internal.

The problem is that the internal restrictions on the conduct of the state are usually in the hands of the political forces within the state. And the sociological realities are implacable. It is relatively easy for a majority to take control over the apparatus of the state, which has the ultimate control over policy. This includes the appointment of judges. Legal and constitutional restrictions are ineffective in the face of a majority that is resolutely determined to deprive a minority of its rights.

The primary legacy of legal positivism was to enshrine the proposition that the political power of the state is legally unfettered.[9] This essentially leaves an oppressive state free of legal constraints in the pursuit of its domestic affairs. But, of course, the Westphalian system has already freed it from legal constraints in the extra-constitutional realm. The real challenge for legal theorists is accordingly that states have carved out a sphere of activity in the international arena that is only subject to political regulation.

There is no disputing the obligations of states. There is no meaningful reason to think, historically or otherwise, that states are above moral prescriptions. We can go further however. There is a broad consensus on many of the moral principles that govern the conduct of states.[10] These principles include an obligation to respect fundamental rights. The problem is that these obligations are political rather than legal obligations. As a result, they are of little utility in situations where the political forces inside and outside the state have no interest in enforcing them.

There is no defeating the realist position in political theory. There are situations where the polity finds it in the interest of the state to violate the rights of the minority, at the behest of a majority. This may not be a problem in the ordinary course of government. But it is in these circumstances that the classic problem of secession arises. And the problem of secession lies in enforcing these obligations in situations where the state has an active interest in violating them. The idea that this can be accomplished by political means is naive. The problem in contested cases is that it cannot be accomplished politically.

The purpose of a legal theory of secession is to provide a means for dealing with those cases where a political resolution of the issue is not possible. This requires some recognition of the legal limits of sovereignty, which restricts the enjoyment of sovereignty to legitimate states. Allen Buchanan has frequently argued that the legitimacy of the state and the international system itself is premised on its respect for basic human rights. In his latest book, *Justice, Legitimacy, and Self-Determination – Moral Foundations for International Law*, Buchanan argues for a moral theory of the international law, which would essentially ground the institution of state sovereignty in a moral rather than a political concept of legitimacy.

This is not possible, however, without extending the compulsory concept of law into the extra-constitutional realm where states theoretically exist. The mechanics of such a system are relatively simple. There must be a universal principle of legal justice, which applies in any set of social circumstances. It follows that the actions of the state must conform to such a principle. This principle of justice gives rise to subsidiary principles, which help to enumerate the purpose of the state and set out the legal parameters in which it is entitled to govern. At least some of these subsidiary principles might be found in a concept of natural rights, some notion of majority rule, the satisfaction of legitimate wants or the common good.

Although legislative instruments are necessary, along with a satisfactory institutional structure, a court trying an issue like secession derives its fundamental jurisdiction from the moral sources of the law. The natural source of a court's jurisdiction in deciding questions with regard to the title to the sovereign power is the principle of justice and our personal rights. This is partly because the competition in such cases is between the state and individual persons, standing together or alone. But it is also because these rights are morally obligatory and possess the same compulsory character as the law.

The limits on the authority of a court's ruling on a state's title to the sovereign power are accordingly determined by the legal principle of justice. This provides the foundation for a mandatory principle of legal legitimacy, which determines the legal validity of the state's title to the sovereign power. The development of this aspect of the law has been hampered by the lack of an adequate legislative framework and the relatively arcane process of formulating policy at the international level. There are, nevertheless, many signs that the more overtly moral aspects of the international law are acquiring a new prescriptive force.

This is where legal positivism falls short. The moral jurisdiction of the courts is inherent: it derives from the moral character of the law and not from political sources. This explains the compulsory jurisdiction of the ordinary courts, which has its roots in fundamental moral principles rather than a statutory warrant. It is the moral sources of the law that guarantees the independence of the courts and gives them the capacity to decide the legal legitimacy of the state's conduct. A body with the authority to override the wishes of institutional political actors cannot receive its authority from the institutions that it supervises.

The common law makes the same distinction. It is usually said that superior courts have an inherent jurisdiction, which does not derive from legislation. This gives them the authority to hear any matter that arises within the geographical jurisdiction of the court. It also gives them the authority to decide points of practice. The significant feature of this jurisdiction is that it is in the keeping of the superior courts, which decide the limits of their own jurisdiction, in accordance with those legal principles that determine the proper parameters of the judicial exercise.

The jurisdiction of a court that tries an issue like secession emanates from the same legal and moral principles, which extend into the extra-constitutional realm. This is apparent in the decision of the Supreme Court of Canada in the *Secession Reference*. Although the court traced its ruling to 'underlying constitutional principles', the decision steps into the extra-constitutional realm for its authority. This may be inevitable, since a court cannot deal with secession without ruling on matters that fall outside the ordinary legal and political orders. It nevertheless illustrates the existence of a moral law that binds the state.

The Supreme Court ultimately relied on the principle that political actors are obliged to respect the rights of minorities. This is a universal principle that extends well beyond the explicit provisions of the Canadian constitution or the issue of secession. The court's position would at least implicitly place fundamental moral limits on the exercise of political authority in any human circumstances. If there is a compulsory body of law in the realm outside the ordinary legal and political orders, it would apply universally.

This would include situations where there is no credible sovereign power. A court with the inherent jurisdiction to decide questions concerning the title to the sovereign power would logically have the authority to deal with other situations where the domestic order is in question. This includes any inchoate or lawless condition, such as war or revolution. It would also have the authority to decide questions that arise in the hiatus between two legal orders. There are many developments in the extra-constitutional realm that lend credence to such an idea. One is the development of an international criminal law and the idea that there is universal jurisdiction to try crimes against humanity.

There may be objections that this would place the judiciary in a position to rule on political matters. There are different ways of phrasing such an objection. Harry Beran has taken a stand against the notion that there are epistemological elites, who are in a better position to make ethical or political decisions than ordinary people. This criticism does not attach to the judicial inquiry, which is merely to determine whether a particular properly constrained conclusion can be deduced from accepted legal principles. Judges have no warrant to substitute their moral or political views for those of other people, who are rightfully consulted in the political inquiry.

There are natural limits on the power of the courts. The restrictions on the judiciary can be provided legally and institutionally, however, without giving the political order ascendancy over the legal order. The courts have a legal obligation to respect the legitimate authority of political institutions. The sovereign power remains a political power and cannot be exercised by the courts. This is a cardinal legal principle in any system that gives the courts the jurisdiction to decide such an issue. The formulation of policy is a political responsibility and the judicial task does not extend to political questions, which are a matter of opinion rather than inference.

There is less reason to be concerned about the powers of the courts than political institutions, since the courts have none of the brute powers of government. Indeed, the larger part of the authority of the courts comes from the fact that their orders are obeyed. This is a moral feature of the law, which goes to the legitimacy of the legal system. It will be the international community and states themselves that ultimately decide whether they are willing to accept a world in which there is a binding law of states. But the failures of a system that relies on political regulation to resolve matters like secession cannot be corrected by more of the same.

A Legal Theory of Secession

The fundamental premise in any legal theory of secession is that sovereignty is legally limited. An illegitimate state is not entitled to the attributes of sovereignty. In its most rudimentary sense, this is a matter of saying that the political authority of the state cannot be used to justify itself. A state that manifestly violates the rights of its population, in contravention of the principle of justice, will lose its legal title to the sovereign power.

This is enough to provide the conceptual foundation for a legal theory of secession. There are, nevertheless, two other theoretical matters that must be dealt with before setting out the details of a legal theory. The first concerns the title to the sovereign power. The second concerns the existing legal and political order.

Title

The first matter is a technical issue. There cannot be a transfer of the sovereign power without a legal title, an abstract interest that can be notionally passed from owner to owner. The title to the sovereign power is in the nature of a grant. It may be exclusive and extend in perpetuity but it is essentially a right to something, which derives from a superior power.

A title is not sufficient in itself. There must also be an underlying title, which vests in some undisputed source of authority. The obvious example is the underlying title to land, which historically vested in the sovereign. This gave the sovereign the prerogative to alienate and dispose of real property within the borders of the state. The idea is that all other titles derive from the interest held by the sovereign. The underlying title cannot be alienated from such a personality.

This may be the most difficult aspect of secession in political terms, though the issues that it raises are primarily explanatory. There must be a conceptual authority that holds the primary interest in the sovereign power. It is some aspect of this interest that is transferred from owner to owner. This repository of authority moreover cannot be the state. The sovereign power cannot be alienated from the state if that is where the underlying title vests. Nor is it possible to trace the original title to the people, since that leaves it in the hands of the majority. This is of no assistance, since it is the stewardship of the majority that is being called into question in secession.

The legal and political sources of the state's authority accordingly diverge in any legal theory of secession. The political justification of any government is internal: the realm of politics is governed by the principle that the people must consent to government. This is a political and sociological principle. It is also a matter of justice. The emergence of political institutions like regional parliaments or a world assembly may create a more complex situation. This would presumably be on the basis of some division of powers, however, and does not affect the principle that political authority within the state comes from the people.

It follows that the political justification of the state is internal. The legal and moral justification of the state is external however. This is an attribute of the mechanics of title: if the state holds a title to the sovereign power, the underlying title must vest in some personality outside the state. It is of little consequence how this personality is described, but it must be a superior authority, which brings together all of the legal interests engaged by secession. This includes the interests of individuals and minorities, as well as the state and the international community as a whole.

The legitimacy of the legal title to the sovereign power depends upon its pedigree. This pedigree originates in some corporate human personality, which holds the underlying title to the sovereign power. The state receives a licence or legal warrant to govern from humanity as a whole, which grants the state a subordinate title in the sovereign power. This changes the historical formula: on this account, the state's ownership of the sovereign power becomes a legal rather than a political fact. It can therefore be alienated from the state, and implicitly from the people. Although the title can only be returned to the people, it can first be formally removed, divided and transferred to a reconstituted majority.

It is humanity then that holds the underlying title to the sovereign power. There is a sense in which the underlying title to the sovereign power is absolute and unconditional. Here at least, the sovereign power simply is. Although this is where sovereignty accordingly lies in the traditional sense, unfettered by positive law, this is simply a way of saying that there are no legal restrictions on its existence. It is a mistake to think that the sovereign power is unlimited. This merely reflects the fact that it must logically exist before any legal constraints are placed upon it.

There is no need to postulate an explicit grant of the legal title to the sovereign power. It is enough if the grant is implicit. There is nothing untoward in this: the consent of the people to the political power of the state is also implicit. The grant of legal title is nevertheless sufficient to place legal conditions on the exercise of the sovereign power, which is subject to the principle of justice. This is a condition placed upon it by humanity and derives from the moral consensus that provides the source of legal authority within the state. Humankind has an inalienable right to intervene in the internal affairs of a state in order to halt fundamental abuses of the sovereign power.

The legal authority of this corporate humanity is justified on the political side by the superior power of the rest of humanity, which comes with moral obligations. Power has its responsibilities. The more fundamental theoretical observation however is that humanity shares some of the attributes of a society, with the same right to protect itself and its members. Whatever the sociological dynamics of the modern state, the reality is that human societies live collectively and not apart. It is the historical idea that human societies are discrete that is fallacious. There is a common good, shared by all, which reflects the overriding interest of humanity in a just, peaceable and well-ordered world.

The legal title to the sovereign power has the quality of a trust in many respects and is held for the benefit of all. This naturally includes minorities. There is a corresponding political prerogative, which is contractual. This derives directly from the people. These two aspects of the sovereign power exist together. It follows that there are contractual and fiduciary obligations that come with the exercise of such a power. If there is a serious breach of these duties, a minority may apply to repudiate the political contract.

Incorporating a Legal Theory into the International System

The second theoretical matter is more pragmatic. It is necessary to determine how a legal doctrine of sovereignty can be formally incorporated into existing legal systems. The first question that arises is whether questions regarding the title to the sovereign power should be dealt with in a domestic or an international venue. The answer appears to be that secession raises domestic legal issues, which must nevertheless be dealt with in the international realm.

Although the law is available to any competent tribunal, the idea of asking a domestic court to determine the validity of the constitutional order from which it derives its own authority is inherently problematic. This is because domestic courts have at least historically operated on the premise that the state has a valid title, since that is what gives the law its authority. There are also practical reasons that make it difficult for domestic courts to decide a contest over the title to the sovereign power. It is better to leave such details to judges who will not be affected by the success or failure of the action before the court. Indeed, it is better for the judiciary.[11]

This leaves the international law. There are many difficulties that arise in this context. The most practical difficulty is that there is no legal machinery outside the state with the authority to determine the validity of the state's title to the sovereign power. The more general difficulty derives from the fact that the international law has historically limited itself to the relations between states. Nor is it compulsory. Although both of these aspects of the international law are changing, they reflect the fact that it was never designed to regulate the internal affairs of the state.

The international law as it presently exists is law in the weakest sense. It has a didactic rather than a legal character and leaves the real authority in the international system firmly in the hands of states. As a result, the only real alternative to a compulsory law of secession lies in the political actions undertaken by other states. These actions are regulated by the international law, but on a normative rather than a compulsory basis.

There is a simple choice that must be made in this regard. We can either leave issues regarding the title to the sovereign power to the norms of the existing international law, which have a pronounced political character, or we can recognize that there is a compulsory extra-constitutional law and create an international court with the jurisdiction to deal with such matters. This would finally introduce the rule of law into the international arena.

International recognition

The literature suggests that there are two ways of regulating secession through the existing international law. The first is to develop the rules for the international recognition of states to deal with those states that violate fundamental rights. This poses many difficulties. For one thing, these rules were developed to determine whether emerging states are entitled to international recognition. The idea that they can now be used to somehow retract that recognition and deprive a state of its membership in the international community seems dubious.

The theoretical problem is that the moral regulation of states is a legal rather than a political matter. This is problematic, since the system of international relations was designed to serve political needs. It accordingly operates on a political and factual foundation: the realist argument is presumably that the rules of international recognition cannot be altered without falsifying the world in which we live. It is no reduction to assert that states are recognized by virtue of the fact that they exist. In this sense at least, states are like individual persons. Their conduct may be regulated by law, but the fact of their existence is a social and physical fact rather than a legal fact.

There is a serious philosophical question here, which goes to the roots of the democratic process. It is the exercise of political will that determines the existence of a state, rather than a set of legal conditions. This does not prevent a legal or even a political body from supervising the exercise of political power and placing legal limits on the actions of a state, but the idea that the state comes into being legally is an erroneous thought that only interferes with the natural and proper workings of the political system.

There is, nevertheless, a well-intentioned argument that states which persistently and flagrantly violate the rights of minorities are inherently illegitimate. Since they are illegitimate, they are not entitled to the privileges that the international community accords to sovereign states. It follows that the international community should refuse to recognize them. In *Humanitarian Intervention*, for example, Fernando Tesón argues that 'a government that engages in substantial violations of human rights betrays the very purpose for which it exists and so forfeits not only its domestic legitimacy, but its international legitimacy as well' (p. 15).

Allen Buchanan has now provided us with a moral account of 'recognitional legitimacy', which would set normative standards for the recognition of states.[12] This is in keeping with more recent criteria, he writes, which hold that a new state 'must not have breached a (basic) rule of international law' in coming into being (p. 50).

> There is evidence that international legal doctrine and practice are gradually adding moral content to the criteria for recognitional legitimacy, so that mere 'effectivity' eventually may not be regarded as sufficient. For example, resolutions of the U.N. General Assembly refused to recognize Rhodesia on the grounds that its basic political and legal institutions systematically discriminated against non-whites. (p. 50)

The political problem does not lie in the principles used to make such decisions, however, so much as the partial and selective manner in which they are employed.

Buchanan argues that the 'moral goals' of the international legal system are 'not only peace, but also justice' (p. 47).[13] He defines 'the minimal requirements of justice as being respect for basic human rights, both within the state and in the state's interactions with those beyond its borders' (p. 47). This adds a constitutional element to the process and places moral conditions on the state's enjoyment of its sovereign status. Buchanan does not contemplate a binding law of states however, and leaves the concept of recognitional legitimacy in the international political arena.

Samuel Barkin makes a related argument in *Millenium*, where he argues that sovereignty has always been subject to 'legitimising principles'. This gives sovereignty constitutional attributes: 'Sovereignty tends to convey upon the state the authority to do as it sees fit internally, except when such action compromises the legitimating constitutional features of sovereign statehood.'[14] Barkin argues that the Peace of Westphalia essentially created a legal order in the international realm, which constrained the actions of individual states.

The criteria of legitimacy have changed over time. Barkin writes that nationalism eventually replaced religion as a legitimating principle in determining the sovereignty of states under the Westphalian system. This led to the 'reification' of borders after the Second World War: 'National borders in this system, as agreed upon in the immediate post-war settlement, came to be sacrosanct in and of themselves, to be taken as prior to the operation of international politics. Except under the most extreme of circumstances, they could not be altered' (p. 244). This arguably reflects the failures of the international system, rather than the presence of a legitimating feature in the international order.

Barkin nevertheless suggests that the principle of borders is in the process of being replaced by a democratic standard, which emphasizes individual rights.

> A norm that has begun to replace territorial legitimation as a defining feature of the constitution of legitimate sovereignty in international relations is the norm of human rights. This norm includes civil and political rights, a set of relations between the state and each of its individual citizens that guarantees to each citizen certain political rights against the state, but not to economic, social and collective rights. (p. 246)

This is too rigid. There is no theoretical reason why social and collective rights need to be excluded from such a norm, which is of no assistance in the case of secession unless it extends to groups.

The fundamental thesis is that the constitutional constraints on sovereignty have now been extended to human rights. Those states that fail to respect these rights throw their legitimacy into question and jeopardize their sovereign status. There are many problems with this line of reasoning. For one thing, it rests on the premise that a state acquires sovereignty by virtue of its recognition by other states.[15] This may be true of some of the external aspects of sovereignty, but not of the sovereignty that it exercises in its internal affairs. It also suggests that those states that have been recognized by other states are internally legitimate. This is simply untrue.

These are two questions of legitimacy that need to be separated here. When we speak of the legal legitimacy of the state in the context of secession, it is for the purpose of examining the state's title to the sovereign power. This is internal and originates within the state. The issue of legitimacy that arises in the context of international recognition is external. Although it may theoretically have a legal element, it is predominantly political. The problem, however, lies in dealing with the internal issue.[16]

There is no denying that the ultimate goal of a seceding minority is an independent state, which is recognized by other states.[17] The process of international recognition only recognizes the fact of secession after it has taken place, however. This is notable in the instance of secession primarily because it deprives an embattled minority of a prospective right to secede. There is very little in such a system to provide effective assistance to a minority that finds itself trapped in an oppressive state. The rules of international recognition merely keep the matter out of the reach of the compulsory law and allows an obstinate state to use the full force of its authority in dealing with the matter.

The more theoretical problem is that international recognition is a matter of agreement among individual states. This will always be governed by political and factual considerations. Barkin acknowledges that there are 'illegitimate states' that have been historically recognized by the community of states and there are many arguments that this remains the case.[18] Whatever norms emerge in the international sphere, the idea that states will restrict themselves to moral principles rather than their own interests in reaching such decisions is not worthy of consideration. The rhetorical use of the concept of human rights, to cite one example, has made it relatively easy for states to promote their geopolitical interests under the guise of larger humanitarian concerns.[19]

Although there may be good reasons to accept the judgement of the international community on the question of legitimacy, this is a matter of agreement rather than a factual inference. It does not have the attributes of a legal finding. The idea that the international community can diplomatically divest a state of its sovereign status without a legal ruling merely subjects the international legal order to the vagaries of politics. The process of recognizing states can never supplant the need for an independent apparatus to deal with legal issues.[20]

The historical criteria for international recognition have a positivist turn. Under these criteria, a state is entitled to recognition if it has effective control of its territory and can enter into relations with other states. The philosophical position behind such a view is that questions relating to the political legitimacy of the state must be decided internally rather than externally. It may seem regrettable that there is nothing in this position to prevent a state that is internally illegitimate from claiming international recognition. But the real significance of such an observation is simply that it must be decided in another forum.

The work of Barkin and other authors is nevertheless significant in promoting the idea that a state should only be recognized if it is internally legitimate. This is apparent in Barkin's comment that sovereignty 'tends to convey upon the state the authority to do as it sees fit internally, except when such action compromises the legitimating constitutional features of sovereign statehood' (p. 239). Both Buchanan and Barkin envisage a limited concept of sovereignty, which is subject to political constraints in the international realm. This is part of the enterprise of developing a concept of sovereignty that is amenable to legal constraints.

Humanitarian intervention

The second way of regulating secession – if regulating is the right word – is to let individual states intervene in the affairs of states that violate the fundamental rights of minorities. This now appears to come within the doctrine of humanitarian intervention, which historically held that states have the right to protect their nationals when they are persecuted or mistreated by another state. This was originally seen as a questionable form of moral rescue, which could only be justified in the most extraordinary circumstances.[21]

The idea of humanitarian intervention is relatively elastic, however, and now provides a rationale for military actions against states that violate the basic rights of their peoples. This has implications for questions like secession: if voluntary military action on the part of states is now permissible, the doctrine could be used to protect the rights of minorities that find themselves persecuted by a state. This would presumably give individual states the right and even the duty to rescue minorities that have been oppressed by other states. These minorities could then be allowed to exercise the right to self-determination.

The antecedents of the modern doctrine can be found in relatively early theories of the international law. The Swiss jurist Emerich de Vattel argued that foreign states have a right to assist a people who have revolted against the 'unsupportable tyranny' of a prince.[22] This may seem paradoxical, since the reigning principle in the Westphalian system is that states are entitled to pursue their own affairs without interference from other states. The doctrine of humanitarian intervention has many of the characteristics of a defence, however, and essentially provides a state with a recognized excuse for contravening the most basic principle in the Westphalian system.

The military actions in Kosovo provide a good example of the new doctrine, though they were conducted by a group of states ostensibly acting under the auspices of the North Atlantic Treaty Organization.[23] The arguments in favour of intervention usually treat it as a moral necessity. Tesón for example argues that the international community must act 'to combat massacres, acts of genocide, mass murder and widespread torture'.[24] This kind of reasoning has become a common means of defending independent military actions in various states. The possession of weapons of 'mass destruction' and the export of terrorism has apparently been added to the list of conditions that require a response. The vagueness of these terms reflects their use in the political arena.

Necessity is usually a last resort in law and politics, and justifies actions that cannot be justified by other means. This kind of reasoning often appeals to the kind of raw emotions that serve political interests. The problems with such an approach can be seen in the historical response of the international community to human rights violations, which has always been selective. There is a more fundamental objection to such a line of reasoning however. Although there may be cases that require intervention, Tesón neglects the real issue, which is that there is no legal machinery to regulate the state.

The arguments in favour of humanitarian intervention implicitly assume that there are no other ways of dealing with these matters. But that is only because there is no legal means of doing so. It is distinctly odd that this should lead to arguments in favour of independent action on the part of individual states. Properly construed, this calls for a compulsory international law, rather than gratuitous action on the part of individual states. The doctrine of humanitarian intervention can never provide anything more than an *ad hoc* system of justice, enforced by vigilante states outside the rule of law.

This is no substitute for an institutional system of justice. The humanitarian problems that call for intervention arise from the fact that states are free actors in the international system. The logical response is simply that states should be subject to the rule of law. This is not a matter of ruling out force or concerted military action. It would be naive to think that questions like secession will never require some use of force. There is a distinction, however, between the use of police or military force pursuant to a legal ruling and within the ambit of a legal order, and the gratuitous acts of individual states.

It is true that there are political restrictions on the actions of individual states. It is now accepted that states should obtain something in the nature of a Security Council resolution before intervening for humanitarian purposes.[25] This is an important development and the actions that are taken pursuant to such resolutions can claim the wider political legitimacy that comes with the endorsement of the members of such a body. The Security Council is not a legal body however, and this kind of norm does not address the legal question of legitimacy. There is nothing in the decision making process of the Council that guarantees the legality of its decisions and the lack of judicial scrutiny is troubling, even when the actions seem justified.

Daniel Philpott has tried to put the best face on the 'nascent norm' that allows the Security Council to authorize humanitarian intervention. In his view, this

> ... actually gives individuals and peoples legitimate claims against state institutions, although these are only exercised in extreme disasters. The sovereignty of the state is becoming less than absolute, the Westphalia paradigm is being weakened and the state is again, at least to some degree, problematic.[26]

This misses the fact that the actions in question are the actions of individual states, acting on their own initiative. The political reality is that this kind of norm merely gives larger and more powerful states a licence to use force outside their domestic borders.

The idea of a posse is a reasonably accurate metaphor for some of the recent actions by individual states in the international arena. There are many reasons to be worried about a system in which individual states take it upon themselves to decide whether they should intervene forcibly in the domestic affairs of other states.[27] It has been argued domestically and internationally that the stability of the international order is already at risk. As Barkin writes, the international state system has progressed to the point that 'territorial adjustments *per se* are no longer thought of as inherently illegitimate' (p. 250).

There have been attempts to set out a more formal doctrine of humanitarian intervention, which would restrict its application. The report of the self-styled International Commission on Intervention and State Sovereignty recognizes that there are situations where the 'responsibility to protect' takes precedence over the principle of non-intervention.[28] This is limited to grievous circumstances such as insurgency, repression, mass murder and genocide. The problem is that the doctrine of intervention remains permissive: these criteria are open to interpretation in a political context and may be applied in the most selective manner.

Legal remedies

The current developments in the international arena nevertheless illustrate the most fundamental fact in any legal theory of secession. This is that external remedies are needed to deal with the state's abuse of its domestic powers. The legal difficulty is that the kinds of remedies that have been discussed are political in nature. Whether they are available to a minority will depend upon the view of other states in the international community.

It is important to separate the legal and political standards of legitimacy. The decisions of the Security Council and the General Assembly over the international community may reflect the view that a particular state is illegitimate. This is a matter of agreement among states, however, rather than a legal judgement. The purpose of the diplomatic process is presumably to determine whether there is some level of consensus on such an issue. This consensus will inevitably reflect the interests of more powerful states and a variety of international actors.

The political process that exists in the international realm is not designed to determine whether a particular resolution can be justified on the basis of substantive principles. These principles have an important part to play in negotiating such a resolution. Their role in the political process is instrumental and explanatory, however, and it is the will of individual states that generates the course of action taken by states. Legal and substantive principles may elucidate the fact of agreement but it is the wants of states and those in political power that decide its terms.

The legal legitimacy of the state's title to the sovereign power is not directly litigible at this point in time, inside or outside the state. The historical international law does not reach into the internal affairs of the state, where the title to the sovereign power lies. It may be possible to apply for a ruling from an international legal body with the declaratory authority to rule on the kinds of violations that might give rise to a right to secede. These kinds of rulings are incidental, however, and do not affect the fundamental authority of the state.

There is no escaping the fact that the existing international law is based on agreement and contract rather than a superior moral order. This perpetuates the idea that states are sovereign in some absolute sense. The international humanitarian law still relies on the fictional belief of states in holding that the customary law is legally binding. The international humanitarian law still obtains its force from the idea that states have accepted it. There is a fundamental body of law, in contrast, that derives from the substantive principles that have been accepted by humanity at large. The force of this law does not derive from the fictional beliefs of states. It accordingly provides an extra-constitiutional source of the law that is needed to determine the legal question of legitimacy.

The practical problem with the historical international law is much simpler. The purpose of a legal right to secede is to deal with contested cases. The most obvious fact that a legal theory of secession must deal with is the stubborn reality that the legal right to secede arises in exactly those situations where the state is determined to resist it. The idea that one can rely on a legal system based on convention and the will of states in such circumstances is simply naive. The legal right is unnecessary in uncontested cases, which can be resolved by political means.

There is no reason, in principle, why states should not be subject to compulsory legal constraints. Although the international law developed on the understanding that states exist in the state of nature, it has always been recognized that the state is subject to moral constraints. Fernando Tesón writes that Hugo Grotius and Emerich Vattel tried to place 'moral limits' on the notion of sovereignty (p. 54). Grotius accepted that secession is available to a population that 'cannot save itself any other way'.[29] This is a right of self-defence, which arises when the people are oppressed.[30]

It follows that there is a moral right to secede. There is a simple reason why this has not made its way into the customary international law. It is that the customary law is the preserve of states, which have reserved the loyalties of their members to themselves. The historical power of the state is predicated on the exclusiveness of its domestic authority. This is one of the more inveterate realities of the state system, which inevitably places those who actively pursue the right to secede on the wrong side of the civil law.

The current law of states does not recognize a formal right to secede. Antonio Casesse is undoubtedly right, in expressing pessimism about the prospect of any changes in the status quo.

> Since most sovereign States – the legislators responsible for the development of international law – are heterogenous, the international community undoubtedly will continue to reject any proposals ... likely to empower individual sectors of their populations and to threaten their territorial integrity; secession is thus certain to remain an anathema.[31]

There is no escaping the 'tenacity' with which existing states guard their territorial integrity

The irony is that this only demonstrates why a normative legal remedy is of no real assistance in the case of secession. Rather than confront the problem, Cassese argues that there is an alternative to the legal right to secede. This consists of narrowing the right of self-determination in the international law, so that it includes those minorities that find themselves within a state.[32] This would guarantee 'internal' rather than 'external' self-determination, and protect the right of national or ethnic groups within the state to assert some degree of 'autonomy' over their affairs, without giving them the right to secede.

David Miller makes a similar distinction between the internal and external facets of sovereignty, and argues that the claims of minorities can be satisfied within the domestic order.[33] The idea of national self-determination does not require that states 'rigidly demand complete sovereignty over their internal affairs' (p. 101). It is possible to divide the powers of the state in such a way as to give minorities some authority over their own affairs, without depriving the state of its external sovereignty. This kind of reasoning will be familiar to anyone acquainted with the arguments for a federal state.

These kinds of political proposals miss the fundamental issue however. There is little reason to discuss this division of powers in the existing international system, since that merely lets the state determine whether such a division is appropriate. This is pointless. It is naive to think that states with a long history of enmity towards particular minorities will voluntarily devolve their powers to those minorities. The idea that there might be international guarantees of 'internal sovereignty' is of no assistance unless it is compulsory.

Cassese recognizes that there are 'exceptional cases' where an internal principle of self-determination is insufficient.

> When, in a multinational State, armed conflict breaks out and one or more groups fight for secession, it may be that it is too late to plead for a peaceful solution based on internal self-determination. Similarly, when the central authorities of a multinational State are irremediably oppressive and despotic, persistently violate the basic rights of minorities and no peaceful and constructive solution can be envisaged, it seems difficult to imagine that those central authorities would be willing to grant autonomy, or participatory rights. (p. 359)

Here Cassese confronts the classic problem of secession, which only arises because the state has the final authority in its internal affairs. Faced with the bare logic of such a situation, Cassese is essentially forced to argue that a minority has a legal right to secede. There is simply no alternative.

The explicitness of this position is a new development. It does not affect the historical situation however, and is better seen as a statement of principle. This speaks to the larger epistemological problems with a normative system of law. It is a conceptual error to speak of a legal right to secede without a body of law and a judicial apparatus to enforce such a guarantee, and the right to secede that Cassese postulates is notional at best.

The legal realities are stark and dramatic. The most primitive legal principles establish that there are cases in which a minority has a legal right to secede. This leaves us with a simple choice. We can neglect the fact that this right is exercisable against the state, or finally recognize that this calls for a new world order in which states are subject to law.

Notes

1 Aquinas, *Summa Theologica*, I-II, q.96, a. 1. There is a constitutional side to the medieval conception of justice, which is rarely appreciated.

2 Finnis, *Aquinas*, p. 289.

3 See Connolly, in the Introduction to *Legitimacy and the State*, at p. 3: 'Perhaps the church will occasionally charge the secular authority with overstepping its divinely established

limits; maybe a maverick philosopher will justify tyrannicide. But the very grounding of political authority, the basic character of established custom, and the existence of finely drawn hierarchies are not treated as variable conventions in need of legitimation. They provide the settled and unquestioned matrix within which issues of politics and legitimacy are marginalized.'

4 Camilleri, 'Rethinking sovereignty in a shrinking, fragmented world', p. 16. The quotation from Jacques Maritain is from Richard O'Sullivan (ed.), *Man and the State* (London: Hollis and Carter, 1954), at p. 31.

5 Vattel makes this explicit in *The Law of Nations*, at §39: 'A good prince, a wise conductor of society, ought to have his mind impressed with this great truth, that the sovereign power is solely intrusted to him for the safety of the state, and the happiness of all the people; that he is not permitted to consider himself as the principal object in the administration of affairs, to seek his own satisfaction, or his private advantage; but that he ought to direct all his views, all his steps, to the greatest advantage of the state and people who have submitted to him.' Vattel is justifying a right of revolution and implicitly traces the sovereign power to the people. See §51: 'If the authority of the prince is limited and regulated by the fundamental laws, the prince, on exceeding the bounds prescribed him, commands without any right and even without a just title: the nation is not obliged to obey him, but may resist his unjust attempts.'

6 Locke, *Second Treatise of Government*, §222.

7 Gilbert, 'Community and civil strife', p. 10.

8 See Gilbert, at p. 13, where he quotes Henry Sidgwick, in the *Elements of Politics*, at p. 648: 'I think it important to dispel the illusion that any form of government can ever give a complete security against civil war. Such a security, if attained, must rest on a moral rather than a political basis ... it cannot be found in any supposed moral right of a numerical majority of persons inhabiting any part of the earth's surface, to be obeyed by the minority who live within the same district.'

9 There are real limits to liberal constitutionalism, which provides a check on government rather than the state.

10 Liberal theory provides a reasonable model in this context. John Rawls's law of peoples sees nations as contracting parties, who are subject to the principles of justice on which they would hypothetically agree.

11 Since the decision of the Supreme Court of Canada in the *Secession Reference* was only an advisory opinion, the court was spared such predicaments.

12 See Buchanan, 'Recognitional legitimacy', at p. 48: 'The judgement that a political entity is legitimate in the recognitional sense confers the status of being a member in good standing of the state system on that entity, with all the powers, liberties, claim-rights, and immunities that go with that status.' Buchanan elaborates on these views in *Justice, Legitimacy, and Self-Determination – Moral Foundations for International Law*.

13 And see Buchanan, p. 64f.

14 Barkin, 'Evolution of the Constitution of Sovereignty', p. 239.

15 See Barkin, at p. 232: 'An authority is only sovereign in a system of states if other authorities recognise it as such. In Janice Thompson's words, "sovereignty is not an attribute of the state but is attributed to a state by other states".'

16 There is some recognition of this in the literature, but few solutions. Henry Shue agonizes over the failure of the international law to deal with the internal question of legitimacy in 'Eroding Sovereignty'.

17 See Buchanan, at p. 2, where he sets out the attributes of independent statehood: 'The prevalent view among international legal theorists is that this includes the following: 1. the right to territorial integrity; 2. the right to noninterference in internal affairs (internal self-determination); 3. the power to make treaties, alliances, and trade agreements, thereby altering its juridical relations to other entities; 4. the right to make (just) war; 5. the right to promulgate, adjudicate, and enforce legal rules on those within its territory (subject to certain restrictions).'

18 See Barkin's comment, at p. 233: 'This is not to say that the international community will necessarily take decisive and immediate action against an illegitimate state. When dealing with Revolutionary France, for example, the European monarchies clearly had to take France's power into account as well as its legitimacy.'

19 See Barkin, p. 250. There is an unintended hint of this in Buchanan, at p. 23, where he writes: 'Nevertheless, withholding recognition does have important consequences: an illegitimate state or government cannot validly claim that other states are bound to support its exercise of power and that they act wrongly if they provide aid to rebels or secessionists. Also, as Rawls emphasizes, an entity's lack of legitimacy makes it permissible for other states to try to reform it by measures that would be impermissible interferences if directed toward legitimate entities.' The danger in these remarks is palpable.

20 There are good reasons why it must remain apolitical matter. Buchanan argues that a state which 'comes into being by displacing or destroying a legitimate state by nonconstitutional means is itself illegitimate' if there are 'institutional resources' available for constitutional change. But this would create 'illegitimate states' that perform all the functions of government, without participating in the formal world order.

21 Cf. Hannum. *Autonomy, Sovereignty and Self-Determination*, at p. 104, where he refers to 'the somewhat questionable doctrine of humanitarian intervention'.

22 See Vattel, *Law of Nations*, at §56: 'But, if the prince, by violating the fundamental laws, gives his subjects a legal right to resist him, – if tyranny, becoming insupportable, obliges the nation to rise in their own defence, – every foreign power has a right to succour an oppressed people who implore their assistance.' And see Tesón, p. 55, at note 23.

23 For a contemporary account of the doctrine of humanitarian intervention, see 'The Future of Humanitarian Intervention', a special issue of *American Diplomacy* (July 2001) containing a selection of papers from a conference on the Center on Law, Ethics and National Security (LENS) at the Duke University School of Law.

24 See Tesón, *Humanitarian Intervention*, at p. 4: 'May states unilaterally intervene by force in order to put an end to serious human rights violations? Or should states instead absolutely abide by the prohibition of the use of force embodied in article 2(4) of the United Nations Charter, and thus refrain from forcibly intervening in such cases? The first horn of the dilemma opens the door for [an] unpredictable and serious undermining of world order. The second horn of the dilemma entails the seemingly morally intolerable proposition that the international community, in the name of the nonintervention rule, is impotent to combat massacres, acts of genocide, mass murder and widespread torture.' But Tesón's definition of 'humanitarian intervention' is much more permissive than this kind of moral argument would suggest. See p. 5: 'I define humanitarian intervention as *proportionate transboundary help, including forcible help, provided by governments to individuals in another state who are being denied basic human rights and who themselves would be rationally willing to revolt against their oppressive government.*' There is no real way around it: this definition is full of moral and legal evasions, and serves the needs of intervening states.

25 Though the current military actions in Iraq were taken without such resolutions.

26 Philpott, 'Sovereignty', p. 368.

27 Cassese appears to take the view, in *Self-Determination of Peoples*, that this was the basis on which the West intervened in northern Iraq, to protect the rights of the Kurdish minority. It is ironic that he dismisses this, before the recent invasion, as an 'exceptional' case (p. 361).

28 The report of the Commission, entitled 'The Responsibility to Protect' and dated December 2001, is available on its website: http://www.dfait-maeci.gc.ca/iciss-ciise/report-en.asp.

29 From Grotius, 2 *De Jure Bellis Ac Pacis Libri Tres*: 6, 4, as translated by F. Kelley and quoted in Buchheit, *Secession*, p. 50f. And see the sentence on the same page: 'Employing the "organic" terminology, "the right which the part has to protect itself", he argues, is greater than "the right of the body over the part".' This seems to miss the thrust of the classical argument, which is that the part is nothing without the body. It is interesting that

Grotius believes such a right must be exercised in accordance with the common good. 'I should hardly dare', he writes, to 'indiscriminately' condemn a minority that 'availed itself of the last resource of necessity in such a way as meanwhile not to abandon consideration of the common good.'

30 See Buchheit, *Secession*, p. 53.

31 Cassese, p. 349.

32 See Cassese, at p. 350: 'As long as self-determination is perceived primarily as a right to independent statehood it will remain more a source of conflict than a substantive component in the settlement of disputes. States will continue to oppose with force peoples invoking their right to self-determination, characterizing the members of liberation groups as terrorists intent on dismembering the country. At the same time, those entitled to self-determination will lean towards rigidity and intransigence; convinced that the right to self-determination entitles them to absolute independence, they will be reticent to negotiate if sovereignty does not immediately appear in the offing.'

33 See Miller, *On Nationality*, at p. 99, where he writes that states 'are said to be sovereign internally in so far as they are recognized as the final authority on all matters that arise within their boundaries; and they are sovereign externally in so far as their decisions cannot be overridden by any other body, whether another state or an international institution'.

Chapter 5

Existing Theories of Secession

This chapter reviews the philosophical literature, which essentially contains two kinds of theories. The first is based on the right of self-determination. The second is based on the notion of a just cause, which gives a minority a moral right to a remedy. These kinds of theories can be classified as theories of secession based on the political and legal concepts of legitimacy.

Allen Buchanan makes a related distinction between two kinds of theories that would support the existence of a 'general' or inherent right of secession. 'Remedial Right Only Theories assert that a group has a general right to secede if and only if it has suffered certain injustices, for which secession is the appropriate remedy ...'[1] The second kind of theory, which Buchanan describes as Primary Right Theories, premise the right of secession on the political right of self-determination. As a result, primary right theories 'assert that certain groups can have a (general) right to secede in the absence of any injustice'.

Other authors have made the same dichotomy. In *Secession: The Legitimacy of Self-Determination*, Lee Buchheit suggests that there are two possible approaches to secession. The first approach sees secession as a means of protecting a group that has been oppressed by an overholding state.

> From the indications now available ... the concept of 'remedial secession' seems to occupy a status as the *lex lata*. The focus of attention here is on the condition of the group making the claim. Remedial secession envisions a scheme by which ... international law recognizes a continuum of remedies ranging from protection of individual rights, to minority rights, and ending with secession as the *ultimate remedy*. (p. 223)

This sets out a moral issue, which rests implicitly on the argument that a state that oppresses a minority loses its legal legitimacy.

Buchheit describes the second approach, which is not accepted in international law, as a 'parochial' model of secession.[2] 'The underlying force' of such a view 'rests upon the urge to be governed by those like oneself; it is unconcerned with the relative merits of the alien rule because ... the mere *fact* of alien domination is the basis of the complaint' (p. 223). This approach rests on a distinctly political right, which arises from the freedom of association. This raises the question of political legitimacy, which rests on the consent of individuals.

Daniel Philpott writes that philosophers have provided two answers to the question whether self-determination can be justified.

> The first ... argues that a group attains a moral right to self-determination (to secession, in Buchanan's version) when it has suffered certain kinds of threats or grievances, including 'historical grievances', such as previous invasion or annexation, as well as threats to its cultural preservation, threats of genocide, and finally, 'discriminatory redistribution' ...
>
> The other type of answer argues ... [that] self-determination is a basic right, rooted in liberal democratic theory, available to any group the majority of whose members desire it. Threats and grievances are unnecessary to establish a claim.[3]

Christopher Wellman adopts a similar position, in arguing that the source of a right of secession can be found in choice or justice, or some amalgamation of the two criteria, as the basis for a right of secession.[4]

Wayne Norman divides contemporary theories of secession into 'nationalist', 'choice' and 'just-cause' theories, but recognizes the affinity between nationalist theories and those based on choice, which can be seen as 'nationalist theories shorn of the moral complications of ethnicity'.[5] Buchanan divides primary right theories into 'Ascriptive' and 'Associative' theories on the same basis. Although most theorists include conditions relating to ethnic origins, there is nothing that restricts either type of theory to groups of people who share a national or cultural identity.

Political Theories

Association

It is accepted that a state is politically legitimate if it receives the consent of the population.[6] Theories of secession based on the right of self-determination generally measure this consent on a democratic basis. On this view, a state loses its title to the sovereign power when the majority removes its consent. The simplest example of such a theory is probably what Buchanan calls 'the *pure plebiscite theory*' (p. 39), which simply gives a majority of the population in any region a right to secede. The issue is whether the individuals within a specific territory wish to govern themselves.

Harry Beran, for example, takes the position that individuals have a moral right to decide their political relationships. As a result, he writes, 'any group is justified in seceding if (1) it constitutes a substantial majority in its portion of the state, wishes to secede, and (2) will be able to marshal the resources necessary for a viable independent state'.[7] 'Democratic liberalism', he argues, 'is committed to the view that any territorially concentrated group within a state should be permitted to secede if it wants to and it is morally and practically possible.'[8] These are major qualifications, however, which introduce a legal element into the question of secession and seem sufficient to curtail most of the attempts to exercise such a right.[9]

Beran's theory provides an example of an 'Associative' theory, which simply holds that the right to secede can be traced to our freedom of association. Authors like Christopher Wellman and Daniel Philpott see this freedom as the source of a right of political self-determination that in turn gives rise to a right to secede. Wellman recognizes that claims for secession that are 'grounded in past injustices' may give rise to claims that have all the hallmarks of a movement for self-determination. This nonetheless seems incidental to the deeper claim that individuals acting collectively are entitled to decide for themselves whether they are subject to the authority of the state.

Wellman argues that the legal view curtails our political rights:

> The traditional view suggests that to be legitimate, a government need not function exactly as all citizens would want, but it must treat its citizens in a minimally just manner. If a state has a valid claim to the territory it occupies as long as it avoids injustice, though, it is difficult to see how an individual or group can have rights to political self-determination. (p. 147)

And similarly:

> ... the traditional account of political legitimacy, coupled with the standard interpretation of the principle of national self-determination, leaves no room for political self-determination as such, only room for a right to be spared political injustice and a derivative, remedial right of self-determination when the exercise of this latter right is the only way to redress this injustice. (p. 149)

This seems to raise a philosophical question as to the origins of the right to self-determination.

Whatever the differences, all of the theories of secession based on self-determination seem to push us towards the 'plebiscite' model of secession endorsed by Beran and criticized by Buchanan. Wellman argues that the notion of consent does not provide a satisfactory conceptual basis for a theory of secession because it 'allows a virtually unlimited right to secede from states not grounded in consent' (p. 151). This overstates the usual meaning of consent and calls for a more explicit expression of approval than the historical literature. If we accept this democratic rider, it is certainly evident that these theories would at least implicitly deprive many existing states of their legitimacy.

Wellman seems to solve this problem by assuming that the citizens of a state will not arbitrarily withhold their consent. If we accept this, the suggestion appears to be, the notion of consent is sufficiently compelling to provide the basis of a state's legitimacy. Wellman actually borrows from the legal view in setting out his own theory, which combines the fundamental aspects of the consent model with a 'teleological' approach that recognizes that a state 'has a valid claim to its territory by virtue of the security and efficiency it provides' (p. 157). The function of a state is to secure peace 'without committing injustices' and a state that performs such a function in a satisfactory manner is entitled to retain its jurisdiction over its territory.

These qualifications give Wellman's theory a pronounced legal character. In spite of this, he adopts a liberal view that favours secession: 'We begin with liberalism's presumption upon individual liberty, which provides a *prima facie* case ... *for* the permissibility of secession ...' (p. 161). It follows that a minority 'has the right to secede when its independence will not jeopardize political stability' and 'many groups have a primary right to secede even in the absence of past injustices' (p. 170).

While Wellman bases his theory on self-determination and freedom of association, he is forced to qualify his position in order to protect the interests of other parties. This leads him to a more restricted position:

> Therefore we can conclude that *any* group may secede as long as it and its remainder state are large, wealthy, cohesive, and geographically contiguous enough to form a government that effectively performs the functions necessary to create a secure political environment. (p. 161f)

This would seem to put an onus on the seceding group to demonstrate that secession will not undermine the viability of the remainder state.

There are other theories based on similar principles. Daniel Philpott argues that 'any group of individuals within a defined territory which desires to govern itself more independently enjoys a *prima facie* right to self-determination – a legal arrangement which gives it independent statehood or greater autonomy within a federal state'.[10] In Philpott's view, '[s]elf-determination – again, an actual legal arrangement that provides a group independence or more legal authority within a state – is rooted in moral autonomy ...' (p. 353). By moral autonomy, Philpott means 'individual moral autonomy', which is not possible without political institutions that protect individual freedom, uphold democracy and guarantee a just distribution of goods.

Like Wellman, Philpott bases his theory on the liberal democratic tradition, which guarantees individual rights. Philpott argues that 'any group with a particular identity that desires a separate government is entitled to a *prima facie* right to self-determination' (p. 361). Philpott argues that such a right can only be defeated by 'a manifestly illiberal principle', whatever theory of obligation we adopt (p. 368). Democracy is a matter of 'exercising one's autonomy in the political realm'. Philpott is immediately forced to restrict this right, however, since its exercise may interfere with the autonomy of individuals in the remaining state.

The theoretical nature of Philpott's theory makes it highly speculative. Although he suggests that self-determination will make citizens more autonomous, this is largely an assumption.[11] And it cannot be assumed. The dissolution of a state into smaller states may create puppet states, which are dominated by their neighbours. It may create corrupt local governments or dictatorial regimes, dominated by clans. There is no guarantee that it will increase the autonomy of the members of such a state.

The principle of self-determination may actually diminish the scope in which individuals can exercise their autonomy. The more narrowly we define a self-governing group, the more likely it is that the demands for conformity among the members of the group will be intensified. The subdivision of existing states into smaller states may also bring new minorities into the foreground and create new possibilities of persecution. This is a concern in the work of Donald Horowitz, who has argued that successful movements for self-determination tend to create residual minorities who are victimized by the new majority.[12]

These kinds of criticisms are not enough to defeat the general principle of self-determination. If a large majority of people in a particular territory desire secession, and secession does not imperil other interests, it is difficult to see why they should not be permitted to secede. This is a fundamental political right, which exists independently of any legal right to secede. There is no reason why a legal theory of secession would displace such a right. Indeed, one of the purposes of a legal regime would be to recognize the legal validity of a minority's attempt to exercise such rights.

Like other authors, Philpott is essentially forced to accommodate the legitimate interests of existing states and is careful to distinguish between the right of self-determination and a right of secession. In point of fact, he argues that there should be a presumption against secession, which is only justified if there is a manifest injustice. This gives his theory a legal and remedial character.

Ascription

There are other political theories of secession that ascribe the right of political self-determination to ethnic minorities and similar groupings of individuals. These theories seem to have received the endorsement of history, which provides many examples of national movements seeking independence from an existing state.

David Copp, for example, argues that a group claiming the right to secede must qualify as a '"society" in a relevant sense'. This requires some degree of cultural or ethnic autonomy.

> Examples are French society, Puerto Rican society, and the Cree living in northern Québec. In the relevant sense, a society is a group comparable in size and in social and economic complexity to the population of a state; it has a multi-generational history; it is characterized by a relatively self-contained network of social relationships and by norms of cooperation and coordination that are salient to its members; it is comprehensive of the entire population of permanent residents of a relevant territory, with the exception of recent arrivals who may not yet fit into the group's network of social relationships.[13]

There are elements in this concept of a society that distinguishes these groups from mere associations.

Avashai Margalit and Joseph Raz argue that the members of an 'encompassing group' like a nation have a right to decide whether they should exercise sovereignty over their own affairs. In their view, the distinguishing features of such groups are social and cultural, and provide some basis on which the members of the group can identify with each other.[14] The crucial claim is that the well-being of the individuals within an encompassing group depends upon the group's ability to preserve its culture. The right to self-determination and any corresponding right to secede can therefore be traced to individual rights.[15]

The fundamental argument is simply that an individual's membership in a cultural group gives value and meaning to that individual's life.

> It may be no more than a brute fact that our world is organized in a large measure around groups with pervasive cultures. But it is a fact with far-reaching consequences. It means, in the first place, that membership [in] such groups is of great importance to individual well-being, for it greatly affects one's opportunities, one's ability to engage in the relationships and pursuits marked by the culture. Secondly, it means that the prosperity of the culture is important to the well-being of its members. (p. 449)

It follows that political arrangements that improve the 'prosperity of the culture' will improve the well-being of the group's members.

Margalit and Raz essentially take it as a given that there are 'many circumstances' where self-government is necessary 'for the prosperity and dignity of encompassing groups' (p. 460). Since it is the individuals within the group who receive the benefits of membership in the group, Margalit and Raz argue that it is those individuals who are 'best placed to judge whether their group's prosperity will be jeopardized if it does not enjoy political independence' (p. 457). This is fine as far as it goes, though it does not deal with the adverse effect of secession on those individuals whose interests are in conflict with those of the seceding group.

Margalit and Raz recognize the need to consider other interests and restrict the right of secession to a group with a substantial majority in the relevant territory, 'for the purpose of protecting the culture and self-respect of the group'. This is subject to the additional proviso 'that the new state is likely to respect the fundamental interests of its inhabitants, and provided that measures are adopted to prevent its creation from gravely damaging the just interests of other countries' (p. 457). These restrictions raise the question of legal legitimacy and implicitly acknowledge that the relevant moral concerns take priority over political considerations.

There are other ascriptive theories. David Miller, for example, argues that national communities 'have a good claim to political self-determination'.[16] He distinguishes between a national and an ethnic identity, however, which does not extend beyond its cultural character.

> The problem of secession arises only in cases where an established state houses two or more groups with distinct and irreconcilable national identities – irreconcilable because, for instance, each takes a different religion to be constitutive of its identity, or because each includes as part of its historical self-understanding its separation from, and antagonism towards, the other; a case such as that of the Jews and the Palestinians in Israel. (p. 113)

In Miller's view, this kind of claim only gives rise to a right of self-determination when the group in question exercises authority over the territory that it wishes to occupy.

Miller recognizes that secession tends to inflame the tensions between national groups in the resulting states. As a result, it is necessary to consider whether the resulting states are likely to respect human rights in determining whether a particular claim to secession should be upheld. There may also be cases where secession deprives a parent state of some advantage that is essential to the well-being of its citizens. Miller therefore accepts that we need to consider the viability of the remaining state, in determining whether a minority is entitled to secede.

Miller is willing to take the principle of nationality much further, however, than many authors. In some cases, he writes, the hostility between two groups may be so ingrained that secession may not be feasible without an actual 'exchange of populations' to prevent the creation of minorities in the resulting states. Without legal supervision, however, this runs the danger of rewarding the two groups for their failure to respect the rights of the minorities in question.

The ascriptive approach is naturally appealing to those who actively support national causes. Kai Nielsen, for example, argues that human beings cannot flourish without 'a secure social identity', which is found in an attachment to a local identity 'and not just to humanity in general'.[17] This culminates in national attachments: 'We are, to put it crudely, lost if we cannot identify ourselves with some part of an objective social reality: a nation, though not necessarily, a state, with its distinctive traditions' (p. 32).

Nielsen argues that multinational states have failed to provide adequate protection for minority cultures. As a result, national identities are 'only secure' under modern conditions 'when people with these national identities gain control of the conditions of their existence by having the power that goes with having their own state: a state which protects and actively furthers these national aspirations' (p. 32). This is an ascriptive argument, but Nielsen's theory has a remedial justification, since it traces the peremptory right to secede to the inherent failure of states like Canada to protect the rights of its minorities.[18]

The difference between a legal and a political theory of secession in this context is primarily strategic. From an evidentiary perspective, Nielsen's theory places the burden of proof on the federal government, which is essentially obliged to rebut a presumption in favour of secession. He is careful, however, not to give the same presumptive right of secession to national minorities in the province. Although Quebec must exercise any right to secede without violating 'anyone's rights', the implication is that these minorities would have no right to secede without just cause.[19] There is a 'sturdily democratic' history in Quebec, which is sufficient to protect the rights of minorities.[20]

Legal Theories

There are also legal theories of secession. These theories take the position that the powers of the state are subject to moral constraints. The right to secede of self-determination is a remedial right, which only arises when the state loses its legitimate right to govern. This raises the legal question of legitimacy, which must be decided on the basis of the principle of justice rather than the principle of consent. The literature seems to assume that any remedial right is restricted to national minorities.

Henry Sidgwick takes a remedial stance in *The Elements of Politics*. Any 'right of disruption' like a right to secede, he argues, must be based on something more than the interests of those seceding, or the 'sentiments of nationality'. There must be 'some serious oppression or misgovernment of the seceders by the rest of the community, – i.e., some unjust sacrifice or grossly incompetent management of their interests, or some persistent and harsh opposition to their legitimate desires, – would be usually held necessary to justify the claim' (p. 226). Sidgwick essentially calls for a finding of oppression. This enters into legal territory and separates the moral and the political questions.

Allen Buchanan is the most prominent exponent of a remedial theory of secession in the contemporary literature. He has summarized his position in an article in *Philosophy and Public Affairs*, where he argues that a group has a right to secede if either of the following conditions have been satisfied.

> 1. The physical survival of its members is threatened by actions of the state (as with the policy of the Iraqi government toward Kurds in Iraq) or it suffers violations of other basic human rights (as with the East Pakistanis who seceded to create Bangladesh in 1970), *or*
> 2. Its previously sovereign territory was unjustly taken by the state (as with the Baltic Republics).[21]

This gives rise to a general right of secession that is available to any aggrieved minority.

Buchanan envisages other situations, where there might be a special rather than a general right of secession. Remedial theories would recognize:

> ... *special* rights to secede if (1) the state grants a right to secede (as with the secession of Norway from Sweden in 1905), or if (2) the constitution of the state

> includes a right to secede (as does the 1993 Ethiopian Constitution), or perhaps if (3) the agreement by which the state was initially created out of previously independent political units included the implicit or explicit assumption that secession at a later point was permissible (as some American Southerners argued was true of the states of the Union). (p. 36)

It is notable that these special rights raise discernible legal issues and call at least implicitly for a legal regime that subjects the state to binding legal constraints.

Per Bauhn, who adopts a remedial stance, argues that a minority may have a right to secede on cultural grounds. This is based on the larger principle that the state has an obligation not to discriminate against minorities. Bauhn uses the example of a cultural subsidy:

> What if the government strongly subsidizes the cultural practices of the dominant cultural group and gives nothing at all to the members of the cultural minority (who still are obliged to pay taxes just like all other citizens)? Does this constitute a just ground for secession?[22]

On the face of it, Bauhn writes, the answer to such a question is no. The state has a general right to subsist and a minority has an obligation to seek other solutions, such as a democratic change of government.

This does not leave the minority without recourse. Its members 'are no longer obliged to be fully loyal' and 'are justified in refusing to pay taxes to a state which is deliberately unfair to them in its distribution of its fiscal resources' (p. 111). This seems to provide the beginning of a predictable series of events that leads relentlessly towards secession. If the state responds

> ... by increasing repression, so that state officials either refuse to protect the basic rights of the members of the minority culture (to life, freedom, physical and mental integrity), or actively violate these rights, then secession is morally justified, since the state no longer performs those protective functions which justify the loyalty and obedience of its citizens in the first place. (p. 111f)

Bauhn's conception of justice is dynamic, since the state has an active obligation to redress inequities. If it fails to do so, an oppressed minority has a right to reject its authority and secede. This is a last resort.

Separating the Legal and Political Questions

There is no clear separation between legal and political theories in the literature. The restrictions that the proponents of political theories of secession place on their own theories often seem to outweigh the rights that they grant. Although the moral and legal question takes precedence over the political question, there is no reason why a legal theory of secession would prevent a minority from asserting a political right to secede. Such a right would nevertheless be subject to legal constraints.

The distinction between the legal and political questions is blurred by the fact that the issues that arise in a political context of consent have a moral character of their own. It is difficult to imagine a plebiscite succeeding unless there is a perception of injustice. Wayne Norman expresses this rather well in the draft of a paper, where he criticizes the abstraction of choice theories:

> Choice theories hold, with some limitations, that if a majority in a region want to secede then they have a right to ... But people who actually want to secede almost always want to do so for certain reasons, and it is these reasons they cite as the moral justification for their movement. It is these reasons they advance to their fellow citizens in order to get them to join the movement or at least to vote for secession in a referendum. People do not merely proclaim that they should secede because they want to.[23]

It follows that theories of secession that ignore the dynamics of existing conflicts are unlikely to provide a compelling account of the right to secede.

The legal and political questions nevertheless need to be separated. The political question is whether a minority wishes to secede. The issue is whether the minority has withdrawn its consent to government. This does not provide an intelligible basis for a legal ruling and cannot be answered in a legal forum. It is much like asking whether spouses should divorce. The legal theories in the literature accept that this can only be determined on a democratic basis, usually by holding a plebiscite.

The political right to secede is more a statement of will than a right, properly speaking. It arises when a minority expresses its political resolve, in an appropriate political forum. This does not decide the legal question, which requires an institutional act by an appropriate legal body. The legal question is clearly whether a minority has an enforceable right to secede. This is problematic in the existing international order. The reality is that none of the major theories of secession would be effective without a binding legal regime. It is universally accepted that states are obliged to exercise the powers of government in accordance with the principle of justice. The literature in the area is replete with remarks that at least implicitly accept that individual states are subject to an overarching, enforceable moral order.

This consensus surfaces in the belief that legal restrictions must be placed on the seceding state. Allen Buchanan for example writes that:

> ... other conditions ought to be satisfied if a group that suffers any of these injustices is to be recognized through international law or international political practice as having the right to secede. Chief among these is that there be credible guarantees that the new state will respect the human rights of all its citizens ...[24] (p. 37)

This can be seen as a matter of consistency, since a minority cannot claim a legal right to secede when it has been oppressed without granting the same right to other minorities.[25] But the crucial observation is that there are no credible guarantees without a compulsory legal regime.

There is at least some recognition in the literature that the legal and political questions of secession raise different kinds of issues. This is apparent in the distinction between the use of a substantive and a procedural process in deciding whether a minority has a right to secede. Allen Buchanan has drawn an analogy between a substantive process and a 'fault model' of divorce.[26] A substantive process would award a minority a right to secede when it establishes that certain grounds have been met, such as historic unfairness, unsettled territorial claims or the failure of the state to redress institutional inadequacies.

The idea of a purely procedural process seems problematic. The important point is nevertheless that it does not require a definitive answer to a specific moral question. The literature draws an analogy between procedural models of secession and 'no-fault' models of divorce, which do not require grounds like cruelty or desertion. This is a helpful analogy, though it glosses over the substantive role of the courts in such situations. The use of a procedural process primarily determines whether a minority wishes to secede. The most prominent proponents of a procedural approach have probably been Avashai Margalit and Joseph Raz, who argue that the members of a minority have the right to decide for themselves whether they want independence.[27] This raises questions of preference and choice, and can only be addressed by an act of the popular will.

Those authors who favour a procedural process have argued that a judicial body would have difficulty deciding whether a minority is justified in seceding. Wayne Norman for example submits that the major advantage of such a process is that it keeps the question of secession in the political arena.

> Secessionists and unionists are likely to disagree about what kinds of incidents or events can give just cause to secede, about whether such events have occurred, about whether they have been or could be rectified by measures short of secession, about whether the particular violations were significant enough to justify secession, etc. We could never expect criteria for just cause to be spelled out in law, and this is yet another reason why we would not expect a tribunal or court to produce a decision that would not be open to doubt.[28]

Norman's concerns are less significant in morally compelling cases. That raises other issues, however, and he is right in thinking that a court would not be able to formulate the reasons that might justify the decision of a minority to withdraw its consent to government.

David Miller takes much the same position in suggesting that a constitutional provision that dealt with secession would have to favour procedural criteria.

> ... the conditions justifying secession would need to be stated in a form that a judicial body could apply, and this immediately slants the discussion in favour of

> certain criteria and against others. For instance there is likely to be a bias in favour of procedural criteria (is there a majority in favour of secession in the territory in question?) whose application is relatively uncontroversial, and against substantive criteria whose application may depend upon difficult and contested matters of judgement (is the existing state suppressing or eroding the distinct culture of the minority applying to secede?).[29]

This deals with the political rather than the legal question of secession.

Miller is right in suggesting that the decision to secede is a matter of preference and does not provide the proper subject matter of a legal ruling. The reasons behind such a decision are matters of opinion and are usually not litigible. The problem is that preference is not sufficient in itself to decide such matters. Henry Sidgwick recognized this 100 years ago, when he complained that any attempt to incorporate the 'divine right of majorities' into political theories would unravel the entire state system. A simple majority principle 'would lead naturally to an indefinite disintegration of political societies; since a faction that was in a minority in the whole state would probably be in a majority in some districts, and might accordingly, on this principle, claim to be governed according to its wishes in these districts'.[30]

Sidgwick himself takes a substantive position. It is the failure of the state to respect the substantive rights of a minority that gives rise to the legal right to secede. This right cannot be awarded without proof and explicit findings of fact. It requires a neutral process to try the matter, presided over by an independent and impartial tribunal. A good deal of the difference between the procedural and substantive processes can be found in the difference between what is in keeping with opinion and what can be deduced from principle. The factual issue that arises in the legal process is whether a government has breached its fiduciary duties to a minority. This is well within the normal ambit of the legal process.

The question that determines whether a minority has a legal right to secede is roughly whether the minority would be morally justified in seceding. This is what gives it the legal right to decide whether to do so. The question before the court requires a substantive answer and cannot be decided by consulting the will of the parties. A political act like a plebiscite merely establishes whether a majority within a particular group wishes to secede. This brings in all the problems of a majoritarian democracy and cannot guarantee the morality of such a decision.

The legal right of secession is an extraordinary right, which arises independently of the political process. It will only arise in situations where the conduct of the state takes the issue of secession outside the ordinary parameters of the political arena. The more common means of secession remains in the political realm. Nor is there any reason why a minority needs to apply for a legal ruling in order to lawfully secede.

The legal process is nevertheless there, in the face of disagreement among the parties. There are many reasons why a vote in favour of secession may require moral ratification from a court, which formally acknowledges the legal validity of such a decision. Some of these reasons are political, since a decision from a legal body may be helpful in establishing the neutrality of such arrangements. In addition, there are many legal issues that arise in the normal course of implementing a decision to secede. This invokes the supervisory authority of the courts, however, rather than its original jurisdiction.

Determining which Minorities Have the Right to Secede

There are a number of related questions in the literature. The most fundamental is whether the right to secede should be restricted to nationalities. This has been the subject of considerable debate.

The contemporary argument against giving any special status to nationalities is philosophical. Contemporary liberals are uncomfortable with the idea that there is a vague collective good, which takes priority over individual rights. There is an opposing argument from within the liberal ranks however, which sees national or ethnic rights as a necessary facet of our personal autonomy. Without such rights, the argument goes, an individual who is a member of a national minority cannot enjoy the cultural or social benefits that accrue to the majority.[31] This raises a question of discrimination.

One of the standard defences of nationalism is that nations provide the cultural values with which individuals make their personal decisions. Although Margaret Moore acknowledges the attraction of such an argument, she argues that the academic literature fails to distinguish between culture and identity.[32] This is a significant distinction, which undermines the argument that nationality is a repository of cultural values. Many national groups have retained their identity in spite of profound changes in their cultures.

Moore also reviews the argument that national identity provides individuals with the psychological motivation to act in the interests of a common good. The argument is that this promotes feelings of fellowship, which permit the redistribution of wealth and the implementation of social programmes.[33] Moore submits that similar kinds of identification have occurred on a more global level, at least in the instance of natural and humanitarian disasters. Nor is it clear that an individual's identification with an ethnic or national group and a larger multinational state need exclude one another.[34] This would seem to run against the existence of pluralistic democracies, the idea of federalism and the successful emergence of multinational associations like the European Union.

The place of nationality in the formation of personal identity has been disputed. Jeremy Waldron argues that individuals do not need a sense of belonging to a particular national or ethnic culture in order to make meaningful choices in their lives. The existence of an increasingly fragmented modern lifestyle, which borrows its cultural traits from diverse sources, demonstrates that nationality is not a necessary part of human life.[35] On Waldron's view, there are individuals who refuse to be defined by location, ancestry, citizenship or language.[36]

It is necessary, however, to separate the question whether nationalism is a positive or necessary feature of human society from any question about its place in a theory of self-determination. Moore writes that the question:

> ... is not ... what way of life is existentially attractive, as a way of life, but rather what is the appropriate response to the fact that many people do have national identities and attachments. This second question takes it as an empirical given that national identity is important for most people, in conditions of modernity.[37]

It follows that there is a heavy onus on those who reject national attachments to establish the moral and practical efficacy of their own position.

The right answer in law is the pragmatic one. The legal question is merely whether national identity is such a fundamental feature of human society that legal theories must accommodate it. The answer seems relatively simple. At this point in history, the reality is that individuals define themselves in a way that takes much of its colouring from their national or ethnic identity. Since most claims for secession come from national or ethnic movements, it does not seem realistic to construct a viable theory of secession without recognizing the part played by a national or ethnic good in such a process.

Notes

1 Buchanan, 'Theories of secession', p. 35.
2 At p. 224, Buchheit states that the claim of the parochialist 'ultimately rests on the association of certain transcendent benefits which attend self-rule'. These 'metaphysical advantages' do not lend themselves to a judicial analysis.
3 Philpott, 'Self-determination in practice', p. 80.
4 Wellman, 'A defense of secession and political self-determination', p. 142. And see ibid., footnote 2, where Wellman recognizes the distinction that David Schmidtz has made between *emergent* and teleological justifications for the state.
5 Norman, 'The ethics of secession', p. 37.
6 Beran discusses some of the variations in theories of consent in chapters 4 and 5 of *The Consent Theory of Political Obligation*, at pp. 56–77.
7 Beran, *The Consent Theory of Political Obligation*, p. 39.
8 Beran, p. 41.
9 Beran argues that the existing state should be accommodated by placing conditions on the new state, rather than by restricting the right of secession. This presents many legal and practical difficulties.
10 Philpott, 'In defence of self-determination', p. 353.
11 See Philpott, ibid., at p. 360: 'In sum, [the citizens of Utopia] may now more directly pursue their Utopian causes as Utopians, without outside interference or burden. Participatory Utopians now participate more effectually in Utopian affairs, their efforts no longer truncated or attenuated.' These statements are mere abstractions.
12 And see Buchanan, at p. 45: '[in the first place,] when an ethnic minority secedes, the result is often that another ethnic group becomes a minority within the new state. All too often,

the formerly persecuted become the persecutors. Second, in most cases, not all members of the seceding group lie within the seceding area, and the result is that those who do not become an even smaller minority and hence even more vulnerable to the discrimination and persecution that fueled the drive for secession in the first place.' This is accompanied by a reference to the work of Donald Horowitz.

13 Copp, 'International law and morality in the theory of secession', p. 227f.

14 So the first two features are that the group 'has a common character and a common culture', and that 'people growing up among members of the group will acquire the group culture, will be marked by its character'. Margalit and Raz, 'National self-determination', p. 443f.

15 See Margalit and Raz, p. 450.

16 Miller, 'Secession and the principle of nationality', p. 65. In *On Nationality*, at p. 27, Miller sets out five criteria for a national identity. 'These five elements together – a community (1) constituted by shared belief and mutual commitment, (2) extended in history, (3) active in character, (4) connected to a particular territory, and (5) marked off from other communities by its distinct public culture – serve to distinguish nationality from other collective sources of personal identity.'

17 Nielsen, 'Secession: the case of Québec', p. 31. Nielsen is relying on the work of Johann Göttfried Herder.

18 And Per Bauhn adopts a remedial stance in *Nationalism and Morality*, where he contemplates a right of secession based on the kind of cultural grounds advanced by Nielsen in the instance of Quebec.

19 An act of secession that did not respect the rights of minorities in the province, Nielsen writes, 'would not have legitimacy' (p. 30).

20 And of course the same logic would naturally apply to Canada.

21 Buchanan, 'Theories of secession', p. 37.

22 Bauhn, *Nationalism and Morality*, p. 111.

23 Norman, 'Domesticating secession', p. 5.

24 This kind of restriction is attractive to many authors because they comport rather well with a liberal conception of justice, which emphasizes individual rights.

25 Cf. Nielsen, at p. 29, where he states that 'persons who are extensively predominant in a distinct territory' have the right 'to determine their common destiny provided they do not violate the civil liberties of others, including, of course, minorities who live in the same territory'.

26 Though Buchanan also remarks, at p. 36, that there is no requirement that a substantive model use the concept of fault. A constitutional regime that recognizes the need to preserve a culture as a legitimate ground for secession 'need not imply that anyone, including the state, is at fault for the precariousness of the group's cultural survival'. This is unclear. It might always be said that the fault lies elsewhere, in history for example.

27 For Margalit and Raz, the question is whether independence would improve the 'prosperity' of a minority's culture. Though the word 'prosperity' seems unfortunate and a word like 'viability' may be more appropriate.

28 Norman, 'The ethics of secession', p. 37.

29 David Miller, 'Secession and the principle of nationality', p. 63

30 Sidgwick, *The Elements of Politics*, p. 648. It is nevertheless apparent, Sidgwick adds, that those who rest the legitimacy of government on consent do not 'shrink from drawing this inference'.

31 As a result, the liberal tradition has shown considerable historical sympathy to claims for national independence. Will Kymlicka writes that one of the hall-marks of the liberal tradition is its respect for the principle of self-determination. See *Multicultural Citizenship*, for example, at p. 49: 'For most of the nineteenth century and the first half of the twentieth, the rights of national minorities were continually discussed and debated by the great liberal statesmen and theorists of the age.'

32 See Moore, *The Ethics of Nationalism*, where she canvasses a variety of liberal arguments in favour of nationalism. The 'cultural argument' suggests that nationality provides the

context in which individual people make choices and pursue their well-being. This promotes their autonomy.

33 See Moore, at p. 80, where she discusses William Galston's book, *Liberal Purposes: Goods, Virtues, and Diversity in the Liberal State* (Cambridge: Cambridge University Press, 1991). As Moore puts it: 'In Galston's view, the sacrifices necessary for the realization of the common good require an emotional identification with the state and its members.' David Miller advances a similar argument about redistribution in *On Nationality*.

34 This was a source of controversy among the American pragmatists. See the discussion, for example, in Nancy Fraser, 'Another pragmatism: Alain Locke, critical "race" theory, and the Politics of Culture' and Ross Posnock, 'Going astray, going forward: Du Boisian pragmatism and its lineage', in Morris Dickstein, *The Revival of Pragmatism: New Essays on Social Thought, Law and Culture* (Durham, NC, and London: Duke University, 1998), at pp. 157–75 and 176–89.

35 In *Multicultural Citizenship*, at p. 85, Kymlicka suggests that Waldron is confusing ethnic cultural traits with national or 'societal' cultural traits.

36 Waldron, 'Minority cultures and the cosmopolitan alternative', p. 95.

37 Moore, 'The limits of liberal nationalism', p. 7.

Chapter 6

Institutional and Legal Issues

This chapter reviews a number of legal and institutional issues that need to be considered in setting out a legal theory of secession. There are at least three different areas of concern. Donald Horowitz has criticized the philosophical literature for its failure to take account of the sociological dynamics that govern secession. Allen Buchanan, Wayne Norman and a number of other authors have argued that it fails to address the realities of international law. It is apparent, finally, that existing theories have yet to deal with the limitations of the legal process in deciding a question like secession. This raises a question of justiciability, which has been neglected in the theoretical literature.

There are additional problems in asking a domestic court to rule on events that occur largely outside the domestic legal order. These concerns are evident in the common law tradition, which contains a significant case law on revolution. Although domestic courts have a limited power to decide the factual issue whether the political order has changed, they have generally declined to rule on the source of their own authority.

Institutional Issues

In 'Theories of secession', Allen Buchanan suggests that there are two different philosophical questions that arise in the context of a right of secession. The first question asks us to identify the circumstances under which a group of people have 'a moral right to secede' (p. 31). The second question asks us to identify the circumstances under which there is a legal right of secession. It is the first question that has dominated the discussion in the area, and few authors, on Buchanan's analysis, have even begun to describe the way in which their proposals might be 'incorporated into international legal regimes' (p. 33). Wayne Norman and a number of other authors have also recognized that there is a need for a theory of secession that provides a legal or institutional authority with the criteria to adjudicate such issues.

This calls for a theory of secession, which sets out the institutional means that could be used to determine whether a minority has the right to secede. Those theories that fail to address the prevailing legal and political realities are of little assistance in developing legal rules and principles. The issue is not so much what an ideal world would look like – from the perspective of the law, that is the wrong endeavour – but how we should incorporate general principles into the existing order of things.[1]

As a whole, the theoretical literature exhibits a surprising indifference to the realities in which such claims arise.[2] Donald Horowitz complains that philosophers have ignored the sociological aspects of secession.

> ... if interest [by philosophers] in the problem is driven by events, the methodology is not, for much of the literature thus far often displays a thoroughgoing ignorance of the complexities of ethnic interactions. To say this is not to exhibit hostility to the efforts of philosophers on such issues in general – for moral reasoning is needed – but *a priori* methods that seem appropriate to other issues are utterly unsuitable to this problem.[3]

It is the abstract accounts of the right of political self-determination in the philosophical literature that attract this criticism.

Most of the complaints lie on the institutional side, however. In 'Self-determination in practice', Daniel Philpott argues that it is time for theories of self-determination to address the 'institutional question' that arises when we consider how a right of secession might be introduced into international or domestic law. The fundamental problem is that the existing international order does not have the capacity or the resources to regulate a question like secession.[4] At this time, it is by no means clear how the right to secession might be exercised in international law, particularly if we wish to give it meaningful force in a domestic context. It does not seem sufficient to speak of international conventions, which operate by agreement between states.

Buchanan argues that remedial theories are preferable to primary rights theories precisely because they satisfy realistic criteria and contemplate a right of secession that is in keeping with the norms of international law.[5] It will come as no surprise that these norms, which have been created by states, run strongly in favour of maintaining the integrity of existing states. The usual argument is that such a right would undermine the stability of the international order, but the political obstacle seems to lie in the fact that any developments that give minorities independent political rights threaten the integrity of the state.

Before considering the specific issues that might arise in litigating a question like secession, it is necessary to step back and consider whether the existing literature has the resources to meet the needs of legal practice. There is some appreciation of the fact that current theories have tended to ignore the needs of legal or political institutions, and cannot be implemented in the existing international order. However, no one has seriously examined how a theory of secession might be applied in a legal setting or looked at the needs of an adjudicative model in the area. This requires some knowledge of the natural parameters of the legal inquiry and the process of taking evidence.

Wayne Norman writes that the moral guidelines in the literature have yet to provide a cogent philosophical response to the existing political process, which 'is crying out for a legal framework'.[6] This, in his view, requires a different kind of ethical evaluation, which reflects the institutional needs of a legal system. There is an important methodological issue here, which arises out of the conventions of legal practice rather than the philosophical literature. From the perspective of the common law, at least, the law already exists, and simply must be found.[7]

If we are going to incorporate a right of secession into the general law, we accordingly need to find those aspects of the law in which it might reside. The theoretical question is not whether there is a legal right of secession. The question is how the existing law might be developed to deal with a new legal problem. This reflects the kind of pragmatic approach that might be taken by a judge in deciding the issue, who must find the right in the existing canons of the law. The source and location of the right will play a large part in determining its substantive contents.

This does not call for a separate inquiry under different regimes of law. It is less important to look at the international law, with all its idiosyncrasies, than to look at the principles of ordinary adjudication. This has generally taken place in domestic courts and tribunals, which only deal incidentally with the international law. It is these courts and tribunals that have dealt historically with the demands of a fair process, the difficulties of proof and the determination of appropriate remedies.

The major questions in the development of an institutional right of secession have as much to do with pragmatic concerns as with anything else. The issues that arise in the context of questions like jurisdiction, forum, grounds and enforceability, ultimately raise a larger question of justiciability. And since it is domestic systems of law that provide the forum in which these questions are answered, these systems should be consulted in establishing the parameters of justiciability. The common law and civil law systems are more significant in this regard than the historical international law.

One of the methodological assumptions that sustains the domestic law is the idea that the entire corpus of the law can be seen as a coherent whole. As a result, a judge who makes use of a hitherto unrecognized legal principle must trace the pedigree of such a principle to the theoretical underpinnings of the existing law. Ronald Dworkin has described this aspect of the judicial process in *Taking Rights Seriously* and *Law's Empire*, where he uses the metaphor of a 'chain novel' to describe the entire body of case law. There are many concerns that inform the judicial task and one of the primary purposes of the legal process is to reconcile the apparent conflicts between competing values, rights and principles.

The common law has developed by inference, and the courts continually return to the origins of the law in order to determine the legal force of specific principles. This is also a question of unearthing, re-examining and exploring the moral foundations of the law, however tentative they may be. The case law generally proceeds by a process of discovery, in which the significance of different aspects of the law are reassessed and brought to the fore. The courts are required to continually reinterpret individual aspects of the law, as successive changes in the law register their effect. This provides the natural means of developing a legal right of secession.

The Presumption of Legitimacy

There is a philosophical issue that seems to lie under these criticisms of the existing literature. The initial question, at least legally, is not whether a state has a moral right to secede, but whether the state is inherently legitimate or illegitimate. This is important because some of the contemporary work in political theory, which is based on a personal right of self-determination, at least implicitly rejects such a view. Remedial theories, on the other hand, retain the presumption that the state is legitimate, but place moral and political conditions on the ownership of the sovereign power. Although the state has original authority, it is the principle of justice that provides the continuing source of its legal powers, and a state that acts unjustly may lose its warrant to pass and enforce the law.

In the remedial view, the decisive issue is whether the existing state has conducted itself in a manner that requires a moral remedy. The legal right of secession arises in those circumstances where the state loses the benefit of the moral presumption that its authority is legitimate. The essential problem with theories of secession based on self-determination is that they implicitly do away with the presumption. Such theories suggest, at least, that the state does not possess any original authority and receives its authority by delegation from individuals.

One of the major difficulties is that the term 'legitimacy' has been used indiscriminately in the literature. Although the legal sense of the term finds its way into the discussion of theories of secession based on self-determination, this confuses the legal and political aspects of the term. Harry Brighouse, for example, sets out three conflicting conditions of legitimacy in an article entitled 'Against nationalism'.[8] But the real difficulty lies at a deeper level, in the use of consent as the criterion of political authority, when states actually function without the consent of a significant portion of the population.

Theories of secession based on self-determination ultimately trace the right of secession to the withdrawal of consent by the populace rather than the moral character of the state. On such a view, the authority of the state is always delegated, rather than original, and the state has no inherent right to govern. The practical problem, all moral issues aside, is that the political process cannot function on the basis of consensus. There will always be individual and collective differences of opinion among the population and some degree of dissent. As a result, theories based on self-determination inevitably justify some form of a majoritarian democracy, in which the legitimacy of the state depends upon its success in obtaining the consent of a majority.

There is nothing in such an arrangement to deal with an unjust state, as long as it acts in accordance with the wishes of the majority. Thomas Pogge recognizes that this leaves a moral lacuna in a footnote to an essay criticizing nationalism, even in its 'bland and conservative' manifestations. 'It is of the essence of justice', he writes, 'that a majority's consent cannot lend *moral* legitimacy to the mistreatment of a minority.'[9] This identifies the moral and legal question of legitimacy that comes to the fore on both sides of secession, since the democratic impulse that expresses itself in the campaign to secede often finds subsequent expression in the oppression of the new minorities in the seceding state.

The literature does not deal adequately with the problem of an unjust majority, which does not present the same problem in the theoretical realm. Any theory of the state based on the common good will presumably include some remedial principle, since a state that acts in a way that is manifestly unjust towards any of its citizens cannot be said to be acting in accordance with the interests of the community as a whole. This includes the majority. The argument that the majority has no interest in the rights of minorities simply fails to recognize our obligations to other people.

The difficulty lies in providing a practical means for the exercise of any rights that flow from the remedial principle. The reality of the political process simply misses the issue. The problem of secession is a problem of minorities, which arises because the political issue of consent can only be decided on majoritarian grounds. Instead of being regulated by moral principles, this principle postulates that the state is regulated by the popular will, in whatever way it manifests itself. This introduces an element of moral uncertainty into the political realm, which is at the mercy of popular prejudice. If the majority in a state is antagonistic towards minorities, the democratic nature of the state will not be sufficient to preserve its moral legitimacy.

It follows that some form of legal regulation is necessary to remedy the deficiencies in the political principle of legitimacy. This regulation must be compulsory for the obvious reason that it may oblige the state to act against the wishes of the majority. We can presumably start with the premise that the state derives its legal and coercive powers from its title to the sovereign power. This is subject to conditions of good ownership, however, and only gives the state the authority to act in the interests of everyone within the community. It follows that a state that treats minorities in a substantially unequal manner has stepped outside the legitimate sphere of its authority.

This sets out a simple legal framework, under which the state's powers of government are subject to the legal principle of justice. There is, accordingly, an overarching standard, which applies to both the overholding and the seceding states. This brings in the legal principle of legitimacy, which would give an oppressed minority the right to secede. If the seceding state oppresses the remnants of the original majority, it would conceivably give the new minority a right of its own to secede.

There are few alternatives to such a scheme. Those who favour a political resolution of the question might argue that there are political means for dealing with the problem of majorities outside the domestic sphere. There is nothing inherently wrong with such an idea, which raises the external question of political legitimacy that forms the basis for the recognition of states. The moral uncertainties associated with a political conception of legitimacy apply as much in the international as the domestic arena, however, and this does not address the legal question of legitimacy. The informal political process in the international realm does not provide the moral guarantees of the legal order.

The moral deficiencies of the political process also manifest themselves on a more practical level. Although the decision to secede is a political decision, which can only be decided on an electoral basis, the procedural aspects of such a decision raise moral and legal issues. The decision cannot be made by the voters in the overholding state, since that would allow the majority to decide for itself whether it has oppressed a minority. There must therefore be some means, as Gilbert suggests, of specifying the population that is entitled to decide the question.[10] This may ultimately determine the final result. These kinds of issues raise moral concerns that cannot be adequately addressed by the political process.

International Law

Although it is not possible to discuss the international law in any significant detail, the subject needs to be addressed. Allen Buchanan and Wayne Norman are right to question the failure of the philosophical work on secession to take the international law into account. The larger problem, however, is that the international law does not recognize the right to self-determination, as that right is understood within the philosophical literature.

This is in spite of the wording in statutory instruments like the *International Covenant on Civil and Political Rights* and the *International Covenant on Economic, Social and Cultural Rights*, which seem to guarantee such a right.[11] As Lee Buchheit writes, quoting a commentator, the debates in the United Nations Human Rights Commission 'made it clear that the principle of self-determination would be invoked only for the liberation of colonial peoples and territories'.[12] Although the covenants protect minority groups, they have not been interpreted in a manner that envisages a larger right of secession.

There are international instruments like the *Charter* of the United Nations that might seem to extend the principle of self-determination beyond these narrow constraints. Most of these instruments have been drafted and interpreted, however, in a manner that excludes any right of secession.[13] The view of the Supreme Court of Canada in the *Secession Reference* seems accurate:

> The international law principle of self-determination has evolved within a framework of respect for the territorial integrity of existing states. The various

> international documents that support the existence of a people's right to self-determination also contain parallel statements supportive of the conclusion that the exercise of such a right must be sufficiently limited to prevent threats to an existing state's territorial integrity or the stability of relations between sovereign states.[14] (p. 282)

This is trite law. The rights under international law that might permit secession, in an extreme case, arise out of the protections given to fundamental human rights rather than the right of self-determination *per se*.

Antonio Cassese seems to favour an extension of the principle of self-determination in *Self-Determination of Peoples: A Legal Reappraisal*. He is unable however to marshal any law stronger than the 1970 *Declaration on Friendly Relations*, which might give rise to a limited right of secession. On the contrary, he acknowledges that the overwhelming consensus among states is that there is no right of secession in international law. '[I]t cannot be denied that State practice and the overwhelming view of States remain opposed to secession. Indeed, it seems that this is one of the few areas on which full agreement exists among all States.'[15] As a result, any attempt to devise a legal theory of secession requires fundamental changes in the international law.

Cassese also is forced to acknowledge that an act of revolution or secession is not subject to international legal standards.[16]

> As we saw above ... international law does not ban secessionism: the breaking away of a nation or ethnic group is neither authorized nor prohibited by legal rules; it is simply regarded as a fact of life, outside the realm of law, and to which law can attach legal consequences depending on the circumstances of the case ... (p. 340)

The most that can be said is that other states may refuse to recognize a new state or impose conditions on its entry into the international community. These are political decisions however, made after the fact, which do not affect the legal character of secession.

Cassese nevertheless wants to argue that there is a limited and remedial right of secession in the international law. The strongest grounds for such an assertion lie in the *Aaland Islands* case, which arose after the first World War. In that case, the League of Nations appointed three jurists to determine whether the inhabitants of the Aaland Islands had the right to secede from Finland and join Sweden. After the Committee of Jurists ruled that the dispute fell within the jurisdiction of the League of Nations, a Commission of Rapporteurs was appointed 'to recommend a programme of action' (p. 29).

Both of the legal bodies in the Aaland Islands case recognized that there are situations where

> ... the State at issue has manifestly abused its authority to the detriment of the minority, by oppressing or persecuting its members, or else proved to be utterly powerless to implement the safeguards protecting the minority. In such cases, according to the Commission of Jurists, one must regard the dispute as no longer

> coming within the purview of domestic jurisdiction ... On the same issue, the Commission of Rapporteurs took a bolder view and stated that, when confronted with the cases at issue, one ought exceptionally to admit the right of 'separation' of the minority from the State.[17] (p. 31)

There are a number of problems with any use of these decisions as the foundation of a right of secession at international law. The two reports were advisory opinions and the comments on which Cassese relies were inessential, since both reports stressed that the solution to the conflict concerning the Islands lay in the protection of minority rights, rather than the relinquishment of Finnish sovereignty.

Cassese also argues that the *Declaration on Principles of International Law Concerning Friendly Relations and Co-operation among States in Accordance with the Charter of the U.N.*[18] implicitly allows secession 'when very stringent requirements have been met' (p. 118). He is careful to use hypothetical language in making these arguments, however, and the position that he sets out seems weak.

> It can therefore be suggested that the following conditions *might* warrant secession: when the central authorities of a sovereign State persistently refuse to grant participatory rights to a religious or racial group, grossly and systematically trample upon their fundamental rights, and deny the possibility of reaching a peaceful settlement within the framework of the state structure. (p. 119, italics added)

It is true that this contains the elements of a remedial theory:

> Thus, denial of the basic right of representation does not give rise *per se* to the right of secession. In addition, there must be gross breaches of fundamental human rights, and what is more, the exclusion of any likelihood for a peaceful solution within the existing State structure. (p. 119f)

The problem is that there is no legal mechanism to enforce such rights, which can only be asserted by rebellion.

Cassese derives a similar right of resistance from the *Algiers Declaration on the Rights of Peoples*, but the *Algiers* document is merely the expression of 'a private group of politicians, trade-union leaders, representatives of liberation movements, and intellectuals from various countries' (p. 277). The argument is rather convoluted here, since it rests on Article 21 of the *Declaration*, which holds that the rights of minorities are subordinated to the principle of territorial integrity *if* those rights are respected by the state in question.[19] More objectively construed, this kind of conditional is a guarded reiteration of the historical rights of the sovereign state, rather than a positive assertion of a legal right to secede.

The legal significance of the *Algiers Declaration* is dubious.[20] This is the right line of legal reasoning however, and ultimately traces the right of self-determination to the principle of justice. On this account, the legal right of self-determination is a remedial right that flows from the obligation of the state to respect the fundamental rights of the person. The state has no choice in such a matter: a minority whose rights have been violated has an enforceable right to secede and even a subsidiary right to take up arms.

Although the international law has recognized that the state is obliged to respect the fundamental rights of the person, the reality is that there is still no means of intervening legally in the internal affairs of a recalcitrant state. There is always the possibility of 'humanitarian intervention' or the licence provided by a resolution from the Security Council, but these forms of recourse contemplate voluntary actions on the part of individual states. Without an external system of adjudication, which allows the affected parties to challenge the legality of such actions, they are only incidentally justified in law.

The international law is more helpful in setting out the means by which the right to secede must be exercised. Whatever the place of democracy in the world order, Cassese takes the position that a minority cannot legally secede under the international law without a referendum.[21] He suggests that this is illustrated by the case of Quebec:

> Although ... the legal rules do not grant any right to self-determination, international law has already played ... a role as a guiding standard, in that all the parties concerned in Canada agree at least on one issue: any decision as to the future of Québec must be taken by the people of the province by means of a referendum. (p. 254)

This neglects the democratic tradition within Quebec and Canada however, which is far more significant in determining the consensus on the issue.

Cassese also relies on the position adopted by the European Community in setting out the conditions for recognition of the republics of the former Yugoslavia. The Badinter Committee, he writes, saw 'the holding of an internationally monitored referendum involving *the whole population* as an indispensable element for the granting of international recognition of Bosnia-Herzegovina as an independent State. The Committee thus elevated the referendum to the status of a basic requirement for the *legitimation of secession*' (p. 272). This is helpful, in setting out the legal requirements for a political resolution of the question. It does not however address the question whether a minority has a legal right to a plebiscite in the first place.

Natural Law

There is therefore no means, at this point in time, of trying the legal question of legitimacy that arises in the context of secession. It does not seem possible to use the international law for such a purpose without giving the *jus cogens* the obligatory force traditionally reserved for the natural law. This suggestion is probably in keeping with any remedial theory of secession. Allen Buchanan espouses a remedial theory for example that recognizes a right to secede in circumstances where the state has failed to respect the human rights of a group of people with a claim to part of its territory.[22] The significance of Buchanan's theory, like other remedial theories, is that it places moral restrictions on the political order and the principle of political legitimacy.

The concept of the natural law has lost much of its force in ethical and political theory, but remains prominent in philosophy of law. This is because it postulates a moral law above the positive law, which determines whether positive laws are valid.[23] This is of considerable assistance in explaining the dynamic of the constitutional process in determining the validity of domestic laws. It is of little import legally whether such a law derives from religious sources, some form of social consensus, the common features of the human psychology, or some other source. The consensus that allows us to identify such precepts clearly evolves over time.

As Norman Kretzmann writes, the idea of a natural law has a long history.

> There are references to a universal or a natural law in Aristotle's *Rhetoric* and the doctrine was familiar to the ancients. Cicero speaks of it as the law of God, 'everlasting and unchangeable, extending to all nations and all times, with one common teacher and ruler of all'. Those 'who formulated wicked and unjust statutes for nations', he writes, thereby breaking their promises and agreements, put into effect *anything but laws*.[24]

The matter is a relatively simple one: any government is subject to ethical restraints, which ultimately determine the validity of its laws. These restraints must leave enough scope for a state and government to exercise the ordinary political prerogatives.

This brings in the legal concept of legitimacy. The same idea is found in Augustine, and Aquinas, who writes that human law: 'has the nature of law in so far as it partakes of right reason; and it is clear that, in this respect, it is derived from the eternal law. But in so far as it deviates from reason, it is called an unjust law, and has the nature, not of law, but of violence'.[25] Aquinas held that the first precept of the natural law arises from our inclination to preserve ourselves.[26] This gives rise to the concept of self-defence, which provides the most obvious foundation of any remedial right of secession.

This is a place, interestingly, where the medieval view seems to capture more of what we experience than the contemporary view, which falls back on relatively weak assertions that people have a right to self-determination. The idea of choice often seems trivial in the circumstances of secession and it seems more accurate to say that a minority that has suffered severe abuses is *obliged* to defend itself. This is an important consideration legally, since it brings in the doctrine of necessity and suspends ordinary legal restrictions.

Thomas Hobbes develops the medieval position in *Leviathan*, where he essentially holds that the individual right of self-preservation gives rise to a right of association, which provides the basis of political authority. This is a contractual relationship, which is contingent on the provision of the peace and protection that the individual is seeking. Thus, if the enemies in a war 'get a finall Victory; so as ... there is no farther protection of Subjects in their loyalty; then is the Common-wealth DISSOLVED, and every man at liberty to protect himselfe by such courses as his own discretion shall suggest unto him'.[27] In this view, the authority of the political order ultimately derives from the consent of individuals, rather than from the powers of the state.

The legal significance of this position derives from the fact that it separates the interests of the individual and the community at large. Once we have separated these interests, the problem is that they will inevitably conflict. We are accordingly left with two alternatives: we can give the interests of the individual ascendancy over the interests of the community, or vice versa, without recognizing that they share the same interests. If there is a legal argument against contemporary liberals, it is that they take the former position, which traces the authority of the state to the consent of the populace and at least implicitly deprives the state of its original jurisdiction.

Although John Locke takes a similar view of the origins of political authority, he adopts a remedial view of revolution. In a well-known passage near the end of the *Second Treatise*, he argues that the people have a natural right to defend themselves against a government that has become an adversary.

> ... whenever the Legislators endeavour to take away, and destroy the Property of the People, or to reduce them to Slavery under Arbitrary Power, they put themselves into a state of War with the People, who are thereupon absolved from any farther Obedience, and are left to the common Refuge, which God hath provided for all Men, against Force and Violence.[28]

This is a remedial view, albeit a political one, which holds that an oppressive government is illegitimate and loses its title to the sovereign power.

The same reasoning would provide the basis for a remedial right of secession in the instance where a state oppresses a minority. Locke does not believe that a ruler is free to act as he wishes, since he is still subject to the natural law and must be cognizant that this gives rise to the right of revolution. There is no conflict between the individual and collective interests in society in this regard, since the natural law gives the individual a right to preserve the community as well as himself.

> ... having in the State of Nature no Arbitrary Power over the Life, Liberty, or Possession of another, but only so much as the Law of Nature gave him for the preservation of himself, and the rest of Mankind; this is all [a man] ... can give up to the Common-wealth, and by it to the Legislative Power, so that the Legislative can have no more than this. Their Power in the utmost Bounds of it, is limited to the publick good of the Society.[29] (§135)

On Locke's reading, the state has an ethical mandate, which incorporates each individual good in a larger common good. This must include the rights of minorities.

Locke's position in this regard derives, however, from the more basic premise that governments 'are dissolved from within', by various abuses of their powers (p. 425). The right of revolution only arises after the government has lost its legitimacy and is no longer governing in the common good. This tacitly assumes that government has an original jurisdiction, which does not derive from the people. The assumption, in the instance of existing states, is that they are entitled to maintain their authority until such time as they oppress the people and contravene the natural law. The recognition of an international authority to prosecute crimes against humanity can certainly be seen as a step towards some recognition of a doctrine like the natural law in the international jurisprudence.

Locke's argument is still a part of the discussion in political theory. R.E. Ewin, for example, endorses a remedial theory of secession that gives a people the right to reject the authority of a central government. The right to secede, he writes,

> ... might be thought of as something derived from the right of individual persons not to be unfairly persecuted. If they are treated sufficiently badly, then, the argument might go, they will be in their natural condition with respect to the government, no longer bound to obey it, and therefore justified in setting about establishing a new state with whomsoever they choose, using whatever means are reasonable in the circumstances.[30]

From this perspective, it is most convenient to see the right of secession as one facet of a larger question of legal legitimacy. This places moral parameters on the actions of a state, which loses its authority when it oppresses a minority. This gives rise to a political right of revolution, or secession, which exists outside the realm of law.

The problem with the argument that the right to secede arises in this manner, in the state of nature, is that it is the state of nature which requires regulation. From a legal perspective, it does not seem possible to bring events like revolution or secession within a legal regime without moral or legal principles that transcend the normal constitutional order. If they are to have any force, these principles need to apply in the unregulated political realm where revolution and secession occur.

This is in keeping with our moral instincts on the subject of secession. The fact that there may not be any constitutional protection for the rights of a minority within an oppressive state does not seem to affect its right to secede. This is because the illegitimacy of an overholding state derives from a moral order that transcends the constitution. It is this body of substantive principle that would provide the natural source of authority to decide such a question.

The general right of revolution is of no assistance in the classical instance of secession, since a minority's claim to the right usually arises out of the fact that the majority of the populace support the illegitimate actions of the government. This is complicated by the fact that there are many situations where the accidents of geography or the random distribution of population make it impossible for a minority to lay claim to a particular region or locality. There is a broader ethical issue here. It is offensive to suggest that the moral or legal validity of the state's conduct depends on whether the members of a minority are distributed randomly throughout the larger population.

This goes into a more general issue of oppression. On the question of revolution, the truth is simply that the legal right to secede will usually arise in circumstances where there is no realistic prospect of overthrowing the apparatus of the state.[31] This is because states are forced to negotiate a political resolution of such a claim in situations where their authority is seriously contested. As a result, the ligitible cases of secession generally arise in those circumstances where there is no meaningful right of revolution.[32]

In spite of these differences, it is evident that secession and revolution present the same legal problem. In both instances, this arises from the legal fact that it is impossible to form a new state without terminating the existing constitutional order. This disrupts the continuity on which the law relies in determining legal claims and creates a hiatus between the new legal order and the previous legal order. In the common law, as we have seen, this occurs entirely within the political realm, outside the ordinary legal and political orders.

This raises any number of practical questions. Which statutes and regulations, for example, remain in force under the new constitutional order? To what extent do litigants retain or lose their status under the old order? How far back do we trace the origins of a valid title to land? These kinds of issues are difficult to deal with if there is a legal discontinuity because the courts determine the status, rights and obligations of the parties before them from rules and principles that are assumed to exist at the time when the relevant events occurred. The judicial task accordingly proceeds on the basis that the existing constitutional order reaches back in time and extends into the future.

Secession and revolution are extremely difficult concepts, from this perspective. That is because it does not seem open to a court to apply a previous constitutional standard without abandoning the constitutional order from which its own jurisdiction derives. And if there is no nexus between the earlier order, and the subsequent order, there is nothing that guarantees any of the rights that accrue under the older order. This raises the essential problem of secession, since it is impossible to decide these legal issues, or rule on the question of secession, unless there is a higher, overarching legal order, which abridges both regimes.

There are at least two possible answers to the question how this higher, extra-constitutional order might survive the transition from one political regime to another. One is that the sovereign power is an inherent feature of any government and is somehow transferred intact from one state to another. Although this is the kind of view that Carl Schmitt appears to espouse, it runs into difficulties when there is an intervening state of anarchy or civil strife between the termination of one state and the inauguration of another. The other possibility is that the sovereign power has its source in a higher order, which continues without interruptions. If the sovereign power is suspended or ceases to exist, it can therefore be renewed or resurrected. Nor is there anything to prevent the creation of a new sovereign power, outside the ordinary legal and political orders, which is entitled to the allegiance of the courts.

The first possibility, then, is that the sovereign power never ceases to exist. The second is that the source of the sovereign power continues to exist, throughout any hiatus between the two legal orders. Both of these possibilities go against the view that a successful revolution takes effect as a fait accompli that occurs in some inchoate region, outside the ordinary legal order. This would provide the basis for an extra-constitutional legal order, which survives any dissolution of the ordinary legal order.

Leslie Armour takes up this kind of question in an essay entitled 'Law and revolution', where he argues that the concept of law adopted by Ronald Dworkin raises the possibility of a legal revolution.[33] This is because Dworkin believes that the law is made up of principles as well as rules, which are often indistinguishable from moral precepts. Unlike rules, 'principles are guides, may be balanced off against one another, and have their origin in widespread common agreement'.

> There is nothing in Dworkin's thesis which prevents the principles from surviving the dissolution of the legal system – guiding, indeed the departure of the old and the ushering-in of the new. So far as I can tell, one might appeal to general principles to determine, on Dworkin's account, whether a revolution was 'principled' or not – and so it would, in one sense at least, be fair to ask about the legality of revolution.[34] (p. 80)

This is the essential legal question posed by revolution or secession: if we want to bring such events within the rule of law, we need a supervening legal order, which survives any dissolution of the constitutional order.

We cannot speak about a legal transfer of the sovereign power to a seceding state without a set of legal rules and principles to regulate the possession of the legal powers of the state. This is an important and neglected question. E.P. Papanoutsos argues in an older article that we need to distinguish between revolutions which create valid laws and revolutions which do not. 'The only revolution that creates law is one which is morally authentic, with roots deep in the community and historically justified by its own deeds ...'[35] It follows that the only way to introduce the concept of legality in these situations is by falling back on substantive moral views.

This does not exclude the use of the ordinary legal principles that have been developed in the context of the transfer of land or chattels to determine whether the state has a valid title to the sovereign power. These principles must be found however within the fundamental extra-constitutional law that governs the political events that occur between the dissolution of the overholding state and the formation of the seceding state. As we have seen, this exercise is not possible without placing the source of the constitutional and legal order under some form of enforceable moral constraints. At this time, there is little in the international law that would provide the apparatus needed to regulate events that occur within the hiatus between the former legal order and the legal order that replaces it.[36]

We have already seen that the legal consensus in the common law is that the courts have the prerogative to decide for themselves whether they will accept the authority of a revolutionary government. There are at least some moral considerations that enter into such a decision. This gives the courts a residual power, at least, to reject the new political order. The significant suggestion is that there is a moral order above the constitutional order, which determines the validity of the new political order. The importance of such an order is that it transcends any particular set of circumstances and is not subject to any interruptions. The question is whether this might provide the basis for a set of extra-constitutional legal principles, which could be used to regulate events in the instance of a disruption in the political order.

The most difficult issue in this context is how we resolve legal claims that originate in a legal order that has now expired. Since political events occur with remarkable alacrity, in comparison with legal developments, this is difficult without making some use of the prior order. Thus the *Britannica* tells us that judges in the period after the Russian revolution 'were directed at the beginning to apply Russian imperial laws, but only to the extent that they had not been revoked by the Revolution and were not contrary to the revolutionary conscience of the judges'.[37] This is only a temporary, *ad hoc* solution, which does not address the theoretical problem. In addition, the problem created by a discontinuity is far more pronounced in Western legal systems, where individuals and groups have more extensive legal rights.

The constitutional hiatus created by an illegal act of secession was considered by the United States Supreme Court in *Texas* v. *White* 74 U.S. 227 (1869), where the state of Texas moved to recover federal bonds that had been sold by the military authorities of the state during the civil war. The court had no hesitation in holding that the state's secession from the union had no legal effect, and the legislative and executive actions of the rebel state 'were absolutely null. They were utterly without operation in law. The obligation of the State as a member of the Union, and of every citizen of the State, as a citizen of the United States, remained perfect and unimpaired' (p. 238). The court accordingly ruled that the 'Rebel Government' of Texas, which had joined the Confederacy, had never existed as a lawful or *de jure* government of the state.

The question was whether the *de jure* state, now resurrected, was bound by the actions of the illegal, intervening state. The Supreme Court held that some

Acts of the unlawful and revolutionary government, exercising powers akin to a *de facto* government, must be regarded as valid. In the words of the Chief Justice, at p. 240:

> It may be said perhaps with sufficient accuracy, that Acts necessary to peace and good order among citizens, such, for example, as Acts sanctioning and protecting marriage and the domestic relations, governing the course of descents, regulating the conveyance and transfer of property, real and personal, and providing remedies for injuries to person and estate, and other similar Acts, which would be valid if emanating from a lawful government, must be regarded, in general, as valid when proceeding from an actual, though unlawful government ...

This was of no assistance to the defendants, since the court was of the view that the bonds were sold by the military authorities in furtherance of the war, and any actions in support of the rebellion were invalid on their face.

It is significant that the Supreme Court ultimately turned to equitable considerations, in deciding whether to annul the actions of the insurgent government.[38] It is these equitable considerations, moreover, which explain the spirited dissent by Justice Grier, who saw the matter as one of fairness. 'A court of chancery is said to be a court of conscience; and however astute may be the argument introduced to defend this decree, I can only say that neither my reason nor my conscience can give assent to it' (p. 242). Counsel for one of the defendants had argued that, even if there was a legal vacuum, the doctrine of estoppel was sufficient to restrain the power of the state and prevent it from repudiating the contract entered into by the rebel authorities (p. 232).

It follows that the existence of a legal discontinuity is significant theoretically because it leaves the courts with no alternative but to turn to larger ethical considerations. This raises a question as to the contents of any extra-constitutional legal order, which would govern the transition from one constitutional order to another. Although Leslie Armour sees a problem with the natural law, which cannot be ascertained with any certainty, he falls back on a related concept. Above the constitutional order, there is simply the understanding of 'the people': 'there comes a point at which, it seems, there is no appeal except to the common understanding of principles commonly held' (p. 85). It is important to make a distinction, however, between a legal and a political standard. The question, legally, is not what the people wish, but what follows from the principles on which they agree.

Ronald Dworkin seems to adopt a similar standard in arguing that the notion of a 'legitimate' community is based on shared principles: the members of such a community recognize that their 'fates are linked ... by common principles, not just by rules hammered out in political compromise'.[39] This is impossible unless the members of the community share the same moral understanding, which provides the essential basis of any adjudicative process. This is also where the difference between the legal and political process manifests itself. Although it may not be possible to obtain a consensus on the exact question of secession, this does not prevent us from obtaining a consensus on the general principles that form part of the extra-constitutional order. There is therefore nothing to prevent a legal authority from appealing to the views generally held in society.

The fundamental point is that the legal issues that arise on secession need to be decided on moral principles, which are shared equally by the majority and the minority. This is crucial, in determining the fairness of the process and avoiding controversy. There are subsidiary issues here, and the most important consideration may lie in determining the population that should be consulted on a plebiscite. It is apparent that it will be necessary to decide such an issue on legal grounds. At some point, the reality is that we have no choice but to fall back on accepted moral or legal principles, in order to maintain the fairness and efficacy of the political process.

Justiciability

One of the deficiencies in the theories of secession in the philosophical literature is that they fail to recognize the limits of the legal process. This deserves attention. Legal bodies are usually charged with two fundamental tasks: one is to find the facts in the case; the other is to determine and apply the law to those facts. The overriding practical difficulty, with most of the theories of secession in the academic literature, is that they fail to appreciate the limits of the fact-finding process.

This is true for substantive and procedural models of secession. A substantive regime based on historical injustice, such as Buchanan suggests in *Secession: The Morality of Political Divorce*, would require that a court adjudicate on complex historical and political issues that lie outside the normal province of the judicial process. This is a problem, for any legal theory. The answer to the question whether Québec has been treated unjustly in the Canadian confederation is a matter of opinion, which will always be open to debate.

It is one thing to prove a specific historical event by which the state has oppressed a minority. It is another thing to review the historical record and determine whether the injustices perpetrated on a minority outweigh the benefits of government. Whatever their normative implications, legal questions generally require some degree of provability and many cases of political injustice are beyond proof.

This kind of evidentiary problem arises in the context of most theories of secession in the literature. Kai Nielsen, for example, suggests that national groups are entitled to secession unless the existing state demonstrates that it will treat the group fairly. But this is not a simple matter: it may be difficult to prove a past injustice, but there is a historical record, however partial or contested, and facts can be investigated and confirmed. The future is relatively empty and it is impractical to expect a court to make such a momentous legal decision on the basis of these kinds of predictions. It is clear, moreover, that this kind of task is self-defeating and will eventually embarrass the process, since mistakes will be made.

Authors like Avashai Margalit and Joseph Raz put similar conditions on any right of secession. 'The right is conditional on its being exercised for the right reasons, i.e., to secure conditions necessary for the prosperity and self-respect of the group. This is a major protection against abuse.'[40] This is a rhetorical constraint, which is not amenable to proof and does not provide a realistic legal standard.[41] It is impractical to expect a court to determine, as a factual matter, whether the new state is 'likely to respect the fundamental interests of its inhabitants' (p. 457). David Copp introduces similar elements into his legal theory of secession, arguing that the legal right to secede would only arise in situations where secession is 'intrinsically feasible'.[42] This asserts an unenforceable legal test.

There are similar problems with Copp's observation that an international court would have a residual right to deny a minority the right to secede, in an instance where there were legitimate humanitarian concerns.

> A fair implementation of the right to secede in international law would permit the legal right to be overridden as well. For example, in some cases, secession by a group would predictably lead to human rights violations of various kinds; in still other cases, the group would not have qualified as territorial except for human rights violations, such as 'ethnic cleansing'. In such cases, the International Court ought to have the power to refuse to take the final step of according to a group the legal right not to be interfered with in forming a state unless the group implemented a constitution that guaranteed human rights, or unless it corrected the injustice. (p. 237)

This is a relatively naive suggestion, which seriously overstates the speculative powers of legal institutions. Without a compulsory international law, moreover, the implementation of a liberal constitution is of little real significance and will not guarantee the rights of a minority.

There are similar problems with the test proposed by Lee Buchheit in *Secession: The Legitimacy of Self-Determination*.

> Because secession inevitably involves a change in the status quo and any such change is a disturbance of sorts, it would be more realistic to approach this question from the perspective of whether secession, or a continuation of the present union, would be more disruptive of the general international harmony.[43] (p. 231f)

This was published in 1978, well before many of the changes that have occurred in the practice if not the theory of sovereignty. The growth of a global economy, the implementation of free trade zones and other multilateral initiatives have left the matter more complicated than it was when Buchheit wrote his book.

It is extremely difficult to apply such a standard in a legal context, moreover, since most of the factors that Buchheit refers to are matters of opinion, which are not justiciable under ordinary standards of proof. One of the traditional ways to ensure the efficacy of a legal process is to keep it as close to the facts of each case as possible. Although expert evidence is permitted, more and more, in the common law courts, those opinions must be based on facts that have been formally proved.

The same kind of problem arises in the context of theories of secession based on self-determination. Christopher Wellman, for example, recognizes that a theory of secession based on self-determination must consider the fact that secession may be detrimental to the interests of the original state. Daniel Philpott adopts a general standard of justice, which would restrict the application of the right to cases where 'the group's likely potential for justice – that is, its degree of liberalism, majoritarianism, and treatment of minorities – is at least as high as the state from which it is gaining self-determination; its claim is enhanced, and more justifiably takes the form of secession, when it suffers threats and grievances ...' (p. 382).

The standards that this sets are impractical. These kinds of conceptual tests go directly against the evidentiary principle that the courts should not make findings on speculative matters. As a general rule, a party's opinion with respect to the consequences of secession cannot be expressed with the kind of certainty needed to provide the proper basis for a legal decision. This is particularly difficult when a party is a collective or corporate entity, like a state or a diffuse minority, composed of individuals with a wide variety of interests and inclinations.

There are serious limits on the kinds of issues that a decision-making body can fairly try and there are good reasons why courts generally operate *ex post facto*. The certainty required of legally binding decisions is not available in a process that asks a court to predict whether the state will treat a minority unjustly. As Donald Horowitz writes, in 'Self-determination: politics, philosophy, and law': 'The inability to forecast the emergence of an illiberal regime with any degree of reliability renders this qualification on the right of secession illusory' (p. 198). The trial of such uncertain issues is easily influenced by the errant political considerations that affect so many decisions in the political arena.

This is a general problem with theories of secession that are based on self-determination. This is because these theories usually contain qualifications, in the interests of consistency, that restrict the right of secession to those circumstances where a minority is willing to respect the rights of the minorities within its population. This not only requires a court to predict the course of future events: it also raises questions about the seceding group's motivations, which are often not susceptible to proof.[44] It is a mistake to expect a court to enquire into a party's motivations in anything but the most obvious circumstances.

It is possible to take some measures to try and address these kinds of concerns. If there is a serious concern about the effect of secession on the viability of remainder states, for example, a seceding state might be required to provide specific guarantees that would leave the remainder state in a position to maintain itself. It is difficult to see how such guarantees can be properly enforced, however, without introducing a compulsory legal element into the existing international order.

There is a natural correlation between the kinds of moral considerations that provide a justification for secession and the moral factors that arise in the context of revolution or historical doctrines like *jus ad bellum*. It may be relevant, for example, whether an existing state and the movement that opposes it have popular support, or whether other states have interfered in the matter. These kinds of analogies are limited however and are only of general assistance. Since the fundamental purpose of a legal theory of secession is to provide a relatively peaceful means for resolving such conflicts, a legal remedy should be available before conditions have deteriorated to the point of war or revolution.

It is also important to recognize that the natural scope of a legal theory of secession at this stage in history falls well short of those situations where there is open warfare between a state and a minority. As Abeysinghe Navaratna-Bandara writes, there is a point where the process of civil disintegration seems difficult to stop. 'A determined secessionist campaign may lead to a lengthy social and political crisis at all levels of society. Militarization of political and social life may become unavoidable. As a result government will become ever more authoritarian and repressive. And the secessionist movements may *intend* just that.'[45] At some point in the contest, the question whether a minority has a right to secede dissipates in the general need to find a peaceful end to the conflict.

The possibility of dealing with such matters under a legal regime for secession depends, to some extent, on the authority that is given to a court with the mandate for resolving such claims. There is no doubt that issues like viability or relief arise in both sets of circumstances and it is the principle of justice that appears to supply the appropriate standard in both situations. If an international court has the inherent jurisdiction that it needs to decide an issue like secession, it would also have the authority to deal with these kinds of supplementary issues.

From an evidentiary perspective, it is the correlation between the legitimacy of the state and the most basic human rights that provides the most feasible grounds for a claim that a minority has a right to secede. That is because the proof of human rights abuses falls well within the ordinary parameters of a legal inquiry and is open to a resolution in a juridical setting. The same cannot be said of the teleological questions proposed by Christopher Wellman and other authors in the area. The members of courts or international tribunals are not well placed to make a finding that a state will or will not function well in the event of secession.

There seems no reason to dispute Buchanan's call for a 'progressive' interpretation of the principle of territorial integrity. This would hold that the principle of territorial sovereignty will only protect those states that respect fundamental personal rights.

> According to the *progressive* interpretation, the principle that the territorial integrity of existing states is not to be violated applies only to *legitimate* states – and not all existing states are legitimate. There is, of course, room for disagreement about how stringent the relevant notion of legitimacy is. However, recent international law provides some guidance: States are *not* legitimate if they (1) threaten the lives of significant portions of their populations by a policy of ethnic or religious persecution, or if they (2) exhibit institutional racism that deprives a substantial proportion of the population of basic economic and political rights.[46]

Although Buchanan's view probably provides the best basis for the development of a legal right of secession, it rests on a benign interpretation of recent events in international affairs. These events raise their own questions of legitimacy.

It is by no means clear that states are prepared to accept the concept of legitimacy set out by Buchanan. The concerns of the USA, for example, with respect to the International Criminal Court indicate the reluctance of powerful states to accept a compulsory law in the extra-constitutional realm. Buchanan's argument nevertheless appears to be the right one, in emphasizing individual rights, and it is the liberal literature that provides the appropriate grounds for a legal right of secession. This is because the legal right of secession arises most conspicuously when a state violates the physical integrity and fundamental rights of the members of a minority.

Notes

1 Compare Margalit and Raz, 'National self-determination', p. 440: 'Moral inquiry is sometimes understood in a utopian manner, i.e., as an inquiry into the principles that should prevail in an ideal world. It is doubtful whether this is a meaningful enterprise, but it is certainly not the one we are engaged in here. We assume that things are roughly as they are, especially that our world is a world of states and a variety of ethnic, national, tribal and other groups.'

2 This is a reflection of broader concerns in the philosophical literature. In 'Justice and the authority of states', for example, Robert L. Simon argues that the ideal conceptions of justice in the academic literature ignore the existence of states and the conditions in the world. As a result, they cannot be applied without compromising our civil obligations to people in our own community.

3 Horowitz, 'Self-determination: politics, philosophy, and law', p. 199.

4 See Philpott, 'Self-Determination in Practice', at p. 8: 'It could be that the world's political institutions, its international law and its domestic constitutions, are, at this stage in history, too blunt-edged, too bereft of judicial clout and enforcement capacity, to propound a law of self-determination that would ... effectively cull the just claims, sift out the unjust ones ... issue the partial and truncated approvals that many imperfect claims will require, determine the extent and amount of settlements, and perform judgments that would be heeded and respected ...' (p. 84).

5 Wayne Norman argues in a similar vein that a modified 'just cause' theory provides the best institutional theory of secession.

6 Norman, 'Domesticating secession', at p. 13.

7 Nor is ethics entirely different: in many cases, moral theories merely serve to explain or justify existing moral views.

8 See Brighouse, 'Against nationalism', at p. 369f: 'Liberals are typically not content with social institutions that merely deliver liberal justice. They usually believe that the state must do more – it must also be *legitimate*. There is no consensus on exactly what constitutes liberal legitimacy. But three features are common to many accounts. The primary concern is with the consent of the governed. If legitimacy rested on unanimous consent, that would give a veto power to the unreasonable, which may, in turn, make it impossible for liberal arrangements ever to be legitimate. So the consent requirement is usually spelled out in terms of some hypothetical contractual condition: the state has to be such that it would be endorsed by all reasonable and well-informed people who are interested in moral terms of association. Just as unanimous consent is too stringent a condition to be plausible, the hypothetical consent condition can look trivial. So it is usually strengthened by some concern that the state aspire to the actual consent of at least a majority, and preferably the vast majority, of citizens. Finally, conditions are placed on the means by which the state can permissibly seek the consent of the governed.'

9 Pogge, 'The bounds of nationalism', p. 489, at footnote 44.

10 See the reference to Gilbert, 'Community and civil strife', p. 90.

11 Section 1 of both covenants reads: '1. All peoples have the right of self-determination. By virtue of that right they freely determine their political status and freely pursue their economic, social and cultural development.'

12 Buchheit, *Secession*, p. 84. At pp. 58–137, Buchheit provides a good if dated introduction to the right of self-determination and secession.

13 See Cassese, *Self-Determination of Peoples*, at p. 40, where he writes that the Committee responsible for the relevant provision of the *Charter* agreed on four points, the second of which was that the principle of self-determination 'conformed to the purposes of the Charter only insofar as it implied the right of self-government of peoples and not the right of secession.'

14 Documents like the *Declaration on Principles of International Law Concerning Friendly Relations and Co-operation Among States in Accordance with the Charter of the United Nations*, GA Res. 2625 (XXV), 24 October 1970, seem of particular note. But see para. 128 of the judgement in the *Secession Reference*, at p. 282f: 'The *Declaration on Friendly Relations, Vienna Declaration, supra*, and *Declaration on the Occasion of the Fiftieth Anniversary of the United Nations, supra*, are specific. They state, immediately after affirming a people's right to determine political, economic, social and cultural issues, that such rights are *not* to be construed as authorizing or encouraging any action which would dismember or impair, *totally or in part, the territorial integrity or political unity of sovereign and independent States conducting themselves in compliance with the principle of equal rights and self-determination of peoples* as described above and thus possessed of a government representing the whole people belonging to the territory without distinction ... .'

And see Cassese, at p. 6, where he refers to 'such documents as the 1970 UN Declaration on Friendly Relations', 'which characterize self-determination with the flowery and loose rhetoric of freedom and liberation and yet couch its operative terms in the dry and tight language of legal disclaimers, substantially excluding secession from existing States'. Or Cassese, at p. 112: 'Before embarking on a discussion of the language employed [in the *Declaration on Friendly Relations*], it must be emphasized that the overwhelming majority of States participating in the drafting of the Declaration took strong exception to the notion that peoples might have a right of secession.' The same is true of other international instruments. At p. 288, for example, Cassese writes that Principle VIII of the *Helsinki Declaration* 'recognizes that self-determination must not disrupt the *territorial integrity of States*'.

15 Cassese quotes a written reply by the British Foreign Minister to a question raised in the House of Commons in 1983: 'It has been widely accepted at the United Nations that the right of self-determination does not give every distinct group or territorial sub-division within a State the right to secede from it and thereby dismember the territorial integrity or political unity of sovereign independent States' (p. 124).

16 The matter is complicated by the fact that colonial peoples have a larger right to political self-determination, which includes some vague and secondary right to the use of force. As a result, 'liberation movements' have rights which are not available to minorities within larger states. See Cassese, at p. 153: 'liberation movements have been given a *legal entitlement* which is less than a *right* proper but more than the *absence of any authorization whatsoever*. This position can be best expressed by holding that liberation movements, although they do not possess a *legal right* to enforce their substantive right to self-determination by resort to war, nevertheless have a *legal licence* to do so. This notion is intended to encapsulate the idea that wars for self-determination are not ignored by international law, or left in a legal vacuum as being outside the realm of law *qua* mere factual occurrences'. But this kind of tortuous reasoning is self-defeating. On a more fundamental level, it merely recognizes that these events occur in an inchoate realm outside the legal order.

17 And see Cassese, p. 360.

18 GA Resolution 2625 (XXV), 24 October 1970.

19 See Cassese, p. 299. Hurst Hannum expresses the situation more accurately in *Autonomy, Sovereignty and Self-Determination*, at p. 116, where he writes: 'The Algiers Declaration also implicitly supports the right of a minority group to secede from the larger political entity if its human rights are denied ... .'

20 Cassese acknowledges that states have 'refused to grant' the right to secede contemplated by the *Algiers Declaration* (p. 302).

21 See Cassese, at p. 334, where he writes that there are no democratic norms in international law. 'In short, the relationship between the whole population of a sovereign State and its government is still regarded by customary international law as coming within the purview of its domestic jurisdiction ...'

22 Although Buchanan restricts the general right of secession, he recognizes that there may be 'special' rights of secession, such as the rights provided by a constitution that permits a particular group to secede. See Buchanan, 'Theories of secession', at p. 34: 'By a right in this context is meant a *general*, not a *special*, right (one generated through promising, contract, or some special relationship).'

23 There are technical reasons why a strict natural law might not seem to provide the best source for a right of secession. See Buchheit, for example, at pp. 46–57. This does not affect the general claim that there are universal moral precepts, which apply in any human society.

24 This is from Cicero, *De legibus* II v 11, as quoted (and presumably translated) by Kretzmann, in 'Lex iniusta non est lex', at p. 100.

25 Aquinas, *Summa Theologica*, IaIIae, q. 93

26 See Aquinas, at IaIIae, q. 94, resp.: 'inasmuch as every substance seeks the preservation of its own being, according to its nature: and by reason of this inclination, whatever is a means of preserving human life, and of warding off its obstacles, belongs to the natural law'.

27 Hobbes, *Leviathan*, p. 230 [174].

28 Locke, *Second Treatise of Government*, §222. The remark that follows immediately upon this suggests that Locke sees this right as a safeguard against tyranny: 'Whensoever therefore the Legislative shall transgress this fundamental Rule of Society; and ... endeavor to grasp ... an Absolute Power over the Lives, Liberties, and Estates of the People; By this breach of Trust they forfeit the Power the People had put into their hands ... and it devolves to the People, who have a Right to resume their original Liberty, and by the Establishment of a new Legislative ... provide for their own Safety and Security ...' Locke places the King under similar restraints.

29 Locke continues, in §135: 'It is a Power, that hath no other end but preservation, and therefore can never have a right to destroy, enslave, or designedly impoverish the Subjects.'
30 Ewin, 'Peoples and secession', p. 230. Ewin postulates a qualified right of secession, since he argues that such a right is restricted to groups who have already achieved some measure of autonomy. This is a reflection of his view that a group becomes 'a people' by virtue of the fact that they are self-governing. There may be room for elaboration here. But this is circular.
31 This leaves out those situations where a minority takes advantage of the break-up of a state to assert its own claim to independence.
32 This is presumably why Allen Buchanan sees a right of secession as a relatively 'moderate' alternative to a right of revolution, when revolution 'is not a practical prospect' (p. 36).
33 Sidgwick expresses the traditional position in *The Elements of Politics*, at p. 645, where he writes that a 'legal or constitutional right of insurrection is an absurdity'. This does not interfere with 'the moral right to resist and overthrow established rulers in extreme cases of misrule, under most forms of government ...'
34 Dworkin is well known for recognizing the role of principles in the common law. And see Cassese, for example, at pp. 128 and 320, where he argues that principles have a singular importance in the development of international law.
35 E.P. Papanoutsos, 'Law and revolution', p. 207.
36 Though this goes a long way in explaining why the concept of the state evolved as it did. See Gierke, *Natural Law and the Theory of Society*, vol. I, at p. 160: 'The principle that a moral person was a unity, which continued to exist through all the changes of its parts, produced, or helped to produce, a theory of the continuity of public rights and duties; and it began to be generally assumed that the State remained the same identical "Subject" of rights not only when there was a change of persons or territory, but also when there was an alteration in the form of the government. A further consequence followed. In cases of the division of an existing State, or the union of several existing States (such cases being held to involve merely "alterations" of the political situation, as distinct from the complete extinction of a State), rules were laid down which secured the transference of the rights and duties of the old "Subject" to the new "Subject" which had taken its place.' It is interesting that the authority of the state on this view transcends the political order, which could not, logically, be used to determine its legitimacy, any more than the domestic or internal law.
37 'The evolution of modern western legal systems' in *Encyclopaedia Britannica*.
38 The majority suggests that the bonds were bought on speculation, in awareness of the fact that they might not be redeemed.
39 Dworkin, *Law's Empire*, p. 211.
40 Margalit and Raz, p. 459.
41 The dangers in this position are evident in the fact that Margalit and Raz take the position that the decision of the seceding group must be respected, 'even if wrong, even if the case for self-government does not obtain, provided the reasons that motivate the group's decisions are of the right kind' (p. 459).
42 Copp, 'International law and morality in the theory of secession', p. 229.
43 And see Buchheit, at p. 227: 'to use the perhaps unfortunate "quantitative" image, the secessionists' demands will be considered legitimate only in circumstances indicating that the general "amount" of world harmony would be increased by accepting secession'. He immediately adds that the violence of 'disaffected groups' is not a factor in such a calculation.
44 At the end of 'Secession and the principle of nationality', David Miller argues that we need to look 'at how minorities are likely to fare under various possible regimes' (p. 17). This is probably enough to render his criteria of minimal use in a juridical setting.
45 Navaratna-Bandara, *The Management of Ethnic Secessionist Conflict*, p. 14.
46 Buchanan, 'Theories of secession', p. 50.

Chapter 7

Philosophical Framework

The rest of the book discusses the legal mechanics of secession. This chapter argues that the legal and constitutional orders rest on a principle of justice. This is an elementary legal principle, which includes a substantive element and a number of subsidiary principles. The most notable of these subsidiary principles in the present context is a principle of equality, which requires that the state treat all individuals and groups with a certain moral deference. The state has a general obligation to act in the common good: although there is considerable room for disagreement on the means of reaching such a goal, this does not permit serious violations of minority rights.

There is enough in this analysis to set out the basis for a legal theory of secession, which would give a minority the legal right to secede when the state fails to govern in accordance with the subsidiary principle of equality. This in turn raises the question of discrimination, which determines when the state has contravened the legal standard of equality. It also requires the development of specific criteria, which can be used to determine whether a state has acted unjustly in a particular situation. The concept of human rights, which has already received wide international recognition, provides the major source of these criteria.

The legal question of legitimacy arises when the state fails to govern in accordance with the principle of justice.[1] This is a legal rather than a political principle and is in keeping with the procedural thrust of contemporary liberalism. That is because it concerns itself with the legitimacy of the state's actions and merely sets the moral parameters of government. It does not infringe upon the right of the political actors to determine the normative question whether the state should pursue a particular policy.

There is a philosophical dispute as to whether the state serves anything other than an instrumental purpose. If nothing else, however, the state is a necessary instrument of social good, which ensures a minimum of justice in the relations between the members of society. So long as it serves such a purpose, in a reasonable manner, it has a legitimate claim on our allegiance. Since a just state has a right to maintain and exercise its legal jurisdiction, it has the right to enforce its laws against majorities and minorities alike.

The best view appears to be that constitutional provisions exist under the auspices of the legal principle of justice. This principle can be seen as the primary article of the state. It provides the touchstone of the constitutional process: legally, the purpose of the state is to secure justice, which lies in maintaining the fairness of the relationships between the individuals and groups within society. The principle of justice accordingly provides the ultimate source of legal validity, supplemented and articulated by the guarantees found in a charter, a bill of rights, or other constitutional documents.

In some respects, the principle of justice serves as a principle of interpretation, which guides a court in applying the provisions of the constitution. This is necessary, if we are to resolve the discrepancy that arises when different parts of the constitution come into conflict with each other. It also provides the basis however on which a court can determine whether legal and constitutional provisions are in keeping with the basic moral rights of groups and individuals. This raises the legal question of legitimacy.

There are at least three sets of prerogatives that must be considered in this context. The first set is composed of individual rights, the second of group rights, and the third of the prerogatives of the state, which ideally correspond with the interests of the community as a whole. The multinational state probably provides the clearest example of a political arrangement in which all three sets of prerogatives come into potential conflict with one another. Any court that rules on secession will have to consider: (1) the legitimate prerogatives of government, which guarantee the existing legal order, (2) the rights of the relevant minority, along with the rights of other groups whose rights and interests may be affected by secession; and more prominently, perhaps, (3) the rights and interests of individuals within the state.

There is an important methodological issue here, which relates to the role of the courts in managing the relationships between the different parties in society. One of the tasks of the courts in applying the principle of justice is to resolve the conflicts between the claims made in all three domains. The fundamental methodological premise is that it is possible to serve all these interests at the same time. It is when the state serves one set of interests to the detriment of others, and the moral equilibrium of the state is lost, that it becomes illegitimate.

The contemporary idea that individuals and society have disparate interests is a philosophical rather than a legal convention. As long as individuals have a social as well as an individual identity, they have an interest in the welfare of the groups and the larger society to which they belong. The legal interests of an individual who challenges the actions of government accordingly merge with the interests of the other individuals in society. This may seem rather notional when a court finds openly against a party, but it is in exactly such a situation that this kind of justification of state power is critical. This is a matter of applying the standards that we hold in common, rather than paternalism.

It follows from a legal perspective that the individual and collective interests of the members of society cannot be definitively separated from each other. A court can only maintain its impartiality by adopting a stance that incorporates the legitimate interests of all the parties before it. Without such a postulate, there is no basis on which an adjudicative body can reach a neutral decision in a contested matter. This means that a judicial decision on secession must be justified on principles held in common by the majority and the minority before the court, if the court is to provide a solution that meets the interests of both sides.

This is a general principle of adjudication. It is fundamental that a court's decision must be justified on the basis of principles accepted by both sides. It is the common good that provides the source of the principles that can be legitimately used in adjudicating the matter in dispute between such parties. This is true, in every case. Even states at war share a common good, which manifests itself in the rules that govern matters like the exchange of prisoners.

As a matter of practice, the judiciary essentially assumes that the interests of individuals, groups and the state converge in some larger, more encompassing collection of interests. There is a theoretical side to the role of the courts, which serves an integrating function in society. The task of the thoughtful judge never ends: it is the responsibility of the courts to continually unearth and reconsider the moral and political consensus on which these different sets of rights are based. This is a larger and more important philosophical enterprise than is generally acknowledged.

From a legal and methodological perspective, it does not seem possible to develop a feasible theory of secession without an assumption that it is in the interests of the majority to protect the rights of minorities. The philosophical arguments that have been made in advancing the cultural rights of minorities are significant because they suggest that it is in the interests of the whole society to respect the rights of minorities. Authors who trace group rights to individual rights have little choice but to take the position that the decision to award language rights, for example, to minorities serves the interests of individuals outside the minority group. This is not possible unless those individuals have a personal interest in the well-being of the minority.

The philosophical basis of such a position can be found in American pragmatism. John Dewey, for example, saw the tendency to separate individual elements from the rest of reality as 'the most pervasive fallacy of philosophic thinking'.[2] As Matthew Festenstein writes, in *Pragmatism and Political Theory*:

> Dewey argues that the individualistic school of England and France in the eighteenth century errs in conceiving of the individual as 'something *given*, something already there', outside of society, and in seeing social institutions as instruments for advancing the interests of pre-social individuals. The school fails to grasp the constitutive role of the institutional and social environment in shaping individual identity.[3] (p. 24f)

There is accordingly a sense in which the identity of the individual is made up of elements in the community from which he takes his understanding of himself and other people.

Festenstein writes that Dewey's commitment to a 'renascent liberalism' 'is supported by a particular view of human flourishing, and by the conviction that the interests of individuals essentially contain 'a regard for the welfare and integrity of the social groups of which we form a part'.[4] Although Dewey was a liberal democrat, it is his concept of the larger good that unites his ethical and political theories. This does not affect his ethical stature as a liberal, who holds that the 'central good' is 'that of individuality or the capacity for autonomous choice'. Although Dewey avoided such abstract definitions of the 'good', there is no reason to dispute the essential point, which is that it is a mistake to see individual and group rights as opposing interests.

Dewey argues that we cannot conceive of individual human beings, as they actually exist, outside a social context. The fulfilment of individuals is dependent upon others, and attributes of social life, like language, are an intrinsic feature of the individual. As he writes, in 'The individual in the new society', a narrow liberal view

> ... ignores the fact that the mental and moral structure of individuals, the pattern of their desires and purposes, change with every great change in social constitution. Individuals who are not bound together in associations, whether domestic, economic, religious, political, artistic or educational, are monstrosities. It is absurd to suppose that the ties which hold them together are merely external and do not react into mentality and character, producing the framework of personal disposition.[5]

This is in keeping with more contemporary arguments, *per* Will Kymlicka, that any meaningful guarantee of individual rights includes social and cultural rights.

Dewey was suspicious of abstractions and wanted a moral theory that would facilitate moral and political decision making, rather than a theory that provided general answers to theoretical questions. As Festenstein writes:

> Social interests 'flourish to some extent in all persons who have not already been warped'. Self-interest and benevolence are 'both of them secondary phases of a more normal and complete interest; regard for the welfare and integrity of the social groups of which we form a part'; and overcoming these secondary phases is 'a condition of mental and moral health'. (p. 60)

It follows that the interests of the individual and the entire community coincide.

Dewey's view is significant from a methodological perspective because it means that the right solution to a social or political problem can meet the interests of the individual and society. This is very much in keeping with the mode of reasoning used in a legal and constitutional forum, which proceeds on the assumption that the legitimate interests of different parties can be reconciled in some larger, overarching good.

Charles Taylor adopts a similar position in criticizing the 'atomism' of the liberal tradition. In one of the essays in *Philosophical Arguments*, Taylor suggests that atomists accept two basic tenets in political theory. They believe (1) that the social aspects of existence should be explained 'in terms of properties of the constituent individuals' and (2), that 'social goods' can be explained as 'concatenations of individual goods'.[6] The major advantage to such a position is that it provides a relatively simple, schematic means of investigating social phenomena, which is more in keeping with the demands of economic and statistical analysis than a traditional philosophical approach.

There is no reason to doubt the benefits of the approach that Taylor is rejecting from the point of view of the social sciences. It runs into difficulties, however, when we turn to philosophy. Like many authors, Taylor argues that society is something more than a collection of discrete individuals, whose interests can be separated from the interests of the larger community. It is in the legal and political arenas that the practical importance of such a view comes to the fore. That is because legal and political institutions cannot function without some means of reconciling individual and group rights with the interests of the larger community.

The point of the critique by Taylor and others is that it is impossible to separate the interests of individuals and the interests of the community. The same position can be extended to groups. This kind of view weighs in on the side of authors, like Allen Buchanan and Will Kymlicka, who see group rights as a necessary part of any comprehensive theory of individual rights. Kymlicka has essentially argued that every individual lives within a national or cultural context and has a personal interest in preserving community values. The same kind of insight surfaces in the more recent work on nationalism, which recognizes that our individual identities derive from the community.

Dewey's position rests on the principle that individuals do not exist in isolation from the community and form a necessary part of some larger whole. We are born into a community, much as we are born into a family, and shaped by its social forces without exercising any choice in the matter. This is a question of context, as much as anything else, and it is naive to think that we can abstract the individual from the community, since it is the community that provides the sources of the individual's identity. The statement that the community is made up of individuals seems incomplete and there is a psychological sense, at least, in which we can say that it is the individual who is constructed from the community.

There are insurmountable philosophical problems with the view that the community and the state owes its existence to the exercise of individual choice. This goes into other issues however, which are beyond the range of the present discussion. There is at least a legal consensus that we are obliged to obey just laws. Whatever we make of personal autonomy, it is a relative concept that does not deprive the state of its right to enforce such laws. Although there are situations where an individual is entitled to reject the authority of the state, the reality is that there is a implicit presumption in the law that runs in favour of the state's authority.

Although it is impossible to work out the details of a general theory of adjudication in such a limited context, one can discern its basic outline. It has already been suggested that one of the purposes of the law is to regulate the relationships between individuals, groups and the state. The first requirement for any legal theory in the area of secession is therefore to provide a theory that can accommodate all three sets of original rights and determine where they converge. This raises the question of justice: it is when a state oppresses a minority and the three sets of interests diverge that a state fails to abide by the general principle of justice and loses its moral legitimacy. It is in these kinds of circumstances that a minority might acquire a right to secede.

The question of legitimacy gives rise to a second order of legal rights. If the right of secession is a remedial right, it is a subsidiary right. That is to say that it is premised on the contravention of other rights, and is not one of the rights that come under the original purview of the principle of justice. In this sense, it is a legal rather than a simple moral right, which repairs the injustice of the state. It will be evident that a court can only adjudicate this kind of issue if it distances itself from the interests of individuals, groups and the state. It will also be evident that the state cannot be judged in this context unless it is in some sense equal to individuals and groups, and has its own rights and responsibilities.

It is the principle of justice that governs the courts in refereeing the relations between the different parties in society. This is a substantive principle, which contains the moral principle that individuals and the groups of which they form a part are equal. In a legal context, however, it gives rise to a more procedural principle of equality, which is probably a necessary feature of any coherent concept of the state. Nor is this a particularly modern concept: in the *Summa Theologica*, for example, Aquinas tells us that an individual is only bound by laws that are 'proportionate' and impose an equal burden on those who are equally situated.[7] If the state comprises a variety of different actors, the only alternative to the principle of equality is to favour the interests of one party to the detriment of others.

There is no real way of separating the substantive and procedural aspects of equality, at least in a legal forum. The contemporary philosophical sees the procedural principle more literally. The issue of equality is nevertheless a central concern in the liberal canon. It is on this basis that Will Kymlicka wishes to argue for group rights, which would rectify the inequality that the members of minorities might suffer in a society where the majority belongs to another culture. Allen Buchanan and Jeremy Waldron argue, against this, that ethnic or national rights essentially discriminate against individuals who do not belong to such communities. It is the concept of equality that provides the premise of both arguments.

The substantive principle nevertheless occupies an essential part of the liberal tradition, since it is not possible to derive a procedural principle of equality without it. If individuals are entitled to the equal benefit of the law, it is because they have the same substantive value as other people. The point is that there is something in the moral content of what we are that is fundamentally the same. There are religious formulas that express these sentiments, such as the statement that we are all equal in the eyes of God.

There is something wrong in the fact that the substantive concept of equality in itself seems to contravene the procedural notion of equality in the philosophical literature. This surfaces in discussions of the good. Since people have different conceptions of the good life, Ronald Dworkin argues, 'the government does not treat them as equals if it prefers one conception to another, either because the officials believe that one is intrinsically superior, or because one is held by the more numerous or the more powerful group'.[8] The *reductio* is simple enough. What of views which hold that people, or the views they hold, are morally unequal?

One is tempted to say that theory is one thing; reality another. To a lawyer at least, this merely demonstrates that an empty principle of equality is of little assistance in a forum where meaningful decisions must be made. There is no obvious reason to shrink from the substantive task: if the principle of equality forms part of a legal common good, it is a substantive principle, which favours some conceptions of the good over others.[9] The idea that a system based on the principle of equality must treat such views equally is extremely artificial. One may have the right to hold such views, equally with other people. But that is another matter.

The contemporary philosophical literature neglects this aspect of the legal process. In *Justice as Impartiality* for example, Brian Barry argues that the conflicts between parties with competing rights must be resolved by an appeal to rational standards, which can be accepted by either of the interested parties. This is fair enough, but if the conflicts are substantive, there is no escaping the fact that these must be substantive standards.

Barry makes a distinction between first and second order conceptions of the good, which are substantive and procedural respectively. Jason West provides a synopsis of the distinction in *The Philosophical Forum*:

> Substantive conceptions are comprehensive in so far as they are general moral theories which try to give principles for deciding how to act or live one's life. Consequently, they are not merely political. Further, according to Barry they are capable of yielding specific resolutions to questions about individual policies. By contrast, second-order conceptions of the good do not specify what the content of the good is.[10]

Barry wants to rest political theory on the second order good of impartiality, which specifies how we should make political decisions but does not stipulate what policy should be followed in a particular case.[11]

Although this is a political rather than a legal argument, Barry takes it with him when he turns his attention to constitutional theory. The first problem with such an approach is that the constitutional law does not restrict itself to matters of process. Barry deals with this issue by arguing that certain substantive goods are common to any first-order conception of the good. They can therefore form a legitimate part of the constitutional order. In point of fact, this resembles the approach taken by the courts, which generally function on the basis of the moral consensus in society. On the more fundamental issue, it acknowledges that we need a substantive standard to decide ordinary constitutional issues.[12]

Barry's primary example is a constitutional provision guaranteeing freedom of religious worship: since the proponents of any conception of the good will claim the freedom to worship, he argues, the principle can serve as a 'substantive rule' of justice. The problem is that this does not provide us with enough substantive content to answer the questions that naturally arise in a legal setting.[13] These questions are inherently pragmatic: 'What do we mean by worship?' 'Does the right to worship extend as far as public prayer?' 'Does this give rise to ancillary rights, like the right to a religious education?' These kinds of questions cannot be decided without employing substantive principles.[14]

The major problem with adopting a procedural view is probably that it conceals the adjudicative standard in difficult constitutional cases. The force of the procedural argument in contemporary thought may derive some of its vigour from the development of the doctrine of 'due process' in American law. This has been complicated, however, by the development of a substantive doctrine of due process.[15] There will be procedural safeguards in any effective legal system, but these safeguards primarily ensure that substantive questions are decided fairly and impartially.

The distinction between a procedural and a substantive principle of equality admits of many degrees. The law concerns itself with the application of general principles to specific cases. This is a procedural exercise in many respects and the question whether a particular principle is substantive is a relative matter. We might say that the English and French populations in a state, for example, are equal under the law. This is unhelpful, however, without the addition of substantive propositions, such as the proposition that national languages should be preserved. These propositions require further substantive content, such as the idea that a language cannot be preserved unless it is a language of instruction in schools.

The principle of justice and its subsidiary principles accordingly take us into substantive issues. This differs from a simple process of ethical evaluation. The role of the courts us to determine whether the actions of the state come within the legitimate bounds of government, rather than whether they are correct. As a result, judicial decisions have a distinctly procedural character and are usually neutral on specific questions of morality.[16] This does not change the nature of the constitutional process, however, and the task of the courts remains substantive. It requires some reference to an independent source of moral authority, which can only be found in a common set of beliefs.

This description of the legal principle of justice runs at least implicitly against the academic literature, which tends to exaggerate the diversity of moral views in society. In *After Virtue*, for example, Alasdair MacIntyre argues that our society has become so pluralistic that it 'cannot hope to achieve moral consensus' (p. 252). As a result, he suggests, the role of a constitutional court has become that of a mediator, which has no recourse to the moral consensus that is needed to reconcile the conflicts which come before it. Thus, in *University of California Regents* v. *Bakke* 438 U.S. 265 (1978), the United States Supreme Court followed 'incompatible principles' in striking down a special admissions programme for minorities, even as it upheld the right of the university to consider race in its admissions process.

MacIntyre essentially argues that this kind of development has robbed the United States Supreme Court of its moral jurisdiction: 'The Supreme Court in *Bakke*, as on occasion in other cases, played the role of a peacemaking or truce-keeping body by negotiating its way through an impasse of conflict, not by invoking our shared moral first principles. For our society as a whole has none' (p. 253). This is a dubious argument in a legal context. In any constitutional jurisprudence, the courts constantly invoke moral values and principles to justify their decisions, on the basis that those values express the general consensus within society.

There is far more agreement on the underlying principles that form part of the legal and constitutional order than the philosophical literature acknowledges. There is an official aspect to the judicial function that is absent in academic work and legal reasoning has its own conventions. The legal inquiry proceeds in a cautious, empirical vein, which restricts itself to the facts of specific cases and does not set out the meaning of terms and concepts before applying them to the facts. This leaves us with a relatively empty conception of justice, which acquires most of its substantive content when it is applied to specific circumstances. The vague legal formulae in a constitution can be interpreted in many ways.

Although there is plenty of room for the scepticism of a jurist like Oliver Wendell Holmes, a judicial system that throws doubt on the moral efficacy of its own rulings has lost its way. The primary requirement of any legal process is the ability to make decisions and it is no use saying that we cannot decide between competing views, since that makes it impossible to resolve the issues that arise in the courts. This requires different strengths than theoretical work and judicial bodies need a far more refined, and extremely graduated, capacity to distinguish between different cases. On the larger issue, however, the simple fact is that decisions must be made, and in many cases, it is impossible to make them without drawing on positive and substantive moral views.[17]

This does not affect the procedural character of the principle of justice, which takes precedence over our specific moral views. In *Planned Parenthood* v. *Casey*, for example, the majority of the United States Supreme Court held that a decision like *Roe* v. *Wade* calls on both sides of a divisive issue like abortion 'to end their national division by accepting a common mandate rooted in the Constitution' (p. 11). The view adopted by the court is markedly neutral, in spite of its substantive effect. The majority at least suggests that those on both sides of such a divisive issue have a common interest in accepting a resolution based on constitutional principles, whatever moral views they hold.

This appeal to larger interests reflects the principle of justice, which holds that the common interest of the parties transcends the specific views on either side of the contest. This is in keeping with the general practice in the courts. As a rhetorical matter, counsel in a constitutional case inevitably try to establish that it is in the larger interest to hold in favour of their clients. The decision in *Casey* also acknowledges the importance of consensus in the law which comes from the judicial obligation to evaluate different cases under the same body of accepted principle. This provides most of the discipline in the jurisprudence and requires considerable elaboration in specific cases.

It is the moral consensus in this body of customary and constitutional principle that maintains the coherence and consistency of the law, and sets out the legal obligations of the political actors in the state. This is evident in the decision by the Supreme Court of Canada in the *Secession Reference*, which holds that there is a constitutional obligation to negotiate any claim for secession in a manner that accommodates the rights and interests of all of the affected parties. Like the judgement in *Casey*, this suggests that the common interest provides the criteria needed to determine the proper disposition in any contest over the exercise of different rights.

The court in the *Secession Reference* spoke of the need to reconcile the 'various rights and obligations' of the parties and recognized that the process of reconciliation is a necessary feature of any resolution of such claims (p. 249). Nor did the court restrict itself to rights: 'In the event [that] secession negotiations are initiated, our Constitution, no less than our history, would call on the participants to work to reconcile the rights, obligations and legitimate aspirations of all Canadians within a framework that emphasizes constitutional responsibilities as much as it does constitutional rights' (p. 273). The exact meaning of the word 'responsibility' is unclear, but it clearly includes the obligation on the various parties to respect the constitutional rights of other participants in the process.

I have already suggested that it is impossible to construct a viable theory of legitimacy from the point of view of adjudication without an overarching view, which unifies all of the competing interests in a single, comprehensive theory. This is a requirement of any satisfactory decision-making process, which brings two competing principles for example into keeping with a third and larger principle. The process of reasoning in constitutional cases is one of inference and the courts generally begin with moral principles that they regard as incontestable. This allows them to evaluate competing claims on the basis of a common standard.

The subsidiary principles of justice express themselves in the moral and political principles on which a constitution is premised. The Supreme Court of Canada considered some of these principles in the *Secession Reference*.

They include a basic respect for the democratic tradition and the need to protect minorities and their rights. There is also an obligation on the political actors to act in good faith, within the rule of law, and introduce any changes to the legal order through negotiation and consensus. In the Canadian context, this includes the principle of federalism, which 'facilitates the pursuit of collective goals by cultural and linguistic minorities which form the majority within a particular province' (p. 252).

The general values and principles on which the Supreme Court relied can be traced to the obligation of the state and government to exercise the sovereign power in the common interest, without discriminating against minorities. The distinctions drawn by government between the different groups in society must be drawn on grounds that further some genuine public interest. It is not enough on this reasoning if a language law is in the interests of the majority of people in Québec. It must also serve the interests of minorities, if only because they share an interest in the well-being of the majority.

These kinds of principles are foundational. As such, they take us into the extra-constitutional realm, where the sovereign power exists. The legal precepts in this realm exist in a hierarchy of increasingly general principles that take precedence over the specific requirements of the domestic law. This kind of legal step seems inevitable in the instance of secession, since the legal precepts in this realm share the general character of universal moral principles. This provides the natural source of the substantive beliefs shared by competing ethnic or religious groups.

There is a related issue here. Since the sovereign power exists outside the constitutional order, any principles that govern secession must also exist outside the state, where the act of secession occurs. Although the court in the *Secession Reference* drew these principles from Canada's constitutional traditions, one can well imagine circumstances in which a constitution conflicts with such principles. This is particularly true in the instance of a state where there is a long-standing hostility between different ethnic groups.

It is the extra-constitutional law that accordingly provides the natural framework in which any legal right to secede must be analysed. There are two sides to such an inquiry: one side of it relates to the provenance of the right of secession, which originates in the failure of the overholding state to respect the moral limits of its authority. The other equally important side of it relates to the legal and equitable requirements of any valid process of secession. It is the latter aspect of the question that the Supreme Court of Canada deals with in the *Secession Reference*.

The Supreme Court holds that the Canadian constitution cannot be amended without a political consensus. It is the question of legitimacy that lies at the root of such a stipulation: 'Refusal of a party to conduct negotiations in a manner consistent with constitutional principles and values would seriously put at risk the legitimacy of that party's assertion of its rights, and perhaps the negotiation process as a whole' (p. 268).[18] While the Supreme Court recognizes the possibility of an impasse, that does not affect the obligation of the political actors to reach an agreement.[19] The relevant political actors must simply negotiate until they reach a solution that meets the interests of all parties.

There is a fundamental issue here, which was not fully considered by the court. On the one hand, the Supreme Court leaves the question of secession in the political arena. At the same time, it holds that political decisions must be made within the constraints of the fundamental legal principles that it sets out. In the court's view, the question of secession is accordingly a political question, but one which must be decided within the moral constraints established by the legal concept of legitimacy. This recognizes that the legal question of legitimacy takes precedence over the political question.

Antonio Cassese seems to take a different view in *Self-Determination of Peoples*. The major issues in Quebec, he writes, 'must be settled at a political level and the law can only intervene at a further stage, when political solutions have already been found and there is a need for their consecration in norms and institutions'.[20] This reflects the traditional view, which reflects the historical doctrine of sovereignty and gives the political order precedence over the legal order. If the *Secession Reference* points us in another direction, it is probably because this kind of abstract view is untenable in a concrete case. The moral concerns that arise in specific cases are enough to force any court concerned with the general well-being to place restrictions on the actors in the political realm.[21]

Rights

The principle of justice is based on the concept of equality. This finds expression in the principle of legal equality which provides the source of individual and group rights. This kind of principle is enunciated, constitutionally, in a provision like section 15 of the *Canadian Charter of Rights and Freedoms*, which states that every individual 'is equal before and under the law and has the right to the equal protection and equal benefit of the law'. This raises the question of discrimination, which is essential in the context of secession, and calls for more specific criteria, which can be used to determine when the state has contravened the standard provided by the principle of justice.

It is beyond the scope of the present book to review the history of the concept of rights, which appears to have developed from the recognition that the natural law gave the individual claims against society. As the *Encyclopaedia Britannica* puts it, the concept of rights has become the *lingua franca* of contemporary debates in moral, legal and political theory.

> Today, the vast majority of legal scholars, philosophers, and moralists agree, irrespective of culture or civilization, that every human being is entitled, at least in theory, to some basic rights ... the last half of the 20th century has seen, in the

> words of human rights scholar Louis Henkin, 'essentially universal acceptance of human rights in principle' such that 'no government dares to dissent from the ideology of human rights today'.[22]

The significant point is that the modern concept of human rights shares the axiomatic character of earlier principles of legitimacy, which were uncontroversial in their time.

This cannot be viewed in isolation. The contemporary commitment to human rights functions within a larger belief that those with moral, social and political rights are entitled to some form of recourse in the courts.[23] The *Britannica* puts the matter as well as anyone in stating that, 'in the real world', it probably makes more sense to say that we have witnessed 'a rising and overriding insistence' on equality.[24] It is not the concept of a right that is so central, as the belief that there is some deep sense in which comparable individuals and groups are morally equal.[25]

This does not reduce questions of human rights to a simple question of parity, since there are substantive rights that stand on their own. The argument is nevertheless that the rights and obligations in society should be equally shared. The legal right to secede grounds itself in the infringement of such a principle. It is this relative apportionment of benefits and burdens that provides the focus of any challenge to the integrity of the state. A minority cannot logically complain that it has been treated the same way as others in society. There is nothing in such a claim that would give a minority the legal right to separate.[26]

The legal right to secede asserts itself primarily as an argument that a group has been discriminated against. The essence of the claim is the contention that individuals or groups with similar features have not been treated equally. This kind of constitutional or extra-constitutional claim follows a familiar format: (1) Since other individuals or groups enjoy certain prerogatives, and (2) since the party before the court shares the relevant characteristics of those individuals or groups, (3) the law must grant them the same prerogatives.

It is necessary to distinguish between a simple moral and a legal right to secession. A higher moral standard is required in a legal forum, where the consequences are so grave. The legal right to secession would only arise in cases of pressing and substantial inequality. This brings in the concept of oppression. It would nevertheless be a mistake to try and specify the precise inequality that would be sufficient to justify a legal order in favour of secession. As a matter of prudence, it is preferable to deal with such issues, after a court has made a finding of fact that requires it to do so.

The legal argument is simply that a state cannot discriminate against minorities. The focus of such an inquiry is not the nature of the inequality, but the burden that it imposes on the members of a minority. At some point, this becomes oppressive. The right of secession arises when the oppression is of such a substantial nature that the person or group is morally entitled to reject the authority of the state. One of the more obvious examples in recent years is the case of East Timor, which was the scene of violence and intimidation.

This is usually expressed as a question of human rights. There may be philosophical issues as to what constitutes a 'human being' or whether the rights that we normally ascribe to human beings derive from other sources. The French phrase, *les droits de la personne*, is historically more accurate than the English term. Since the rights of the person have a legal rather than a natural derivation. The law has traditionally attached rights and obligations to those individuals who are members of society, rather than to individual human beings. This calls for a different kind of analysis than the political inquiry.[27]

Although it is usually accepted that the right to secession is a group right, many authors insist that this kind of group right should be seen as an adjunct of individual rights.[28] Buchanan argues that the matter is simpler in a legal realm, since the legal right to secession can only be exercised by groups.

> If an individual right is one that ... can be exercised independently by an individual, then the right to secede ... is not an individual right. Its exercise requires collective action, even though we can speak of the individual rights that members of the group have to participate in that collective action.[29]

There is nevertheless a primary sense in which it is the rights of individuals that concern us on secession. As Hurst Hannum writes, the question of 'personal security' is foremost in dealing with the question of self-determination.

> Mass and individual killings; torture; arbitrary and indefinite arrests; induced starvation; illegal expropriation of land; and discrimination in employment, housing, and public services are the most common *causes* of the assertion of group rights by the powerless. In addition, they constitute the most common *responses* by central governments to perceived threats to national unity and territorial integrity.[30]

It is individuals who provide the unit of sensation in society and directly experience any discrimination or oppression. It is therefore individuals who 'must be the ultimate beneficiaries of collective rights if the latter are to have real meaning'.[31]

It is now accepted that the rights of the person are foundational. They do not require any further justification. It is exactly this characteristic that gives them the extra-constitutional status that is needed to decide the legal question of legitimacy. They are also well-designed to supply the necessary corrective in the context of secession. The concept of personal rights is an overtly ethical concept rather than a political one, and will often conflict with a principle like majority rule. It accordingly provides a useful source of criteria for determining whether a state is legally legitimate.

There is another factor that is important in a legal context. The concept of rights is inclusive and open-ended: as a result, it is impossible to exhaustively determine our rights or know whether new rights might be used to justify the actions of a minority in seceding from a larger state. This is a necessary attribute of any legal concept, since the courts need considerable room in which to tailor the law to the circumstances that arise in specific cases. The concept of personal rights merely provides a convenient yardstick, by which we can measure whether the state has acted justly in a particular set of circumstances. It would be a mistake to confine the legal meaning of a term like 'oppression' or 'legitimacy' without considering the implications of such a move on specific cases.

This is not the place to enter into a debate as to which rights qualify as fundamental rights of the person, Allen Buchanan nevertheless seems right in arguing 'that there are some candidates for inclusion in the list that are relatively uncontroversial because they are supported by a wide range of moral theories and traditions of ethics'.[32] For the most part, Buchanan adopts the catalogue of rights espoused by John Rawls:

> These include the right to life (understood as a right not to be unjustly killed), a right to liberty that at least encompasses freedom from slavery, from involuntary servitude and forced occupations, a right against religious persecution, and a right to the material conditions of subsistence. I have argued elsewhere that this list should be expanded at least to include rights against discrimination on grounds of gender, race, ethnicity, nationality, and religion, and this expansion accords with the mainstream of modern human rights doctrine as embodied in international law. (p. 53)

Even in those instances where it is contraventions of the right to life, liberty and security of the person that provide the immediate cause for concern, it is the question of discrimination that seems pivotal. It is not the fact of oppression in itself that gives rise to the right of secession, but the fact that the oppression discriminates against a particular group, with the natural right to form its own state.

It is necessary to develop a more integrated view of personal rights, which can deal satisfactorily with the wide range of claims which have been advanced under such a concept. One of the problems that requires more attention, philosophically, is the conflicts that arise between competing rights. As the Canadian jurisprudence illustrates, constitutional guarantees protecting freedom of expression will naturally impinge upon a minority's right to preserve its language and culture. It seems inevitable that an individual's right to property will conflict with another individual's 'right' to equality of opportunity.

It is unrealistic to place restrictions on the personal infringements that might be used to substantiate the claim that the state has oppressed a minority. Still, the distinction between individual and group rights seems to dissolve in this context. There is a sense in which the personal rights of individuals are often more compelling than other rights. Such rights include legal protections against torture, indiscriminate crimes of violence, and the basic right to life, some degree of liberty, and security of the person. As a result, they provide the most likely examples of a cause of action in secession. These rights cannot be given legal recognition without an additional right of due process, procedural fairness, or 'fundamental justice', the equivalent concept in the *Canadian Charter of Rights and Freedoms*.

Having said this, there may well be social, cultural and political rights which might activate a legal right to secede. A minority which was denied the right to vote and participate in elections, for example, would seem to have a *prima facie* case of oppression. There is no need to restrict such rights to individual rather than collective rights and this might include some form of a right to self-determination. There are more concrete group rights, certainly, like the right to certain schools, the right to public services or even the right to a fair share of a federal budget, which could conceivably give rise to a right of secession. The academic distinction between negative and positive rights is of little help in this context and the relevant question seems to be one of exigency.[33]

Although Buchanan is concerned about procedural fairness, he is concerned with substantive rights, which rest on the assumption that human beings are substantively equal. This is evident in his argument for an institutional morality that is 'teleological' enough to see basic human rights as a necessary good in human society (p. 64). The word 'necessary' is important here, since it suggests that the rights that accrue to persons are only incidentally a matter of agreement. For this reason, the position that Buchanan takes provides an alternative to the contractual view of international relations. This view attempts to show that reasonable nations would naturally agree to some form of equality, which permits them to pursue their own affairs without interference from other nations.[34]

The problem lies in the state. History continues to demonstrate that the Westphalian view cannot ensure the equality of individuals within the state. Many states have flagrantly abused the rights of minorities. As the *Economist* reported in 'A survey of human-rights law', at the end of 1998:

> Since 1945 there have been around 100 serious armed conflicts in the world. It would be difficult to name many that did not involve some war crimes or crimes against humanity. In the past decade alone, conflicts in Somalia, Rwanda, Bosnia, Chechnya and Sri Lanka have all involved the large-scale murder or mistreatment of POWS, attacks on civilians and atrocities. (p. 11)

By any conceivable definition, the actions of a state which permits the rape and murder of a minority are oppressive. It is the flagrant situations that need to be addressed before considering more ambiguous circumstances.

We immediately find ourselves in uncharted territory. This is because there is no skirting the fact that the immediate problem in dire cases is one of process. There is no legal means in the present international order of resolving such issues. The first step in the development of a legal theory of secession is accordingly to set out a legal machinery to resolve such conflicts. Here it seems best, as Buchanan suggests, to start with the most common case, which 'seems to be something like that of a national minority with group-claims against the majority nation-state in which it finds itself'.[35] The more complex claims can be dealt with by way of analogy or an extension of the principle used in such cases.

Notes

1 The state is obliged to govern in *reasonable* accordance with the principle of justice.

2 Dewey, 'Context and thought' in vol. 6 of Jo Ann Boydston (ed.) *Later Works of John Dewey, 1925–1953* (Carbondale, IL: Southern Illinois University Press, 1981–92, p. 5, as quoted in Festenstein, *Pragmatism and Political Theory*, p. 25.

3 Cf. Taylor, *Philosophy and the Human Sciences*, at p. 8, where he writes: 'The disengaged identity and its attendant notion of freedom tend to generate an understanding of the individual as metaphysically independent of society. Of course, it can allow for views which see the individual as shaped by his social environment ... But what it hides from view is the way in which an individual is constituted by the language and culture which can only be maintained and renewed in the communities he is a part of' (p. 8).

4 Festenstein, *Pragmatism and Political Theory*, p. 23.

5 Dewey, 'The individual in the new society', p. 410.

6 Taylor, 'Cross-purposes: the Liberal-Communitarian debate', p. 181. The law seems to take a finer view of the issue, in distinguishing between the several and collective interests of a group of individuals. See *Syndicat catholique des employées de magasins* v. *Paquet Ltée.* [1959] S.C.R. 206 (S.C.C.), for example, at 355, where Justice Judson stated that a collective agreement cannot be construed simply as 'the equivalent of a bundle of individual contracts between the employer and employee negotiated by the union as agent for the employee'.

At ibid., p. 185, Taylor argues that there is nothing in the idea that individuals are 'socially embedded' that prevents us from giving 'individual rights and freedom' the same priority that they receive in the atomistic literature. But of course he is working with a much broader different concept of individual rights.

7 And see the discussion in the *Summa Theologica*, at II-II; 57, where Aquinas says that the notions of justice and right rest on the principle of equality.

8 Dworkin, 'Liberalism', p. 127.

9 It is impossible to treat contradicting views equally unless we reject them both. This seems dangerous in a substantive context.

10 West, 'Impartiality and conceptions of the good', p. 24. And see Barry, *infra*, note 11 at p. 133.

11 See Barry, *Justice as Impartiality*, at p.143: 'As far as the great bulk of contemporary legislation and policy-making is concerned, justice as impartiality will have things to say about *how* the legislation or policy can be framed consistently with the demands of justice, but it is silent on the question of *what* the content of the legislation or policy should be. In all these matters, the neutrality inherent in justice as impartiality leads to an insistence on the point that the decision-making process should not give any special advantages to certain conceptions of the good over others.'

12 Nor does Barry take issue with the substantive point. See Barry, at p. 93: 'We cannot, in other words hope to be able to specify the characteristics of a just constitution in purely procedural terms. For we must be concerned with the substantive justice of the laws and

government policies that are produced within the framework for collective decision-making that it provides.'

13 Barry seems to make the mistake of thinking that the bare wording of a constitution is sufficient to decide such issues. This is misleading. Most of the substantive content in constitutional principles like freedom of religion is found in the jurisprudence interpreting the constitution.

14 The *parens patriae* jurisdiction in the common law provides an example of an area where courts are forced to consult substantive moral principles. See the decision in *Re Eve* [1986] 2 S.C.R. 388, for example, where the Supreme Court of Canada relies upon the value of maintaining a person's bodily integrity, the privilege of giving birth, and other moral considerations.

15 The limitations of a procedural principle of equality are illustrated by the notorious Canadian decision in *Attorney-General of Canada* v. *Lavell* (1973), [1974] S.C.R. 1349. See the judgement of Ritchie J., at p. 1373. And note the reference to *Stephen's Commentaries on the Laws of England* at p. 1366.

16 It is for this reason that the contemporary academic literature is more in keeping with legal views than with ordinary ethical or political beliefs.

17 The first sentence in the decision of the United States Supreme Court in *Planned Parenthood* v. *Casey* seems to catch a sense of this: 'Liberty', the court writes, 'finds no refuge in a jurisprudence of doubt.'

18 And see *Reference Re Secession*, at p. 294: 'A political majority at either level that does not act in accordance with the underlying constitutional principles we have mentioned puts at risk the legitimacy of its exercise of its rights, and the ultimate acceptance of the result by the international community.' Though this actually raises two questions of legitimacy: one internal and legal; and the other external and political.

19 See p. 270. There are at least a few instances where secession was not contested. In *Secession: The Legitimacy of Self-Determination*, at p. 98f, Buchheit mentions the dissolution of the union of Norway and Sweden in 1815 and the secession of Singapore from the Malaysian Federation in 1965.

20 Cassese, *Self-Determination of Peoples*, p. 253f.

21 I should point out in fairness that the decision in the *Secession Reference* was issued after the publication of Cassese's book.

22 'human rights', *Britannica*.

23 See Lawrence Friedman, 'Is there a modern legal culture?', at p. 123, where he writes that there is a modern tendency to see law as '*instrumental*': 'By this I mean that people, groups, classes, occupations, strata, all conceive of law, and use law, as a weapon, an instrument, a tool for achieving economic and social ends; what is more, they think it is perfectly proper to do so.'

24 See the *Britannica*, 'human rights': 'In the real world, despite differences in cultural tradition and ideological style, there exists a rising and overriding insistence upon the equitable production and distribution of all basic values. U.S. Pres. Franklin D. Roosevelt's Four Freedoms (freedom of speech and expression, freedom of worship, freedom from want, and freedom from fear) is an early case in point. A more recent demonstration was the 1977 Law Day speech by then U.S. Secretary of State Cyrus R. Vance, in which he announced the U.S. government's resolve "to make the advancement of human rights a central part of our foreign policy" and defined human rights to include "the right to be free from governmental violation of the integrity of the person, ... the right to the fulfillment of such vital needs as food, shelter, health care, and education, ... [and] the right to enjoy civil and political liberties". Essentially individualistic societies tolerate, even promote, certain collectivist values; likewise, essentially communal societies tolerate, even promote individualistic values. Ours is a more-or-less, not an either-or, world.' Many philosophers would do well to reflect on the latter comment.

25 This may seem to come into conflict with the common belief that individuals have special obligations to their immediate family and other members of the same ethnic or national

community. See Weinstock, for example, 'National partiality', at p. 516: 'Recent defenders of nationalism have pointed to the fact that most people feel that their obligations towards their compatriots are either more numerous or more stringent than those which bind them to people from other countries as evidence that something is seriously amiss with the universalism which allegedly underpins liberal theory. That people believe quite strongly that they have such special obligations is taken as a datum for which different theories of justice must somehow offer an account. It is taken to be a measure of the theoretical success of a theory of justice that what we might call the "special obligations thesis" can be derived from it.' There is no obvious reason however why these different obligations need to conflict with each other.

26 Though a minority might seek secession, simply to escape the asperities suffered by the general population. This is a truncated right of revolution, however, rather than right to secede. See p. 227.

27 See the comment of the majority in *Winnipeg Child and Family Services (Northwest Area) v. G.(D.F.)* [1997] 3 S.C.R. 925, at ¶12, where the court dealt with the question whether a foetus can be regarded as a person: 'As this Court put it in *Tremblay v. Daigle*, [1989] 2 S.C.R. 530, at p. 553: "Ascribing personhood to a foetus in law is a fundamentally normative task. It results in the recognition of rights and duties – a matter which falls outside the concerns of scientific classification. In short, this Court's task is a legal one. Decisions based on broad social, political, moral and economic choices are more appropriately left to the legislature."'

28 For a good example of the approach generally taken in the literature, see Darrel Moellendorf, 'Liberalism, nationalism, and the right to secede', at p. 88.

29 Buchanan, *Secession: The Morality of Political Divorce*, p. 76f. The passage continues: 'The same holds true for collective property rights and robust minority language rights. All of these are group rights in the sense specified above: they are ascribed to groups and must be exercised collectively, through political mechanisms, on behalf of the group.'

30 Hannum, *Autonomy, Sovereignty, and Self-Determination*, p. 117. Hannum continues, at p. 117f: 'Such violations are often linked to imposition of states of siege or emergency, and the violation of human rights by members of the security forces almost universally renders the resolution of conflicting assertions of rights impossible through normal legal or political processes.'

31 Hannum, p. 110.

32 Buchanan, 'Recognitional legitimacy', p. 52.

33 This is true more generally: we have come to a point in human history where a starving population has a legal right to assistance.

34 See Tesón's critique of the Rawlsian position at pp. 58ff, which provides a good summary of its major tenets.

35 Buchanan, *Secession: The Morality of Political Divorce*, p. 79.

Chapter 8

A Legal Theory of Secession

A legal theory of secession needs to satisfy at least three requirements. It needs to give us the means for determining when a legal right of secession arises. This must be sufficient to establish the standard in specific cases. It needs to provide the mechanism needed to exercise the right to secede. Finally, it needs to identify the law that would provide the criteria needed to make decisions in the area. This is problematic because it requires a reconsideration of the nature of the legal order and the extension of the law into the international realm.

It is the remedial theories in the literature that provide the natural source of a legal right. One of the reasons for this is that the remedial approach recognizes that we have an interest in maintaining the integrity of the legal and political order. There should therefore be a legal presumption in favour of existing states to preserve domestic and international stability.

There are a number of other issues. The proper cause of action in secession can be found in the doctrine of oppression, which has been applied in the context of the right of self-determination. The use of such a standard prevents gratuitous claims. It is apparent that secession is a remedy rather than a substantive cause of action. The moral and legal force of the argument for secession would strongly suggest that minorities are entitled to other remedies in situations where secession is not a practical alternative.

Since the legal right of secession merely gives a minority the right to exercise a political prerogative, any legal model would have to make provisions for a plebiscite to decide the political issue. The natural analogy is with the law of contracts: if the state breaches its obligations to a minority, it seems fair to say that the minority has a right to revoke the constitutional contract. This is a political matter.

Philosophical Underpinnings

In setting out a legal theory of secession, it is necessary to consider the philosophical underpinnings of the law. This has been neglected in the philosophical literature. Sergio Cotta tells us that medieval thinkers distinguished between justifications of the origins of power (*quod titulum*) and justifications of its exercise, over time (*quod exercitium*). This is a helpful distinction: although the two issues overlap, it is the second issue that raises the legal question of legitimacy. The law favours certainty and there is a legal and moral presumption in favour of the status quo.

Once the social contract is established, it is entitled to the benefits of this presumption. As Lee Buchheit writes in *Secession*, this is reasonably well expressed in the legal maxim '*pacta sunt servanda*', which expresses 'the rather rudimentary proposition that, all things being equal, contracts should be kept'. A minority has no right to disrupt the continuity of the legal order without taking the interests of other groups and individuals into account. 'When a number of groups band together ... they commit themselves to stand by their agreement and remain loyal to the social entity in return for the benefits of life in the larger association' (p. 21). Any unilateral decision to secede is unfair, since other groups are entitled to assume that the state will continue to exist.

As we have seen, the two positions in the literature of secession have different premises. The premise behind the remedial position is that we have a general interest in maintaining the territorial integrity of the state, which can only be challenged in those circumstances where a state seriously defaults on its moral obligations. One of the philosophical tenets underlying such a position appears to be the observation that an individual has no choice but to accept the reasonable constraints of the larger community in which he finds himself. This encapsulates the traditional view of the law. Unlike much of the contemporary philosophical literature, the law operates on the premise that the state possesses some legitimate authority over the individual, with or without the consent of the individual.

The primary legal fact lies in the existence of the sovereign power. This is the source of the legal order and the rule of law, which cannot be disrupted without entering a state of revolution. The law accordingly rests on the presumption that the authority of an existing state is legitimate. This authority comes with important reservations, nonetheless, which reflect the constraints imposed on the state by the conception of justice. Since most states are subject to the limitations of a written constitution, which are often difficult to distinguish from general moral prescriptions, individuals and minorities have a legal or constitutional right to challenge an unjust law. This provides a useful dynamic for determining the issue of legitimacy.

Against this, there is the position taken by those authors who base the right of secession on the right of self-determination. These authors generally accept the liberal view that the state derives its authority from the consent of the individuals under its jurisdiction rather than the existence of a sovereign power. It is the moral autonomy of each individual that gives rise to the political and democratic right of self-determination, through which individuals grant the state the authority to exercise the prerogative of the sovereign.

A number of authors have accordingly argued that any rights held by groups or even the larger community can be traced to the personal right of individuals to freedom and autonomy. If we take such a position, it seems evident that the state derives its authority from the fact that individual citizens have, freely and independently, given it the licence to govern. This reflects the atomism in most of the contemporary work in political theory: as Donald

Horowitz has remarked in 'Self-determination', 'sharply individualistic justifications of a collective right to secede appear to be ascendant' (p. 198). From this perspective, secession is merely a way of repairing the infringement of a collection of individual rights.

The second position is significant, as Christopher Wellman writes, because it does not restrict the right of secession to those situations where the restraints imposed on the individual become unreasonable. The right of political self-determination is meaningless without some freedom of association, which permits individuals to choose who they wish to associate with politically. This view is reflected in the theoretical work on legal and political obligation, which generally focuses on the question whether the individual has agreed to be bound by the political or legal restrictions that the state has placed upon him. The more ontological issues relating to the individual have already been mentioned.

Legally, the important question is one of temporal priority. One of the major problems with the second position is that it does not seem possible to give the individual any legal prerogatives without assuming that the community already exists, since it is the community which grants the individual those prerogatives. The evolution of our rights seems significant here. We are born into families and our parents generally retain their authority over us in childhood, unless they exceed the standards set by society. This authority is lost over time, as an individual approaches and enters adulthood, but our ability to choose the people with whom we associate is always limited. There is never any situation in which the freedom to associate is not free from social and political constraints.

This does not do away with the volitional issue, since individuals retain the right to reject the authority of the state when it places manifestly unjust restrictions on their personal liberties. Although this can be seen as a withdrawal of consent, there is no reason why this kind of right needs to be predicated on the existence of consent. This is a pivotal issue, legally if not morally, and these kinds of arguments suggest that any legal right of secession will depend on whether individuals are entitled to reject the authority of the state. It is important to separate the two positions, here: the legal problem with the idea of self-determination is that it treats the individual in a state as if they are living outside the social contract, without the obligations that come with it. The remedial position assumes that they are subject to it.

The practical distinction between the two positions is reflected in the common law. A contracting party's right to rescind a contract only arises if the other party has already acted in such a way as to repudiate the contract. This may be a question of neglect, as shown by the second party's refusal to perform its fundamental obligations under the contract. This gives rise to a right of election: the first party can then elect whether to terminate the contract, or maintain the existing agreement and sue for damages. Once a minority has established oppression, which constitutes a fundamental contractual breach, the issue is whether it wishes to seek redress within the existing state. This seems to take us into contractual principles, which would hold that it has no obligation to accept the assurances of a state that has already failed to meet its fundamental obligations.

The significance of this in the case of secession is plain. The contractual analysis holds, moreover, with or without the formalities of a constitutional document. However the question of secession arises, it is worth stating that many technical issues might arise in this kind of context. In some circumstances, for example, there may be a question whether the state before the court is the same state that oppressed a minority. It could be argued that there is no continuing identity, as a result of constitutional changes, which makes the respondent state responsible for the actions of its predecessor.

Retaining Sovereignty

This provides the groundwork for a legal theory of secession. The first issue that needs to be considered is the question of sovereignty. There are two factors that militate in favour of a legal presumption that existing states are legitimate. One has to do with the political fact of sovereignty; the other has to do with the role of such a concept in maintaining the legal order.

The first factor is simple enough. Any realistic theory of secession has to recognize that the international political order is premised on the existence of independent states, whose primary interest is to maintain their own authority. This is not a fact that will go away and there is little reason to pursue theories that fail to acknowledge it. Christopher Wellman's contention that 'many' groups have a right to secede 'even in the absence of past injustices' simply fails to acknowledge the social and political realities of the existing state system.[1] The international order may have its deficiencies, but it has a historical rationale and it is naive to think it can be dismantled without major social upheavals.

Allen Buchanan also writes that there are good moral reasons to support the territorial integrity of states:

> ... the recognition of that principle in international law and political practice promotes two morally important goals: (1) the protection of individuals' physical security, the preservation of their rights, and the stability of their expectations; and (2) an incentive structure in which it is reasonable for individuals and groups to invest themselves in participating in the fundamental processes of government in a conscientious and cooperative fashion over time.[2]

There is accordingly much to be said for retaining the ordinary powers of individual states and the balance of convenience weighs heavily in favour of the existing state in those cases where there is no question of injustice. This is not a simple matter of serving the self-interest of existing states.

The territorial idea has made its way into the international law, where it finds expression in the doctrine of *uti possidetis*, which holds that new states retain the boundaries that existed prior to their independence. Joshua Castellino suggests that the doctrine is the major factor in the formation of 'nearly 80 percent of the states that currently exist'.

> Thus, while underlining the principle of stability of boundaries it provides a territorial limitation of the exercise of sovereign power in relation to its neighbours by means of a demarcated boundary line that had existed at the moment of independence. This demarcated boundary line is, from this point onwards declared sacrosanct and given international legitimacy.[3]

The logic behind such a rule is simple enough, since it confines any struggle for independence to the territory within the borders of the original state and therefore maintains the stability of the existing international order.

This raises troubling questions about adopting any theory of secession based entirely on freedom of association. As Wayne Norman writes, any attempt to institutionalize a pure choice theory 'would almost certainly spell the end to the system of states as we know it'.

> ... most states, including the majority of currently undemocratic states, would likely be torn asunder by opportunistic secessionist movements – *including many for which there would have been no natural impetus in the absence of the currency and enforcement of the choice theory itself*. I think this would be so catastrophic in terms of human lives and well-being that the states making international law would never permit it; and not just out of cynical fears for their own dismemberment.[4]

We should be wary of any attempt to let unrestrained choice determine the political order. The concept of sovereignty, which allows the state to preserve itself, increases the stability of most societies. Unless we introduce other kinds of criteria, there is nothing to prevent such a principle from leading to the complete disintegration of the state system.

Lee Buchheit catalogues the 'fear' of secession under six headings, at least four of which reflect the uncertainty that would accompany any erosion of the principle of territorial integrity.[5] Allen Buchanan, in 'Theories of secession', appears to see this as the most serious objection to theories of secession based on self-determination.

> Primary Right theories are not likely to be adopted by the makers of international law because they authorize the dismemberment of states even when those states are perfectly performing what are generally recognized as the legitimating functions of states. Thus Primary Right Theories represent a direct and profound threat to the territorial integrity of states – even just states. (p. 45)

The problem with institutionalizing such a theory is that it is likely to precipitate a wholesale fragmentation of states with an acceptable record of justice, tolerance and human rights.

This kind of criticism would seem to undermine any argument for a legal right of secession based on the moral right of self-determination. David Copp side-steps the issue in 'International law and morality in the theory of secession', where he proposes a right that would not affect the principle of sovereignty. '[I]t is no part of my proposal', he writes, 'that a country that ignored the International Court [of Justice] in such cases would lose its sovereignty. My proposal does not increase the enforcement powers of the Court or of the United Nations. It simply adds secessionist crises to their areas of jurisdiction' (p. 238). Copp has no difficulty with the fact that states are not required to submit to the jurisdiction of the court.

> One might think that the Court ought to be given the power to compel states to accept its jurisdiction, but unless this change were made, there would be no requirement that a state submit to the Court on matters of secession. And the issue whether this change in [the] powers of the Court ought to be made is separate from the issue whether the Court ought to be given a role in disputes about secession. (p. 236)

This would create little more than a notional right, which is of little assistance in the pressing cases that cry out for a moral remedy.

There is no doubt, as Norman observes, that the history of violence that often accompanies secession would seem to justify a general presumption against it. The most obvious illustration of this in recent memory was the break-up of the former Yugoslavia. As Antonio Cassese writes,

> It is well known that in Croatia and Bosnia-Herzegovina, as well as in a few former Soviet republics, secession has rekindled old hatreds and led to *loathsome* bloodshed. The realization of self-determination, instead of gradually unravelling old inter-ethnic enmities and solving deep-rooted conflicts, has triggered a settling of accounts that has been ferociously carried out by force of arms, thus resulting in the negation of the very essence of self-determination.[6] (p. 273)

The most momentous criticism of a loosening of the reins may be that the availability of a remedy like secession reduces the incentives for participating in the ordinary political process of the existing state.[7] From a practical perspective, it may simply be that people who are forced to live with one another are forced to curb their emotions.

It is notable in this context that the status quo does not always favour the existing state, which has legal obligations to maintain its own territorial integrity. Buchheit, for example, writes that states do not have the right to relinquish territory or cede it to another state without the consent of the people leaving in the territory.[8] Antonio Cassese takes a similar position.

> Neither State practice nor resolutions adopted by the United Nations or other intergovernmental organizations has recently laid special emphasis on the principle that in the case of a transfer of territorial sovereignty by one State to

> another, the wishes of the people concerned should always be taken into account. This however does not mean that this has been discarded or neglected by States or international organizations. The truth of the matter is that the concept was simply regarded as obvious ...[9]

This appears to be another place where contractual principles determine the legitimacy of the state's actions. A state cannot legitimately divest itself of the burden of government without the permission of the individuals and groups living under its jurisdiction.

The importance of the principle of sovereignty in maintaining the integrity of the legal system has been neglected in the literature. Copp recognizes this issue when he writes: 'States are important because of the benefits that a legal order can bring to society, and the success of a legal system does depend on the state's having effective jurisdiction over its territory and on its continuity over time.'[10] The sovereignty of the state is significant in this context because it secures the authority of the legal order and underwrites our legal prerogatives. The problem with the right to secede from this perspective is that it undermines the stability of the system.

Placing secession within easy reach would accordingly undermine the domestic legal order and introduce a dangerous element of uncertainty into many decisions concerning the rights and status of individuals. Buchanan goes some way towards recognizing this in 'Theories of secession':

> Individuals' rights, the stability of individual expectations, and ultimately their physical security, depend upon the effective enforcement of a legal order. Effective enforcement requires effective *jurisdiction*, and this in turn requires a clearly bounded territory that is recognized to be the domain of an identified political authority. Even if political authority strictly speaking is exercised only over persons, not land, the effective exercise of political authority over persons depends, ultimately upon the establishment and maintenance of jurisdiction in the territorial sense. (p. 47)

This is in keeping with the history of the common law. In spite of the recent attempts by states to extend the jurisdiction of their courts to offences committed in other countries, domestic courts generally exercise their powers over individuals by virtue of the fact that a person is within the territory over which the court has jurisdiction.[11]

If we wish to maintain some semblance of a legal order, the continuity of legal claims needs to be protected. The ownership of property, for example, is usually decided by the passage of title from one owner to the next, in a chain of transactions ultimately devolving from the sovereign. This can be traced to the hereditary conception of legitimacy: when there are two competing claims, it is the claim with the better pedigree that takes precedence. This gives us a way of deciding who has the superior claim. As soon as the sovereign power is disrupted, this is lost, and there is nothing in which to vest a legal title. The significance of such a factor should not be understated, from a practical perspective, if we are to secure any degree of justice in the ordinary affairs of life.

There is some sense, at least, in which the concept of sovereignty merely refers to the inherent power of the state, which keeps the moral framework of the existing collection of rights, privileges, obligations and responsibilities intact. There is no obvious reason why a concept of legitimate sovereignty would not be sufficient to preserve the necessary degree of order in society. In the advent of a new political order, moreover, we are at least theoretically returned to the state of nature, in which claims under the previous legal order have no authority. It seems clear that a global system that preserved these claims would logically increase the certainty of the ordinary legal order.

Creating a Cause of Action

The first issue is when a legal right of secession would arise. This requires some analysis of the legal concept of legitimacy, which needs further elaboration. The first point, however, is that secession is only one of the means of dealing with situations where a state has overreached its legitimate authority. This is easily illustrated. There are regrettable situations where a state apparently receives the support of a majority of its citizens because it has persecuted a particular minority. If these individuals are located within a particular territory, secession may be an appropriate remedy. If they are dispersed throughout the state, however, there is little, short of external force, that can compel the state to respect their rights.

The importance of the example is that it illustrates how the question of legitimacy raises itself in situations where there is no feasible right of secession. The availability of a remedy like secession does not determine the moral rights of the individuals who have been oppressed. In point of fact, their moral claims are probably more pressing than the claims of a minority that can plausibly secede. This tells us a good deal about the nature of any legal right of secession, which functions more as a remedy than a cause of action. The moral and substantive right to redress is the same, whether a minority is dispersed throughout the state or concentrated in a particular territory. It is merely that the division of territory will not rectify the injustice in the former instance.

The same cause of action would logically lie in both cases and it seems difficult to give a court the authority to decide secession without giving it at least implicit authority to provide other remedies in situations that are morally equivalent. The right to secede is like a right to a *chose in action*, in some respects. It can only arise in situations where the necessary *chose* exists. The legal right of secession is essentially a right to withdraw from an association. This is only possible where the members of a minority are collected within a territory that can feasibly be separated from the existing state. Conceptually, the right of secession should only be seen as one of a number of secondary rights that arise in those circumstances where a state acts outside the scope of its legitimate authority.

It is probably impossible to determine the precise point when a state has lost its right to exercise the legal powers of government in the absence of a specific set of facts. Nonetheless, if a legal theory is going to preserve the powers of legitimate states, a legal right of secession will only arise in circumstances where there is a pressing and substantial breach of such a duty. Although it is the failure of the state to fulfil its moral obligations and satisfy the principle of justice that gives rise to the right of secession, the proof of a negative assertion is inherently difficult. From a probative perspective, the allegation that a minority has been treated unequally accordingly requires positive proof of the state's treatment of the members of the minority.

There are differences between the legal and philosophical account of legitimacy, which does not take the same evidentiary and procedural considerations into account. A court will need some conceptual test, however rough, to determine when the state has acted in a way that generates the right to secede. The legal exercise depends upon the use of mechanical concepts, which lend themselves to the demonstrative exercise of proving a claim. The first and primary aim of a judicial proceeding is to establish the facts of a case, which are poorly served by vague or abstract language. This brings in the doctrine of oppression, which essentially requires that some element of exigency be present in an application. The same standard has been used in determining whether a people has the right to self-determination in international law.

The discussion of the term 'oppression' in an ethical and philosophical context is of limited assistance. Iris Young, for example, writes of 'five faces of oppression' – 'exploitation, marginalization, powerlessness, cultural imperialism and violence' – in discussing feminist concepts of racial and sexual oppression.[12] She suggests that these may be used as criteria to determine whether individuals or a group have been oppressed. This kind of discussion might implicitly inform any legal or political discussion of the issue but the issue in a legal forum is far less theoretical. As a general rule, courts do not comment on the meaning of terms unless they are required to do so, and academic discussions are of limited use in a legal context.

It may be more practical to consult other sources. When Henry Sidgwick used the term 'oppression' to justify secession, he did so on the assumption that the meaning of the word was self-evident. It is exactly this property that characterizes many constitutional concepts and makes them useful in establishing the moral circumstances that give rise to our fundamental rights. The natural comparison is with primitive terms in the area of ethics, which are probably incapable of definition. This does not deprive them of meaning: on the contrary, it demonstrates that we cannot discuss moral issues without making use of the basic concepts to which they refer. Much the same argument applies in both instances: it is the certainty of general constitutional principles that is important in a legal forum and we do not need a precise definition, morally or legally, to develop a functional jurisprudence.

The substantive content of any right of secession can only be worked out over time, by an examination of the facts of individual cases. However unsatisfying it may seem philosophically, it is important to leave the theoretical underpinnings of terms like 'oppression' open-ended in a legal context. This leaves the scope of such concepts relatively unfettered, and reflects the instrumental nature of legal theory, which is open to continual elaboration. It is a mistake to think this is restricted to the common law tradition: any jurisprudence will be continually forced to tailor the concepts that it uses to the facts that arise in novel cases.[13] The courts are primarily interested in moral principles as a means of assessing the specific issues that arise in the cases before them and the ultimate question is whether a particular resolution of a case meets the ends of justice.

This is a pragmatic approach. Theory is never an end in itself and should not be developed in the absence of facts that require such an elaboration. It is better to consider the application of the law in situations where there is a wide consensus and extend the principles developed in such circumstances to increasingly difficult examples. This is a more cautious approach than we find in philosophy and comes from the fact that the decisions of the courts have practical consequences, often unforeseen, which force the judiciary to express itself with considerable reservation. In the context of a theory of secession, this means employing a concept like oppression in situations such as genocide, where a state has manifestly contravened the principles of justice. It is only from there that a court needs to work out the implications of the doctrine in more difficult examples.

As the present discussion illustrates, the idea of oppression is bound up with the idea of a burden. There seem to be two aspects to the question: a minority is 'oppressed' when it is (1) treated adversely, in a substantially different manner than the majority; and (2) when it suffers a burden as a consequence. This is a question of proportionate equality: it does not mean that every group must be treated in exactly the same way. If the burdens in society are distributed improportionately, the laws that enforce such a discriminatory regime are contrary to the general principle that the burdens and opportunities in society should be shared equally.[14]

If it is the principle of equality that provides the relevant standard of legitimacy, the conduct of the state will be oppressive when its positive actions demonstrate that it places inherently less value on the members of a minority. This may require some analysis of what constitutes an unfair or undue burden on a minority. At some point, it will be evident that the distribution of rights, prerogatives, interests, benefits, duties or burdens is so disproportionate that it can be characterized as oppressive. This might include political prerogatives, such as representation in government or the appointment of the members of an upper house. There are many sources in the constitutional jurisprudence that would assist in such an enquiry.

Managing the Political Question

A legal ruling would generally go no further than the declaration that there is a right to secede. The legal process is not designed to determine what lies in the popular will and it is impossible to decide the political issue in a legal forum. The second requirement of a legal theory of secession is to set out the means of exercising such a right.

The question whether a minority should actually secede raises issues relating to freedom of association rather than justice. It is bound up with matters of will and cannot be decided by a simple application of moral principles to established facts. It should therefore be decided in a political forum, outside the legal process. The question whether it is in the interests of a minority to secede is intensely speculative and impinges directly on the personal interests of those within the relevant territory. It must therefore be decided by those individuals.

Once a court rules that a minority has a right to secede, it must accordingly ascertain the wishes of the populace. In most cases, this would require an order that a plebiscite be held. This would not always be the case: if there are electoral results that clearly establish the will of the people, those results might be sufficient. There may also be cases, such as genocide, where the gravity of the conduct of the state is so serious that a plebiscite seems morally and legally irrelevant.

The matter may be complicated by the fact that the claim to a right to secede may arise in a situation where the group in question already enjoys some form of self-government, such as Québec. The question in such an instance relates more precisely to the extent of self-determination. The strongest argument for a referendum in such a context may lie in ascertaining whether the wishes of the individual members of a minority correspond with the wishes of their leaders.

The presumption of legitimacy continues to apply in this aspect of the process. The political issue is accordingly whether there is a consensus that the minority should secede. Any discussion of the dynamics of such a contest is better left to political scientists and sociologists, but one can only assume that this occurs when the state fails, and conspicuously fails, to meet the expectations of the minority. This can only be settled by a democratic process, by those individuals directly affected by the possibility of secession.

Although any political contest will canvass important moral issues, the effect of these issues is difficult to measure. From a political perspective, it is probably enough to say that a state becomes illegitimate when it loses the confidence of the electorate. This is not an ordinary electoral issue, however, and it is the existence of the state rather than a specific government that is in issue.[15] The question is whether the state still enjoys the consent needed to maintain the integrity of the political order.

This raises an important jurisdictional issue. By any account, a court with the authority to decide whether a minority has a legal right of secession will have the authority to decide the legal and procedural issues that arise when it poses the political question. This includes decisions identifying the population that should be consulted. It also includes the authority to supervise the process if indirectly by the appointment of the appropriate overseers. The tallying of votes, for example, requires the supervision of a third party.

The courts have a general authority to supervise the political process. This is a function of the inherent jurisdiction of the courts, which derives from the moral provenance of the law and exists independently of any political authority. It follows that there is a second head of jurisdiction over secession, which extends into other areas. There is no conceptual reason why the authority of a court trying secession would not extend over events that occur entirely within the political arena. The decision of the Supreme Court of Canada in the *Secession Reference* certainly holds that a minority cannot circumvent its legal obligations by dealing with the issue in the political realm.

This is important, since the more conventional means of expressing the aspirations of a nation or ethnic group for a separate state remains in the political realm, at least in those states that enjoy a modicum of freedom. It follows that a minority might have a political right to secede, whether it has been oppressed by the state or not. The political right would give rise to a legal right in an appropriate case, since a state that persistently prevents a minority from exercising its legitimate political rights can be characterized as oppressive. The discrimination in such a case might be found in the unequal weight accorded to the ballots of those who have rejected the idea of secession.

The issues that would naturally come before a court on a political claim are largely the same as those that arise in the context of a plebiscite. A court with jurisdiction over secession would logically have the authority to rule on issues regarding any referendum, such as the wording of any question put to the electorate, and the protocols that should be observed in conducting the vote.[16] This would include the power to stop or annul a fraudulent ballot, though any interventions in the political process should be minimal.

This aspect of a court's jurisdiction is significant because the democratic process does not provide an effective venue to deal with disputes between a majority and a minority. If nothing else, the dynamics of the democratic system encourages posturing by political leaders on both sides. There is a natural process of polarization, which is open to manipulation and it may be necessary to intervene, in order to prevent one side or the other from seeking an unfair advantage. It is easy to imagine a minority in a wealthier territory attempting to secede without accommodating the interests of those within the remaining state.

David Miller argues that a political or procedural theory of secession is unworkable without some form of legal recourse.

> It is in any case implausible to think that a purely procedural theory of secession could be satisfactory. If we say, for instance, that a majority vote to secede is sufficient to justify secession, this immediately raises the question of how the constituency for the vote is to be established, and how the territory which the seceding group would take with them is to be defined.[17]

Even if these matters are left to the parties, there will have to be some legal mechanism to deal with disagreements.[18]

The case of Québec is revealing. There is much to be said for David Copp's suggestion that a referendum in Québec should be subject to international monitoring, if not outright regulation.[19] This is important, since the results of a referendum held by one side or the other will be subject to an attack from interests on the other side. The most troubling issue in the Canadian context is probably whether a referendum held by the provincial government is legally binding, if the federal government refuses to recognize its validity. The government of Canada has actually passed a *Clarity Act*, which provides a succinct overview of the kind of issues that might arise on a plebiscite.[20]

The Law of Secession

This leaves the third requirement, which presents the major difficulty in developing a legal theory of secession. As a matter of practice, legal rules and principles do not stand on their own. They have a pedigree in some other source, whether it is the natural law, a constitution, the dictates of a sovereign or the will of an elected assembly. This is ultimately what gives them their authority.

One of the primary tasks of a legal theory of secession is accordingly to locate the source of the law that would regulate claims for secession. This does not present a difficult theoretical issue. It is apparent, however, that the matter cannot be solved without legal regulation of the state. The outstanding question is whether the international community is ready to accept this. History and the power of the state stand directly in the way of such a development.

The first observation is that a legal right of secession cannot be found in the domestic law. This is because secession requires an examination of the source of the ordinary legal order. This cannot be found in itself. The domestic law cannot be used to extinguish or overturn itself. There is a distinct problem of coherence that arises in this context, since one of the axioms of legal interpretation is that the entire body of the law forms a cogent and consistent whole. Much of the work done by judges is to reconcile those aspects of the law that are apparently in conflict, and courts are naturally reluctant to use one part of the domestic law to overturn another.[21]

Constitutional Sources

There seem to be two other possibilities. The first is to seek a legal source within a domestic constitution. Allen Buchanan has canvassed this possibility in *Secession: The Morality of Political Divorce*. This would at least bring the question of secession within a legal framework and provide a relatively peaceful means of settling such disputes.

But the most obvious problem with such a suggestion is enough to defeat it. This kind of solution is problematic, without good faith on both sides. Although it is conceivable that a state might permit a minority to secede, the idea of entrenching a right to secede in a constitutional framework is only feasible if a state is open to the possibility of secession. The cases that call for a legal resolution, however, arise when such demands go against the wishes of the state. This is the usual state of affairs, as the history of civil strife attests. Even in the best of circumstances, it is difficult if not impossible to guarantee a fair and impartial hearing in a domestic setting.

The technical suggestion that a minority might secede by virtue of an amendment to a constitution also raises difficulties. This is because secession nullifies or rescinds the constitution, at least in so far as it applies to particular territory within the state. The whole point of secession is to create a new constitutional order, which derives its authority from the fact of its own existence, independently of the previous constitutional order. Theoretically, there might be a provision in a constitution that limits its duration, though that is not in the nature of constitutions. In any event, it does not matter: there can be no provision that sets out the terms of the constitution that succeeds it. That requires a new statute entirely, which only puts the matter back in the political realm.

Other authors have nevertheless made similar suggestions. Wayne Norman discusses the components of a reasonable 'secession clause' in 'The ethics of secession and the regulation of secessionist politics'.[22] To begin with, such a clause would have to specify what regions or groups would be entitled to sue for secession. It would then have to formulate the question to be used in any plebiscite, stipulate the majority needed to win any ballot, and provide for adjudication by a third party as to the terms of secession. This seems perilous from a political perspective, since the process of amending a constitution to allow for the possibility of secession may foster exactly those feelings of indignation or injustice that gives rise to movements for secession in the first place.

The legal issue is whether a domestic court has the jurisdiction to decide a question like secession. Much of Norman's argument would seem to support an extra-constitutional solution to the problem. The need for a venue outside the courts, the need for an adjudication by a third party, the need to set the terms of separation, all seem to take us outside the existing constitution. All issues of jurisdiction aside, a resulting state will arguably not be subject to the restrictions in an expired constitution. Nor does a constitutional mechanism provide us with any means of regulating the hiatus in which the act of secession occurs.

There are a number of ways that the issue could be set out. H.L.A. Hart believed that the courts cannot operate without a constitutional principle – a 'rule of recognition', which can be used to determine when a law is valid.[23] For a legal positivist, this can be determined by deciding whether a particular law derives from a valid source of political authority. The question can be enlarged to incorporate the constitutional constraints on government. The issue on secession, however, is whether the source of authority is legitimate and in keeping with the larger moral order. The provisions of the constitution are of little assistance in deciding whether the rule of recognition is legitimate and binding.

There are other ways of demonstrating the problem. The law of contracts provides a helpful means of understanding constitutional matters. Like a contract, a constitution might contain a provision stipulating that it terminates on the happening of some event. There is no obvious reason why a domestic court could not interpret and apply such a clause, on the contractual analysis, though political considerations would weigh rather heavily on such a process. The legal problem comes in asking a court to adjudicate the issues that arise once the constitution has been terminated. This is inherently problematic.

The literature has used the analogy of divorce too frequently.[24] It nevertheless illustrates the primary difficulty in setting out a legal theory of secession. A judge's authority to dissolve a marriage derives from the law under which the contract was made, rather than from the marriage contract. A court may approve of a settlement proposed by the parties and incorporate it in the *decree nisi*, but only if this meets the public interest. It is not the fact that the parties have agreed to a particular resolution that gives the court the authority to decide the issue. The source of the court's authority reveals itself in exactly those circumstances where it goes against the wishes of the parties.

Those authors who make an analogy between secession and divorce have already accepted that we need a legal regime in which to decide such issues. It would be foolish to suggest that the divorcing spouses should police the resulting settlement or mediate the disputes that arise in its interpretation. It is the court that has the final authority to decide custody, access and the distribution of financial obligations. It is the court that has the authority to enforce the resulting order. The same kind of reasoning applies to any legal resolution of the question of secession, which presupposes the existence of a court with jurisdiction over the state and its minorities.

There is an additional conceptual problem with the idea that the authority of a court to deal with secession comes from the constitution of the state. This lies in the nexus between the sovereign power, as the repository of the political authority of the state, and the provisions of a constitution. In the American system, it is the people who are sovereign and theoretically set the terms of the constitution. Although the matter is significantly more complicated in countries with a historical monarchy, constitutions are the product rather than the source of the sovereign power. This puts any question as to the existence of the state and the sovereign power that animates it beyond the reach of the constitution.

There might seem to be other possibilities. There are conventions outside the legal mechanisms of the state, which place restrictions on the exercise of political authority. This is prominent in the English tradition: since the English law emanates from the sovereign, it has historically been difficult to regulate the exercise the sovereign power. As a result, constitutional conventions have developed to govern the actions of the crown in lieu of legal rules. Some of the conventions are fundamental: it is convention, for example, that requires that a government resign when it is defeated at the polls.

The ordinary courts have no authority to enforce constitutional conventions however. In *Reference re Resolution To Amend the Constitution of Canada* [1981] 1 S.C.R. 753, for example, Justice Martland observed that it was the prerogative of the Crown in the person of the Governor General to dismiss a government and that the courts could not correct the failure to do so without 'creating a state of legal discontinuity, that is a form of revolution' (p. 882). The domestic courts cannot interfere in the exercise of the sovereign power without bringing the source of their authority into question and overthrowing the legal order.

Extra-constitutional Sources

There is no clear way out of the problem, unless the law that regulates secession emanates from a higher source than a domestic constitution. The other possibility is accordingly to ground the right to secession in an extra-constitutional body of law, which binds the state.

The basic precepts of this body of law can be found in a common set of extra-constitutional principles, a natural law of states, which places legal constraints on the legitimate exercise of the sovereign power. These are foundational principles, which can probably be derived from any of the major legal and religious traditions. They represent the received consensus of humanity. This body of law presumably includes the *jus cogens*, which serves much the same purpose.[25]

There is a practical dimension to these arguments. Lee Buchheit identifies two concerns with regard to the problems experienced in resulting states, either by minorities 'trapped' in an unfriendly state or by a majority 'stranded' without the resources of the larger state.[26] Both of these concerns are notable because they demonstrate the need for a standard of justice that protects the rights and interests of the entire population. These concerns transcend the boundaries of a particular state. It is evident that they also place limits on any theory based on the right of self-determination. It is not enough that it is in the interests of the seceding group to separate.

This highlights the difference between a strict legal process and a process of mediation or arbitration. Many of the advantages of a fundamental law derive from the authority of the court that applies such a law, which arises from moral principles rather than the agreement of the parties. Although any agreements between the relevant parties must be considered, there are important limits on the scope of such agreements. A court considering a claim for secession should have the authority to overturn any agreement between the parties that substantially impairs the principle of justice.

It is not possible to locate the law of secession in the extra-constitutional realm without recognizing that the legal order extends beyond the domestic sphere. This requires major changes in the international law. We have already seen that any right to secession in the existing international law is extremely restricted. As Daniel Philpott writes, the idea of self-determination

> ... has advanced little beyond that of an inspired principle, enumerated with others in international covenants. In international legal consensus and state practice, there is no 'right' to self-determination (outside the colonial context) strong enough to elicit outside recognition to a people seeking federal autonomy or independence from a state. Self-determination has remained in the long shadow of the stronger principle of state sovereignty.[27]

Although the concept of sovereignty has been weakened by the development of European law, regional trade agreements and the frequent use of multi-national military forces, it still presents the most fundamental obstacle to any viable theory of secession.

Philpott argues that there should be a presumption in favour of federalism, in order to avoid the conflict generated by a process that calls sovereignty into question. Federalism is appealing because it does not threaten the integrity of the state. The negotiation of internal boundaries and the division of powers would seem less difficult than outright separation. There is much to be said for such a view, though a federal system may also exacerbate regional tensions.[28] There are potential problems with such a solution if it takes place under the authority of the overholding state, without the supervision of neutral parties. The introduction of a presumption in favour of a certain kind of political regime also seems to trespass on the right of a people to choose its form of government.

As Philpott recognizes, the strongest argument against using the international law to regulate an issue like secession is the realistic one.

> The final criterion for international law as an instrument of self-determination is whether it might develop in the conceivable future. The prospect appears unlikely. Conceptually, there is no lack of international legal grounds or bases for it, for several UN documents endorse self-determination along with human rights and minority rights. But the same documents emphasize the value of non-interference as well. What would be needed is not the development of new legal doctrines or rights, but a recalibration of the priority of self-determination with respect to sovereignty. The desire to abridge sovereignty, though, is precisely what is lacking.[29] (p. 21)

Most of the existing body of international law seems unlikely to provide an adequate source for a legal right of secession.

The first step towards a compulsory law of states may lie in general recognition of the special jurisdiction of legal bodies like the International Criminal Court dealing with violations of basic rights. The statute creating the Tribunal for the Former Yugoslavia, for example, gave the tribunal a personal jurisdiction over individuals who are responsible for the commission of extraordinary offences like torture or genocide. This does not extend to the personality of states, however, and the tribunal does not possess any inherent jurisdiction over the offences in question.[30] This is a serious shortcoming and out of keeping with the jurisdiction of the courts in criminal matters, which is the most moral of the legal jurisdictions. It is naive to think that contraventions of human rights can always be dealt with by legal actions or prosecutions directed at specific individuals. There are many situations where it is the state in its corporate guise that oppresses a minority.

Without some broader recognition that the courts have their own source of authority, which applies in the extra-constitutional realm, it will not be possible to develop a viable legal theory of secession. This is a moral source of authority, which provides a substantive foundation for the development of a compulsory law of states. Historically, the extra-constitutional realm has been a political arena. The real basis of the existing international law is agreement. This is a political rather than a legal standard and is too rhetorical to be of much assistance in the face of compelling state interests.

As it stands, the international law has developed on the basis that the internal affairs of a sovereign state are not subject to international regulation. Sovereign states have traditionally been regarded as independent actors, much like the theoretical individual in contemporary theories of the social contract, and are not subject to the rule of a higher moral authority. This is where the real problem lies and where it must be addressed. Agreement is a poor substitute for morality. It is the law that supplies this deficiency.

Notes

1 Wellman, 'A defense of secession and political self-determination', p. 170.
2 Buchanan, 'Theories of secession', p. 46f.
3 Castellino, *International Law and Self-Determination*, p. 110.
4 Norman, 'The ethics of secession', p. 6.
5 See Buchheit, *Secession*, at pp. 28–31, where he suggests that the general reluctance of states to endorse a rights of secession is usually justified by: (1) the fear of balkanization; (2) the fear that the process of secession may prove endless ('indefinite divisibility'); (3) the fear that secession will have a detrimental effect on the democratic system by providing an alternative to participation in the political process; (4) the fear of infirm states, which cannot support themselves; (5) the fear of 'trapped' minorities; and (6) the fear of 'stranded' majorities who find themselves impoverished by the loss of resources in the seceding state.

And see Sidgwick, *The Elements of Politics*, at p. 649f, where he argues that there is no reason why a right of secession 'should be limited by any consideration of the size or continuity of the territory in which the seceders were in a majority; consistency seems to require us to allow the whole community to be resolved into a congeries of separately governed groups, each member being free to select his own political government, without changing his residence, just as he is now free to select the ecclesiastical government that he will obey'.

6 And see the reference in Chapter 4, at note 7.

7 See note 5.

8 See Buchheit, p. 25f.

9 Cassese, *Self-Determination of Peoples*, p. 189. And see p. 335.

10 Copp, 'International law and morality in the theory of secession', p. 239.

11 In the criminal law, for example, the general rule is that the courts have no jurisdiction to try an individual for an offence committed entirely in another jurisdiction.

12 Young, 'Five faces of oppression' in her *Justice and the Politics of Difference*, p. 64. And see the criticism of her theory of oppression in Moore, *The Ethics of Nationalism*, pp. 110–19.

13 See Barker's introduction to Gierke, *Natural Law and the Theory of Society*, for example, at vol. I, p. xl: 'When the reception of Roman law began to be achieved in Germany about 1500, and the civil law of Rome became a current law in the Empire and its principalities, the German interest in the *Corpus Juris* became very largely practical. The old Barolist tradition of adapting Roman law to the needs of actual contemporary life (which had been contradicted but not checked by the humanists of the sixteenth century, such as Cujas, who wished to understand Roman law as an historical fact of the past in terms of historical scholarship) assumed a new and vigorous life; and a *usus modernus* – a modernisation of the *Digest* or *Pandects* of Justinian, which its votaries called *Pandektenrecht*, but which a modern scholar has called 'Wardour Street Roman Law' – occupied the attention of scholars.'

14 The issue of proportionality arises on both sides of this question, since the principle of equality includes the corollary that individuals and groups who are fundamentally different should not be treated equally.

15 It is true that it may be difficult to distinguish the two.

16 In the *Secession Reference*, the Supreme Court of Canada makes it clear that these kinds of political decisions are subject to legal constraints.

17 David Miller, 'Secession and the principle of nationality', p. 4. This leaves the decisive moral issues to be decided by 'a background theory about the circumstances which make a referendum on secession appropriate'.

18 The present system seems to deal with this through proxies and political negotiation. In *The Management of Ethnic Secessionist Conflict*, for example, at p. 175, Abeysinghe Navaratna-Bandara examines the role of larger states, 'Big Neighbours', in secessionist conflicts within an adjoining state. After examining the history of the conflicts in Sri Lanka, Lebanon, and a number of comparable situations, he concludes that such conflicts must always be considered '... in the context of the natural power relationships in the regional political environment. In this context, a Big Neighbour has been identified as the main stabilizing force of the external system on the conflict, though the conflicting parties, one way or another, may tend to resist its involvement in the process of conflict management'.

19 See Copp, at p. 236f. The case of East Timor aside, it seems unrealistic to argue that many states would welcome international supervision.

20 S.C. 2000, c. 26. The Act also states that a unilateral act of secession would be invalid.

21 This was enough to defeat the *Canadian Bill of Rights*, which required the courts to give a piece of ordinary legislation pre-eminence over other statutes. Since that time, the Supreme Court of Canada has been forced to develop the concept of quasi-constitutional law to overcome the difficulty.

22 Norman, p. 18ff.

23 See Hart, *The Concept of Law*, at p. 100, where he writes: 'the statement that a particular rule [of law] is valid means that it satisfies all of the criteria provided by the rule of recognition'. And see p. 113, where he holds that a legal system must meet at least two conditions, the second of which is that 'its rules of recognition specify the criteria of legal validity'.

24 See Jason Blahuta, 'How useful is the analogy of divorce in theorizing about secession?' Although Blahuta's article is unnecessarily technical, he is right in arguing that the metaphor of divorce is fundamentally misleading without an 'effective legal regime' in the international arena.

25 See Henry Shue, 'Eroding sovereignty', at p. 344, where he describes the *jus cogens* as 'the legal analogue' of 'an intersubjective, but not necessarily unanimous consensus'.

26 See note 5, *supra*. Sidgwick recognizes the problem in *The Elements of Politics*, at p. 227: 'In most cases, a further strong argument against disruption would arise from the inevitable incompleteness of the local separations between the seceders and the rest of the community: the territory which secession would break off would usually contain a minority of inhabitants loyal to the old government, who would be likely to suffer seriously from the change whether they remained within the disrupted district or migrated from it.'

27 Philpott, 'Self-determination in practice', p. 86.

28 Although I have generally avoided examples, Indonesia provides a case study of a state where the debate concerning federalism seems significant.

29 Philpott, p. 92f.

30 See *Prosecutor* v. *Duško Tadić* [1995] ICTY Yearbook, 54 (App. Chamber), at 59: 'Indeed, the jurisdiction of the International Tribunal, which is defined in the middle sentence and described in the last sentence as "the full extent of the competence of the International Tribunal", is not, in fact, so. It is what is termed in international law "original" or "primary" and sometimes "substantive" jurisdiction. But it does not include the "incidental" or "inherent" jurisdiction which derives automatically from the exercise of the judicial function.' Such tribunals have the character of inferior tribunals in domestic law, which only possess the powers granted to them by their enabling legislation.

Chapter 9

Practice Issues

This chapter considers a number of practice issues that would have to be considered in adjudicating a claim for an order or declaration recognizing that a group has a legal right to secede. This extends to matters like forum, standing, the requisite burden of proof and the question of enforcement. The chapter comments on the legal meaning of the term 'oppression', which has been used to regulate the relationship between minorities and majorities in the corporate law. It also reviews the three basic stages in any application for relief. The speculative nature of such an exercise does not diminish its importance.

Preliminary Issues

Forum

The first issue is forum. The question is what court or legal body should try an action in oppression, with an application for an order in secession? Putting aside any questions of jurisdiction, the possibility of bias seems to rule out any attempt to use domestic courts as a forum in which to try a claim. Although it may be possible to hold an impartial hearing in an individual case, this is the exception rather than the rule. In most cases, a state will exercise considerable control over its legal apparatus, either through the appointments process or more informal means. A minority cannot be expected to seek relief from the courts of the state that has allegedly oppressed it.

The problem that arises in this context goes beyond political intrigues or personal bias. In most cases at least, the instincts of a constitutional court will run in favour of the constitution under which it functions. This makes it unsuitable for the trial of an issue like secession, which takes us outside the constitutional order. There are legal ways of working around such difficulties. It may be possible for a domestic court to rely on the principles, for example, on which a constitution is premised. This was the approach taken by the Supreme Court of Canada in the *Secession Reference*. This is a relatively makeshift measure, however, and a constitutional court will have to go beyond its ordinary jurisdiction in deciding such an issue.

Daniel Philpott raises related issues, in arguing that the difficult task is to determine whether a minority seeking secession will deal justly with other citizens.

> More difficult to judge is whether a group meets standards of liberalism, democracy, and respect for minorities, what its distributive obligations are, and whether it merits the last resort of political independence. These are judgements about the substantive realization of goods, not merely the following of procedures, and given their subjective, contingent, and almost certainly contested nature, a court seems required to make them.[1]

The problem is finding an impartial forum in which to decide these issues: 'here, partiality is more questionable, dependent on the degree to which a court could serve as an independent "third party", rather than represent the interests of the central government' (p. 23).[2]

These arguments run against Allen Buchanan's suggestion that secession could be regulated by constitutional provisions that permit secession. I have already suggested that it is difficult for a constitutional court to make such a decision without overturning the basis of its own authority. This is directly related to the problem of future enforcement. How is a domestic court to settle any outstanding issues after the constitution has been rescinded and there are two sovereign states before the court? There are additional concerns at the level of practice, however. The task of determining whether a remedy like secession should be granted is fundamentally different from the task of interpreting or applying the constitution.

Allen Buchanan acknowledges that the problem of bias within domestic courts may be solved by the appointment of an independent judiciary or the use of an international court. Although there may be aspects of the matter that must be addressed by the domestic courts, an international forum seems more likely to provide an independent referee between the contesting parties. It would also be in a better position to apply the relevant law, which lies in the extra-constitutional realm. The better alternative would accordingly be to give any authority over secession to an international court that already enjoys at least an implicit authority over states, like the International Court of Justice.

David Copp has actually argued that the *Statute of the International Court of Justice* should be amended, so as to give the court a jurisdiction over secession. This would at least entrench the right to secede in the international law and provide a legal framework to resolve such disputes. If this is to be effective, however, it requires fundamental changes in the international law. It also requires major changes in the role and purpose of the court, which has been used more as an umpire between states than an independent legal body. The example of the European Court of Justice seems instructive, since the process of the court is open to third parties.

The legal right that Copp envisages would give minorities the right to appear before the International Court of Justice. This would be a momentous legal development, more akin to the extension of the status of persons in the domestic law than anything else. The International Court of Justice could not rule on the legalities of secession without ruling on the internal affairs within a state. This requires a firm hand and it is doubtful whether a court without a compulsory jurisdiction would have the legal and moral authority to decide such issues in a convincing manner. A weak institutional apparatus may be worse than none and merely legitimize the actions of those states who disregard its rulings. It is impossible to avoid some allegations of bias, since it will usually be in the political interests of a losing side to attack the impartiality of a court. This kind of problem will be intensified if a court has limited powers or derives its authority from its rhetorical or persuasive role.

The process of appointing members to any international court is open to manipulation and the statutory instrument creating such a court would need to address such concerns. The Convention that governs the European Court of Human Rights, for example, stipulates that judges must be nationals of different states.[3] At first glance, it might seem better to give both sides some say in the appointment of specific panels, but that invites partial opinions. This is an unsettling possibility, which lends itself to political manipulation and runs the risk of inflaming the political tensions between the parties. Although the United States Supreme Court often seems to have given up on the possibility of consensus, divisive judgments only undermine the principle of *stare decisis* and complicate the law.

Standing

The next issue is who has the standing to apply for a legal right of secession. The immediate answer is 'minorities'. The legal right to secede is premised on the understanding that minorities have standing in the international law. This could theoretically attract liabilities as well as rights.

There is still the question of what constitutes a minority for the purposes of secession. Lee Buchheit wrote in *Secession* in the late 1970s that the legal right of self-determination has always been limited to sanguine groups.

> The doctrine of self-determination has never been interpreted to mean that *any* group wishing to adopt the title of a 'self' has a right to political independence. Throughout its checkered career, the doctrine has always been understood, variously but consistently, to require a nation, or a people, or a colonial people, or some other category with a similar ethnological basis. It has never been intended to encompass a group of people, for instance, united only by a common economic advantage but otherwise entirely fungible with the other members of society. (p. 228)

Buchheit argues that these 'parochial' factors are necessary because an ethnological group is 'likely to produce government based on consent' (p. 229).

There have been attempts to define the word 'minority' in the international arena.[4] Prescriptive definitions are of limited use in a legal forum, however, and it is a minority's existence as a discernible community that gives it the right of political association. The importance of nationality in this context is illustrated by its role in personal identity. If other groups or minorities can positively demonstrate that they possess the same defining attributes, the right to secede could be conceivably extended to such groups. It is important to discourage errant claims, however, and this could easily lead into psychological and sociological issues that have no place in a courtroom.

David Copp has argued that the legal right to secede should be restricted to cases where a group has a historical claim to autonomy. These societies already possess a political and a territorial dimension and are something more than a collection of individuals. The legal identification of the relevant minority should certainly take the natural lines of cleavage in population and territory into consideration. Legal definitions are pragmatic, however, and are subordinate to the purpose of the legal inquiry.[5] If it is oppression that gives rise to the right of secession, the scope of the oppression will be a significant factor in determining who is included as a member of the relevant minority.

The question of who constitutes a minority must be decided on a case-by-case basis. There is also the more technical question of determining who is entitled to represent a particular minority. At the outset of any formal process, a court may need to determine whether the party applying for a remedy has the status to make the application. An applicant might be obliged to demonstrate that it represents a majority of the members of the minority. This would discourage errant claims, which only aggravate the tensions within the groups inside a state. These kinds of issues should be decided promptly, without formality, since a legal process will not have much success in resolving such conflicts unless it proceeds expeditiously.

There is a related issue here, which concerns the jurisdiction of any court that is given the jurisdiction to try a cause of action. What if a state rejects the jurisdiction of the court and refuses to appear before it? Although there is no satisfactory answer to such a question in the existing international system, there are procedures in the ordinary courts to note a party in default. For all of the institutional difficulties, a legal regime will not be able to deal adequately with the question of oppression unless it has the authority to rule against a state that refuses to participate in the process. The consequences of failing to appear must be too great for a state to ignore.

There is another technical issue that arises in this context. Interveners should be discouraged and severely restricted. The efficiency of the process needs to be protected. It is also a matter of justice, however. Secession remains an internal matter and the parties to the dispute should be allowed to resolve it without interference from the international community. Participation in the process should be restricted to those parties with a live interest in the matter. There should be a mechanism to represent the larger interest, but this can be provided by some form of *amicus*, which answers to the court.

Grounds

There is a legal doctrine of oppression, which simply holds that the oppressed are entitled to legal redress.[6] This provides the grounds of any cause of action. It has already been argued that the legal right of secession arises when a state acts illegitimately, in oppressing a minority.

The concept of oppression is relatively stark. As a result, it is amenable to the requirements of proof and comes well within the principle of justiciability. It also meets the philosophical standard envisaged by so many authors, who premise any right of secession on the rights of individuals. This is because the distinction between individuals and groups dissipates in a probative forum.

The evidentiary process focuses on the experience of individuals, since it is individuals who provide the unit of experience in human events. As a consequence, it is necessary to prove two elements in a cause of action in oppression. The first is that the state has oppressed individual members of the minority in question. The other is that it has oppressed those individuals because they were members of the minority. The essence of matter is accordingly found in the question of discrimination.

There may be situations where the right of secession seems to arise in the absence of discrimination. The most obvious case is where a government that oppresses the general population has difficulty exercising its authority over a region in the state. This raises a question of revolution, albeit one within a particular territory rather than the country as a whole. This is not a situation that would normally give rise to an application for secession, since it would be impossible to grant the application without throwing the legitimacy of the entire government into doubt.

Although the proof of oppression seems straightforward in the most serious cases, it would be a mistake to develop criteria for establishing oppression without examining the existing law. This is in keeping with the legal convention that the entire body of law exists as a coherent whole. As a result, there is a legal tendency to introduce novel principles by developing the theoretical premises of the existing case law. This maintains the coherence of the law even as it changes and provides a more pragmatic approach than the approach adopted in the academic literature.

There are a variety of sources that might inform a court's use of the concept of oppression. There is a considerable discussion of oppressive conduct, for example, in the common law. The word 'oppression' appears in *Company Acts* and has been used extensively in the context of corporations. This case law is helpful because it deals with the questions of prejudice that inevitably arise in the dealings between a majority and a minority. As one of the entries in the American *Words and Phrases* puts it: 'in general, the term "oppression" suggests harsh, dishonest or wrongful conduct and a visible departure from the standards of fair dealing that inure to the benefit of the majority of shareholders and to the detriment of the minority. *Jackson* v. *St. Regis Apartments, Inc.*, Mo. App., 565 S.W. 2d 178, 183'.

The notion of visibility is helpful, since any legal right of secession should be restricted to situations where a minority suffers substantial discrimination. The oppression must be overt and palpable. The ultimate moral issue on an application before a legal body is whether the state has demonstrably wronged a particular minority. The statement of law in *Scottish Co-op Wholesale Society Ltd.* v. *Meyer* [1959] A.C. 324 (H.L.), at 342, provides a convenient point of departure. In that case, Viscount Simonds held that a company acted oppressively in selling one of its assets to a company controlled by the majority shareholder. 'It had the majority power and it exercised its authority in a manner "burdensome, harsh, wrongful" – I take the dictionary meaning of the word.'[7]

Perhaps the most significant development in the corporate law is that the concept of oppression has developed in a manner that consciously includes the concept of discrimination. There are interesting parallels here, since the law recognizes the need to respect the legitimate authority of the majority. In *Brant Investments Ltd.* v. *Keeprite Inc.* (1987) 42 D.L.R. (4th) 15 (Ont. H.C.), at 50, for example, Anderson J. writes that a judge must consider the competing interests on both sides of the issue.

> On the one hand the minority shareholders must be protected from unfair treatment. That is the clearly expressed intent of the section. On the other hand the court ought not to usurp the function of the board of directors in managing the company, nor should it eliminate or supplant the legitimate exercise of control by the majority.

It is not enough that the policies of the company are unpopular with the minority.

The corporate analogy also has its limitations. The concept of 'oppression' has been diluted in the context of corporations and now includes simple unfairness. In *Journet* v. *Superchef Food Industries Ltd.* [1984] C.S. 916, at 925f, for example, Gomery J. states:

> In Canada, the Court need only be satisfied that the business of the Corporation has been conducted in a manner that is unfairly prejudicial to the interests of some of the shareholders, or that unfairly disregards their interest. It is now no longer a question only of oppression: now the Court is asked to judge upon the fairness of the actions of management.[8]

It is difficult to see how this would be enough, in the case of secession, if there is a presumption in favour of maintaining the existing political order.

There is another problem with the corporate suggestion that bad faith is sufficient to establish oppression. This seems gratuitous in the instance of secession and would raise all the difficulties of attributing mental and psychological states to artificial entities. The decisive factor in proving a cause of action in oppression is injustice: the moral issue is whether a minority has been so unjustly treated that it is legally entitled to reject the legal and political order. This requires that a court determine whether a minority is entitled to redress and the motives and beliefs of the actors in the state only seem relevant if they establish the fact of oppression.

The American case law also makes use of the concept of oppression in determining whether punishment, for example, is unconstitutional.[9] This brings in the notion of cruelty, which raises the question of proportionality that surfaces in the context of discrimination. There is a sense of this in the English law, and *Stroud's Judicial Dictionary* makes use of the same concept, in stating that the word 'oppression' refers to 'a disregard of the essentials of justice and the infliction of a penalty which is not properly related to the crime of that the party stands convicted'. The term has accordingly been used in the criminal law and arises, for example, in determining whether a confession is voluntary. As in most legal matters, the question whether there is oppression is specific to the circumstances of the case. It cannot be decided in an abstract manner, without an examination of facts.[10]

From a legal perspective, at least, the creation of a cause of action in oppression is a substantive development. This does not decide the philosophical issue regarding the nature of the principles that give rise to such a finding. If the courts are insistent about the substantive nature of their jurisdiction, it is primarily because they reserve the right to go beyond shallow procedural questions. There is no subtlety here: no court is going to permit an act of secession without inquiring into the 'substance' of any agreement between the state and a seceding minority. This is the essence of the ruling from the Supreme Court of Canada in the *Secession Reference.*

There is still the philosophical issue. As always, the legal process calls for a judgment as to the parameters in which power can be justly exercised, rather than a decision on public policy. The principle of equality is essential in determining whether conduct is oppressive and the legal right to secede arises from the fact that the members of a minority have been treated differently than other people. There are no necessary answers here and there is a deep sense in which the ownership of the sovereign power over a minority is a political rather than a legal question, which can only be decided by the people who comprise it.

Burden of Proof

I have already suggested that the burden in the instance of a remedy like secession must be high, to avoid the wholesale disintegration of states, and the question of legitimacy or oppression will only arise in starker moral cases. The simplicity of the *uti possidetis* rule was probably its most important historical feature and there are many administrative and practical concerns that militate in favour of retaining it, at least as a presumption.

There are three fundamental principles that seem paramount in assigning a burden of proof. The first is caution: it is simply that we should exercise a large degree of caution in instituting fundamental political changes, which threaten the equilibrium in society. Part of this is a matter of keeping contracts: existing political commitments should not be changed without good reasons, particularly when they have been sanctioned by long and uninterrupted usage. There is a sociological aspect to such an argument, since habit and custom are the source of laws.

The second fundamental principle is certainty, which provides the foundation of any legal system. The deeper problem for any theory that derives the right to secede from an unrestricted right to self-determination is that the authority of the law generally derives from the power of the state. As a result, the law cannot operate effectively in circumstances in which the authority of the state is easily questioned. It follows that everyone with an interest in preserving the legal order benefits from the fact that the state's title to the sovereign power can only be challenged in extraordinary circumstances. This may be the most significant legal factor in the context of secession and weighs heavily in favour of maintaining the authority of the state.

The third principle is geopolitical. It is commonly accepted that every state derives advantages from the fact that the existence of other states in the international state system is reasonably secure. It is true that the principle of sovereignty has been diminished by the development of trans-national political associations that curtail the traditional powers of the state. This is apparent in the case of the European Union, which now possesses a Parliament, a bureaucracy and legal institutions with considerable extra-constitutional authority. In spite of these developments, however, the geopolitical principle still enjoys considerable currency and the existing state system should be respected.

All these factors draw our attention to the importance of political stability in the state system. They implicitly support the contention that any legal mechanism to resolve the question of secession should contain a presumption against secession. There are other reasons why there should be a presumption in favour of the existing state, however. It is 'crucial to understand', Buchanan writes, that all of the citizens in a state

> ... have an interest in making sure that secession will not be too easy. As the political sociologist Albert O. Hirschmann has noted, where *exit* from an association is virtually costless, there is little incentive to exercise the option of *voice* – the use of critical dialogue within the association to improve the quality of its performance.[11]

This will be less of a concern when the right of secession derives from a remedial concept, since that will limit the remedy to those situations where the state has seriously defaulted on its obligation to respect the principle of justice.

This deals with the fundamental burden in a case of secession, which lies in proving the alleged oppression. There are separate burdens however, that arise in the different stages of an application to secede. These burdens are set out in the following discussion.

First Stage: Preliminary Inquiry

In the first stage of any formal process, a court would need to determine whether it should entertain the application. This is a crucial aspect of the process, since any application is likely to exacerbate the tensions between the state and a minority, and unnecessary applications should be discouraged. It should also be decided expeditiously, to prevent the relevant political interests from using the existence of a cause of action and the prospect of a hearing to their own advantage. One of the advantages to a legal process is that a party which applies for relief is no longer in a political position to reject a decision that goes against its interests. This would not prevent it from reapplying in appropriate circumstances.

At the preliminary inquiry, a court would have to determine whether there is a prima facie case of oppression. This requires proof of the substantive ground of secession: the applicant must provide evidence that the state has oppressed the minority that is seeking secession. *Webster's* defines the word 'oppress' as 'to crush or burden by abuse of power or authority'.[12] This seems sufficient, as a rough guide, and it would follow that a state oppresses a minority when it violates the legitimate rights and interests of the members of a minority.

There is a second issue that arises more specifically in the instance of secession. This is the territorial issue. The claim to a legal right to secede seems moot, if the minority does not have a claim to territory that would provide an adequate basis for a viable state. This seems extraneous at a preliminary inquiry, however, which should be used to determine whether an applicant can establish the substantive elements of the cause of action, rather than whether it is entitled to a particular kind of relief. This has profound substantive implications, since it has the effect of opening up the process to groups that are not in a position to claim a specific territory and at least implicitly raises the possibility of other forms of relief.

This suggests that the issue at a preliminary inquiry should simply be whether there is compelling evidence that a minority has been legally oppressed. Roughly speaking, the legal question comes in two parts: (1) Is there proof that individuals have been oppressed by the state, (2) on the basis of their membership in a minority? The most compelling case of oppression consists of physical oppression, which includes the failure of the state to respect the physical integrity of the members of a minority. This includes positive as well as negative duties, and goes well beyond abuses like torture and disappearances.

It may be obvious in many cases that the oppression has a discriminatory character and targets the members of a minority. This will not always be the case, however, and the two issues are conceptually separate. These kinds of distinctions may seem rather sterile in a moral inquiry, but they perform a necessary function in separating different legal claims. The same body of evidence will normally provide proof of both elements in the instance of secession.

The burden of proof in the first stage of the process should logically fall on the party claiming that it has the right to bring an application. The party claiming oppression has an obligation to provide convincing evidence that there is a strong *prima facie* case. The question of what constitutes a *prima facie* case is a complicated legal issue, at least in the common law tradition. The technical requirements of proof must be worked out in the jurisprudence, but there should be cogent and credible evidence on all of the essential averments. The question is whether the application deserves serious consideration. Since there is a presumption against secession and serious concerns about the political impact of trying unlikely cases, there must be testimony or other evidence that establishes that there are compelling reasons to inquire into the matter.

This may create difficulties if a minority does not have the resources to present a proper case and there should be provisions to ensure that each of the parties before the court is given a fair opportunity to present its case. There is probably a need for a commission or *amicus curiae* to represent the larger public interest and ensure that necessary arguments are put before the court. The system may also have need of an independent investigative apparatus to investigate the applicant's allegations and provide a neutral recital of the facts before the court. This is particularly important in urgent situations.

If there is to be a commission it should be an advisory agency, which is not entitled to deference from the court. In spite of its larger political significance, the question of secession is a matter that arises between contracting parties, and should generally be settled between them. It follows that the parties should have carriage of the case rather than an independent agency, whose role should be restricted to that of a neutral adviser. It is a mistake to look for contributions from individual states to deal with responsibilities like investigation, legal representation or enforcement. If a system dealing with secession is to be neutral and impartial, it should operate independently of any individual states.

Second Stage: Trial

The plaintiff minority should present its case at the outset of the trial, if not through viva voce evidence, at least with the rights of cross-examination and rebuttal. This can be done by means of affidavits, some form of discovery or interrogatories, as well as testimony before the court. The respondent state would have the right to counter and the applicant a right of reply. This kind of litigation has a strong public interest component and the process in oppression should not be completely adversarial. A court would probably need inquisitorial powers, which give it the capacity to ask questions of either side or require the production of evidence. This is a supplemental authority and should not be allowed to prevent the parties from presenting their cases.

The most important issue in the trial of an action is undoubtedly the question of grounds. It has already been suggested that a right of action would arise when a state oppresses a minority, generally by violating the personal rights of the members of a minority. The prospect of a trial raises legal issues, however, which have been overlooked in the academic literature. It also raises questions regarding the jurisdiction of a court, which would conceivably have ancillary powers to decide other issues that arise between competing groups and states in the political arena.

The assignment of the burden of proof in this stage of the process is relatively simple. The essential issue is whether the state has oppressed the minority claiming the right to secede. The burden on this issue is the major burden in the case and logically falls on the minority seeking secession, which has an obligation to prove that secession is warranted.[13] This is in keeping with the legal maxim *onus probandi actori incumbit*, which is accepted in English and European law, and holds that the party relying on a particular fact has the obligation to prove it. It also protects the integrity of existing states. Since cases should only reach this stage of the process if there is a serious issue, and the minority is only asking for the opportunity to ask the political question – there can be no secession without popular approval – the standard should be a balance of probabilities.

Objections

There is a second question that potentially arises on the trial of an action. That is whether secession would unfairly compromise the interests of third parties. This requires a procedure to try objections from groups or outside interests. These objections should only be heard if the security and well-being of the party in question is directly imperilled by the prospect of secession. Standing should not be granted to groups who are indirectly affected by the possibility. If a court is not disciplined on this aspect of the matter, the process will simply unravel in a morass of speculation and self-interested debate.

There may be a role for an investigative agency in ascertaining the relevant facts in this stage of the process. The question is whether secession represents such a threat to the rights and interests of other parties that it operates as an equitable bar to any application. The burden on this question is reversed and falls on the party that is objecting to the application. The threshold on such an issue should be high. This is because the presumption in favour of existing states on any application for secession would only permit a court to grant a remedy in serious cases of oppression. It goes against justice to prevent an oppressed minority from exercising its limited right of departure without a pressing and substantial reason.

It follows that the interests of a third party that wants to stop the process should not be permitted to interfere with the resolution of the case, if the interests of the party can be accommodated in other ways. This part of the process is more important in setting legal conditions on the exercise of the right to secede than anything else. At least some of the issues that arise in this context can be dealt with by a rearrangement of borders, voting rights, or some other means. There is also the possibility – with all its terrible implications – of exchanging territory or relocating populations. Although these kinds of rearrangements are inherently suspect, an oppressed minority is entitled to the full exercise of its rights. It should not be deprived of relief unless there are no legal alternatives.

Third Stage: Relief

Once there is a finding of oppression, a court must turn to relief. The burden of proof in this phase of the process is relatively complex. Since the minority has established its right to a remedy, its burden should be relatively low. This is open to some refinement. As a general matter, the burden of proof lies naturally on a claiming party, but only on a balance of probabilities. There will be claims and counterclaims, and the burden may shift from issue to issue. The status quo is also significant. The burden of proof on the question of borders, for example, should fall on whatever party asks the court to depart from existing borders.

Territory

The first question is territory. This is a practical rather than a philosophical question, which requires an examination of specific cases. Allen Buchanan, in *Secession*, nevertheless sets out two standards on the question:

> If the state (or, rather, the people whose agent it is) has a valid title to the territory, then only the most weighty reasons, namely, a grievance of state-perpetrated injustice or the necessity of self-defence against threats to the literal survival of the members of the group, can justify secession. On the other hand, if the state's title to at least some of the seceding territory is dubious (as I believe it is in the case of Québec), then the need to preserve a culture can be reason enough to justify secession ... (p. 153)

Although Buchanan does not delineate the nature of the state's claim to territory, his approach seems to draw on the concept of ownership.

Buchanan is not dealing with a formal legal process and seems to be distinguishing at least implicitly between a legal and a political right of secession. From a legal perspective, it is nevertheless a mistake to invoke different standards in different cases. It is also a mistake to see the state's claim to territory as an issue of ownership. Daniel Philpott's account seems preferable. In his view, the state does not 'own' the land that it oversees: 'insofar as the state holds the title to land, it does so as an elected trustee, which owes fiduciary duties to the citizenry' (p. 370). It is these fiduciary duties rather than raw territory that is transferred to the seceding government.

This is a better account, though Philpott, in 'Self-determination in practice', fails to make the point as explicitly as he might, and it is the title to land rather than the land that vests in the state.[14] It is not the state's property in the territory that matters as much as its title to the sovereign power, which gives it the authority to govern. The state is more properly seen as the authority in whom the right to property is vested, rather than the owner of territory. The state may or may not enjoy the prerogatives that ordinarily accompany the ownership of land and merely possesses the authority to regulate the accoutrements of ownership, like the registration and transfer of titles.[15]

Buchanan essentially converts the claim that a minority has been unjustly treated into a claim for compensation. This treats the territorial prerogative as an award to be bestowed upon an injured plaintiff and obscures the jurisdictional issue. The fundamental question is whether the state has a legitimate right to establish and enforce the law within the territory. A court will have to determine whether the state has ethically compromised its authority and has the right to carry out the normal responsibilities of government. This should be treated as a claim to a title in government rather than a title in property.

There are difficult evidentiary issues that require further discussion. These are generally related to the viability of the proposed state. In Buchheit's view, a group that wishes to secede must demonstrate that it is 'capable of independent existence' or 'willing to annex itself to an existing, viable entity' (p. 228). Bucheit suggests rather improbably that the viability of a potential state can be subjected to empirical proof.[16] He is also notably sanguine, in his willingness to entertain the possibility of intervention from other states.

A court may be in a position to decide the explicit questions that arise in the instance of enclaves or isolated regions that do not provide a feasible basis for a separate state. It is not in a position to decide more complex questions, however, such as whether a minority has the geographic or economic resources to secede. This raises speculative issues that are better left in the political arena, even when the public is in a relatively poor position to decide them. The members of a minority have the right to put their collective interests ahead of any economic benefits that they may be relinquishing. It is important to develop a legal test that distinguishes policy issues from issues that are more properly need to be decided in a legal forum. Matters that go to freedom of association and self-determination should be tried in the political arena.

There are two separate territorial issues. The first is whether the minority has a claim to the territory in question. The second is whether the territory that is being claimed will provide the necessary geographic basis for a viable state. The minority has the burden of proof on these issues, though the second issue has a low threshold of proof. Plausibility is sufficient. There will inevitably be disputes as to the natural borders of a seceding state, which may take a court into collateral issues. It is important to avoid gerrymandering, since the claim to a specific piece of territory will be an important factor in determining the population that should be consulted in a plebiscite. These are initial issues, however, and the precise demarcation of contested borders should only be dealt with at a later stage, when it must be decided.

Plebiscites

The second question that arises on relief is whether there should be a vote on the matter. This can only be decided in the political realm and will generally require a plebiscite. By this point, a minority is entitled to a political determination of the question and objections to a plebiscite should only be considered if they raise pressing concerns.

The prospect of a plebiscite raises a number of issues of its own, however, such as the precise identity of the group of people who should be consulted. It will also be necessary to give a neutral agency stewardship of the voting process and provide for a neutral tally of the results. In a highly contentious situation, independent observers would be necessary and there would have to be some method of certifying and publishing the results. There is ample expertise in the international community to deal with any issues that arise with respect to this aspect of the process.

There is also an issue regarding the size of the majority needed legitimately to secede. There is no obvious reason why the size of the majority required on a plebiscite ordered by the court and a plebiscite held under political auspices should be different. The legal right of secession is essentially a means of guaranteeing the political right, and once it has been determined that there should be a plebiscite, the same standards should apply. Although there may be moral reasons behind the decision of a minority, it is the mere fact that the requisite consent has been withdrawn that gives a minority the political right to secede. This is a matter of utility: at some point, a minority's lack of consent is so appreciable that good government becomes impossible.

The answer to the question whether a minority wishes to secede is accordingly determined by the right of association rather than the principle of justice. The fairness and justice of the electoral process nevertheless raise legal issues, which come properly within the supervision of a court. This includes the size of the necessary majority. It is notable that the Supreme Court of Canada was unwilling to take a firm position on the matter in the *Secession Reference*, where it simply held that 'a clear majority vote in Québec on a clear question in favour of secession would confer democratic legitimacy on the secession initiative which all of the other participants in Confederation would have to recognize' (p. 293). Elsewhere in the judgement, the court recognized that a constitution 'is entrenched beyond the reach of simple majority rule' (p. 259).

This became a source of controversy when the government of Québec took the position that a majority of 50 per cent plus one is sufficient to justify a unilateral act of secession. Separatists have argued that this is in keeping with international and domestic norms. A simple majority was judged sufficient, for example, when European states held plebiscites on whether to enter the Maastricht Treaty. This seems a different kind of issue, however, which does not change the fundamental personality or status of the states. The more compelling example is the province of Newfoundland, which joined the Canadian confederation on the same basis. This is a poor precedent, however, and there are many reasons why something more than a plurality should be required for fundamental constitutional changes.

The examples in favour of Québec are not convincing. There is a distinction between the decision to join a political association and a decision to leave it. This brings us back to the contractual analysis. There is a sense in which it can be said that the minority has entered into a contract with the majority in the state. The salient question on secession is accordingly not whether a minority wishes to enter into a contract, but whether it wishes to withdraw from the contract. This is a different issue and calls for a higher standard.

The problem is that there are always other interests that must be considered in deciding such an issue. In the *Secession Reference*, the Supreme Court of Canada expressed concern about the position of internal minorities in Québec. It also recognized, however, that it is impossible for a province to secede without affecting the interests of the other parties to confederation.[17] Although individuals outside the province cannot expect to be consulted in a plebiscite, they have legitimate interests that deserve some measure of protection. These kinds of concerns can be accommodated by requiring a substantial majority on any vote to secede.

There are also more general concerns. The most important of these is the need for a stable political order. The idea that the constitutional structure of a state can be changed by a simple majority divests the concept of a constitution of its primary purpose. The larger moral and institutional concerns that raise themselves in the context of a legal right apply equally in the political realm. As a result, the presumption against secession continues to apply and the size of any majority must be substantial, something well above a bare majority. Wayne Norman has argued that this would enshrine the principle of 'just cause' in such a process, since it will not be possible to obtain the requisite majority without good reasons to claim an extraordinary remedy.

The appropriate majority might vary, as a result of the distribution of a minority. The entire population within the prescribed territory should be consulted, but the real question is whether there is a consensus among the members of the minority. Having said this, a vote of two-thirds of the entire population would seem to be the minimum. This is a question of government.

A state without the consent of the large majority of the entire populace will not have sufficient authority to govern effectively.

Ancillary Issues

The final question concerns the ancillary issues that arise in the context of relief. These issues may also arise independently of any action for oppression, in the course of the political process. The relevant political actors may apply for relief under the general jurisdiction of the courts.

The need for a second source of relief is illustrated by the contractual aspects of secession. The idea that a minority has essentially entered into an agreement with the state is subject to many qualifications.[18] There is, nevertheless, something to the analogy with marriage. It is one of the facts of life that parties cannot be forced to honour a contract against their wishes, whatever its subject matter. This is where the right of self-determination asserts itself in the civil sphere: it is always open to a minority to revoke the constitutional contract and pay damages. This is difficult if not impossible to resolve in a political arena and calls for some form of legal recourse.

The process in an action for oppression is governed by the fact that there has already been a finding that the original state has oppressed the minority. This gives the minority a legitimate right to expect some form of compensation. There may also be punitive issues that need to be considered. The burden of proof on relief would nevertheless fall naturally on the prosecuting party. He who claims must prove. Since the original and seceding states would be equal in law, however, they should be treated as equals in this aspect of the process. The presumption in favour of existing states should no longer apply.

In 'Secession: the case of Québec', Kai Nielsen acknowledges that there must be a legal body, to divide the national debt and distribute property between the resulting states.

> There are requirements of fair treatment and fair division on both sides. Thus the seceding nation cannot just walk away from its previous association ... without there being a fair division of the assets and liabilities of the state they are seceding from. Here, to insure fairness, either the parties must come to an uncoerced agreement or failing that they must abide by a decision from an international court. (p. 36)

Thus, there might be an order assessing costs, distributing moveables or establishing the effective date of any transfer of property. There will also be the claims of individual owners, who may be dispossessed when one state cedes its territory to another. This requires a compulsory legal regime, if it is to be effective in dealing with states that resist such orders.

Enforcement

The most fundamental issue that arises with respect to enforcement concerns an order of secession. David Copp has argued that the Security Council could pass a resolution requiring that an overholding state comply with a legal plebiscite. He also argues in a conventional vein that sanctions might be used to persuade an unwilling state to accept the ruling of an international court. This is fine as far as it goes, and there is no reason to dispute his contention that the use of military force should be avoided in most circumstances.

This ultimately leaves secession in the political arena however, and allows states to decide for themselves whether they will accept a ruling. As long as they are willing to accept the cost of sanctions, there is no means of forcing them to comply with the ruling of a court. Nor does this take us very far in solving the problem of secession, since most of the compelling cases arise in the instance of intransigent states. This kind of strategy can be counter-productive and may actually intensify a state's persecution of a minority.

The real problem lies in exactly those situations where a state refuses to accept its obligation to obey a ruling that has gone against it. This is where the law needs to develop, if matters like secession are to be decided by the legal process. There is no alternative: states must simply be subjected to the kind of compulsory rulings that emanate from domestic courts. This is difficult to foresee at this point in time, though the nature of the international law is visibly changing. The regulation of affairs between sovereign states is a political matter, which is governed by agreements and conventions rather than law.

Copp envisages a situation in which the International Court of Justice has the authority to issue declaratory orders, which establish the legal rights of the parties. There would be no legal mechanism to enforce these orders, however, and a minority would ultimately have to rely on political remedies. The most obvious of these remedies is found in the Security Council: but whether the Council actively enforced such rulings would be dependent on the goodwill and self-interest of its permanent members. If an international court is to issue something more than declaratory orders, and enforce them, there must be some means of executing an order of secession.

The same problems arise in the context of ancillary orders and the truth is that none of the theories of secession in the literature could be realistically applied without some legal means of forcing the affected states to obey the terms of secession. Avashai Margalit and Joseph Raz, for example, in 'National self-determination' have argued that the right of secession may be exercised on the understanding 'that measures are adopted to prevent its creation from gravely damaging the just interests of other countries' (p. 457). Harry Beran makes a similar comment. This is not possible without placing compulsory constraints on the resulting states.

The conduct of the resulting states cannot be realistically curtailed without a binding international law. Daniel Philpott acknowledges these concerns when he writes: 'The question of future enforcement also arises here, for once a region has seceded, the status of sovereignty makes it difficult to enforce compliance with commitments from the outside.'[19] This is an understatement. Agreements regarding trade, demilitarized areas or cross-border rights are of no assistance unless the relevant states are required to honour them. Nor is it possible to enforce arrangements that guarantee the safety of a captive population without intervening in the internal affairs of a state.

These concerns will be more pronounced when a minority is forced to make concessions in negotiating secession. It is quite another matter whether the resulting state will consider itself bound by such restrictions, once it has obtained its independence. A state may easily take the position that it agreed to the terms of separation under duress or out of necessity. And there may be merit in these arguments. This calls for legal recourse, on both sides. There is a host of ways in which a sovereign state can finesse its obligations, and the reality of these kinds of situation renders most of the theories in the literature relatively helpless.

The root of the problem is remarkably simple. Since states are sovereign actors in the international realm, it is political rather than legal considerations that determine whether states will be compelled to live up to conditions that they find onerous or unappealing. As a result, it cannot be predicted with any certainty whether a seceding state and its neighbours will be bound by the kinds of measures proposed by so many authors. This merely takes us back to the thesis of the present book. It is impossible to create a meaningful legal right without extending the compulsory law into the unregulated political realm in which states historically exist. If an international court is going to be effective, there has to be a coercive mechanism to enforce the terms of any secession. The orders of the court must be policed.

Notes

1 Philpott, 'Self-determination in practice', p. 94.

2 Philpott goes on to suggest that an international body might be more appropriate, though it remains 'an even more distant possibility' at this point in time.

3 See the website for the European Court of Human Rights, cited in the Bibliography.

4 See the discussion in Hannum, at p. 60f. The following definition of 'minority' was submitted to the United Nations Sub-Commission on the Prevention of Discrimination and the Protection of Minorities in 1985 by Jules Deschenes but not approved: 'A group of citizens of a State, constituting a numerical minority and in a non-dominant position in that State, endowed with ethnic, religious or linguistic characteristics which differ from those of the majority of the population, having a sense of solidarity with one another, motivated, if only implicitly, by a collective will to survive and whose aim is to achieve equality with the majority in fact and in law.'

5 The legal meaning of the term 'minority' for example may not be restricted to groups smaller than the numerical majority in the state. There may be cases where a minority with control of the apparatus of government is a constructive majority for the purposes of secession.

6 See *Kyllo* v. *Panzer*, 535 N.W.2d 896 (S.D.1995), for example, which struck down

legislation limiting the liability for negligence on the basis that the South Dakota constitution opens the courts 'to the injured and oppressed'.

7 See *Dancey* v. *22981 Alberta Ltd.* (1988), 40 A.L.R. 180 (Alta. Q.B.), at 185.

8 And see *Abraham* v. *Inter Wide Investments Ltd.* (1985), 51 O.R. (2d) 460 (Ont. H.C.), at 468f, where Griffiths J. held that oppression refers to conduct 'under which the shareholder is in effect coerced to submit to something unfair'.

9 See the initial entry under 'oppression' in the American *Words and Phrases*: '"Oppression" means an act of subjecting to cruel and unjust hardship, or unjust or cruel exercise of authority to power, especially by the imposition of burdens. *Roth* v. *Shell Oil Co.*, 8 Cal. Rptr. 514, 515, 185 C.A. 2d 676.' The same source is enough to establish that the term has also been used judicially in the context of political rights.

10 See the comments of Spence J. in *Horvath* v. *R.* (1979), 7 C.R. (3d) 97 (S.C.C.), AT 117, where he quotes from the decision of Sachs J., in *R.* v. *Priestly* (1965), 50 Cr. App. R. 183 (C.A.).

11 Allen Buchanan, *Secession: The Morality of Political Divorce*, p. 134. The reference to Hirschmann is to Albert O. Hirschmann, *Exit, Voice, and Loyalty* (Cambridge, MA.: Harvard University Press, 1970), pp. 33–43.

12 *WWWebster Dictionary*, accessed 16 June 1999.

13 See Kokott, for example, *The Burden of Proof in Comparative and International Human Rights Law*, at p. 13, where she distinguishes between the burdens in 'adversarial civil lawsuits' and a human rights or constitutional forum. The arguments that arise in the latter instance generally favour complainants and run counter to the principle of political stability that is so significant in the instance of secession.

14 The technical nature of the state's authority over land may vary from state to state. And there will naturally be land, and attachments to land, which are actually owned by the state.

15 This explains a doctrine like eminent domain, which is an exceptional doctrine that provides for the seizure and expropriation of land in specific circumstances.

16 This may be a reflection of the period in which Buchheit was writing. At p. 230, note 13, he refers the reader to the 'extreme' claim, in the *Scientific Monthly*, that the capacity for self-government can be measured 'by weighing 350 indices of fitness for self-government derived from an equal number of "objectively observable phenomena"'.

17 The court refers, at paragraph 42, to the historical precedent of Nova Scotia, which attempted to secede from the Canadian confederation in 1867. The Colonial Secretary in Britain rejected the Province's request, on the basis that the province of New Brunswick had entered into the same union 'in reliance on having with it the sister province of Nova Scotia; and vast obligations, political and commercial, have already been contracted on the faith of a measure so long discussed and so solemnly adopted'.

18 There will be situations, for example, where a minority has essentially consented to the restrictions of government under duress.

19 Philpott, p. 94.

Conclusion

Institutional Reform

The starting point of the present book is clear enough: we are in dire need of a peaceful means of resolving the conflicts that have arisen when a minority within a particular state claims the right to secede. These conflicts present a serious threat to global stability and peace.

The central thesis of the book is that a government which fails to respect the fundamental rights of a minority is no longer legally legitimate. It is accordingly open to a minority to challenge the validity of its title to the sovereign power. This is not possible without extending the domestic notion of legality into the international realm. As the legal order stands, states are free agents and there is no source of law from which a legal body can draw the authority to order the division of a state into separate political entities.

The overriding problem with any attempt to develop a legal right of secession is accordingly the simplest. It is that secession, as it has been traditionally conceived, occurs outside the legal order. Although common law courts have exercised a residual power to determine whether the sovereign power has changed hands, this is merely the power to determine as a factual matter who holds the right of government. In spite of the many developments in international law, individual states are still immune from ordinary legal constraints.

The Westphalian argument that states should ignore the oppression within other states is no longer tenable. Whatever the refinements, there are only two arguments against a compulsory international law. The first is simply that political leaders are not obliged to follow the most fundamental moral prescriptions. The second is that there is no way of compelling them to do so. There is a kind of wilfulness in both stances that suggests that the attractions of power lie at the root of such arguments.

The cardinal feature of the Westphalian state system has been that individual states will not interfere in each other's affairs. This is a denial of law and the moral requirements behind it, which present the real answer to the kind of political realism that has governed international relations. The law cannot function, however, without an appropriate institutional structure. A court cannot be expected to resolve the intractable conflicts that arise in the instance of an issue like secession unless its jurisdiction is compulsory.

The international law is already full of unenforceable moral commitments and the brute fact is that it is impossible to develop a meaningful right of secession without giving a court authority over sovereign states. There will always be instances of bad faith and cases that go amiss, but standards of justice and fairness are meaningless if they have no legal force. There is no reason why this needs to deprive sovereign states of the administrative and legislative authority to govern.

None of this rules out the role of a body like the Security Council in policing international rulings. It has already been accepted that any international solution to the violence of internal ethnic conflicts must be underwritten by the threat of force. There are any number of possibilities as to who should have the authority to supply that force and how it might be deployed. The present modus vivendi is not enough, however.

There is some protection for human rights under the existing system and the doctrine of humanitarian intervention. But this merely justifies war and invasion as a means of resolving internal disputes within states and offers a rather reckless alternative to the rule of law. It is simply not possible to formulate a legal theory of secession without altering the concept of sovereignty to encompass the existence of a binding legal order above the state.

Changes in the International System

There are many developments in the relations and practices of states that suggest the international order is changing. This is in keeping with the work in philosophy and political theory that makes a comparison between states and individuals. This work at least implicitly suggests that it is now more appropriate to speak of the autonomy of states than of sovereignty in the traditional sense.

Many political scientists take the position that the traditional concept of sovereignty fails to capture the development of capitalism and international systems of production. Joseph Camilleri writes that the idea of

> ... national sovereignty in an international context has been greatly eroded by a web of mutually reinforcing dependencies and interdependencies ... Everywhere the cohesion of national societies seems likely to diminish, and so too the mobilizing efficacy of national governments. Historically state sovereignty may turn out to have been a bridge between national capitalism and world capitalism, a phase in an evolutionary process that is still unfolding.[1]

There are economic, political, social and technological reasons why the international order has changed.

Cassese suggests that states are experiencing greater integration on an economic and political level, even while the ethnic and cultural differences between minorities become more pronounced. The formation of regional economic associations and the authority of organizations like the World Bank and the World Trade Organization attest to this. There are an increasing number of states that willingly attorn to the policies and practices of the various agencies of the United Nations.[2] There are also strong religious and ethnic sources of identity, such as Islamic fundamentalism or 'pan-Arabism', which seem to raise a challenge to the sovereignty of certain states.

There are corresponding legal developments. The *jus cogens* is ascendant. The International Court of Justice has held that states are legally obliged to respect the basic rights of their populations. Daniel Philpott goes so far as to argue that the concept of sovereignty has itself been modified by the development of minority rights and the principle of national self-determination. The creation of the European Economic Union has created a legal order outside the state, with a supervisory jurisdiction in human rights.

The legal systems of the world are converging in a manner that has led to a greater integration of the domestic and international law. The passage of a European constitution will inevitably erode the powers of individual states and give European courts increasing authority over state governments. The current developments in the international criminal law demonstrate that a global system of justice is emerging, with an independent moral jurisdiction. In the long term, the attempts of the USA to restrict the reach of the International Criminal Court seem unlikely to prevail.

There are contrary impulses in the international realm, however. Anne Bayefsky has argued that arguments for 'cultural sovereignty' in the international arena are part of a larger and relatively successful counter-attack on the concept of universal human rights. The philosophical problem can be found in legal positivism, which has undermined the moral underpinnings of the international law, and 'provides no help in constructing external standards of evaluation'.[3] Bayefsky describes the principle of non-intervention as 'the old keep-out strategy', which merely reasserts the historical doctrine of sovereignty and allows states to disregard international covenants protecting human rights (p. 49).

The historical tenets of the state system remain in place. As a result, the international law has few resources to deal with domestic systems that violate human rights, much less the states themselves. Antonio Cassese may be right in arguing that we have not reached the point where it is possible to move human society beyond the bias in favour of state sovereignty. But it is time that we faced the failures of the international law. It is impossible to move beyond the endless, rhetorical protections that the international law has afforded to human rights without legally subordinating the doctrine of sovereignty and the principle of territorial integrity to the principle of justice.

Establishing a Court

Some facts are clear. The Westphalian concept of state sovereignty has begun to unravel and the international community has recognized that it has an obligation to protect the rights and interests of individuals living in hostile and oppressive states. As long as these obligations are honoured consistently and not selectively, this should be applauded. We do not have the legal means however, to deal with the legal obligations that flow from such developments. There is no legal forum in which a minority can seriously contest the state's ownership of the right to govern.

This calls for the establishment of an extra-constitutional court, of general jurisdiction, to deal with the issues that arise regarding the internal legitimacy of the state. The deeper issue lies in the separation between the legal and political process. There is no escaping the fact that a legal doctrine of secession would place the most fundamental political fact within the state under the scrutiny of an adjudicative body, outside the state. This may be an anathema to those in positions of power within the existing state system. But there are no real alternatives.

Although the establishment of an extra-constitutional court is fraught with difficulties, it is notable most of these difficulties have a political nature. They concern matters like the make-up of a court, the appointment of judges, and attempts to treat the adjudicative process as a forum for political arguments. The legal system is subject to many forms of political interference: this is often difficult to discern, and assert itself in the exercise of prosecutorial discretion, the appointment of panels or the withholding of evidence.

These kinds of deficiencies are an inevitable part of any legal apparatus, however, and the issue is a relative one. It is states themselves that must provide the practical and institutional resources to create the judicial structure that is needed to regulate an issue like secession. This is not possible without some recognition from states and the leaders of states that their actions are subject to compulsory moral restrictions. This is only a way of saying that it needs the general consent of those under its jurisdiction.

If this seems unlikely, it is because the international system favours individual states, who do not feel that it is in their interests to accept such substantive changes in the system. The unfortunate psychological reality is that states have a vested interest in maintaining a system that at least theoretically gives them complete authority in their own affairs. The political will to introduce the necessary changes in the existing international order may ultimately be found in inter-state parliaments and assemblies, like the European Parliament or the proposed world parliament, which are not so easily dominated by state interests.

This may seem to raise vague ideas of world government. That is another discussion, however, which is better left to others. There is a judicial aspect to these developments, which is indispensable in redefining the role of international legal bodies. Some of the impetus for a new legal order will have to come from the judiciary, who would be responsible for the development of the legalities of any action against the state. It is not yet clear that international courts have the confidence to undertake such a momentous task.

Separating the Legal and Political Processes

On the theoretical side, the reality is that the changes in the international arena have outrun our theoretical capacities. The conceptual apparatus that has traditionally been used to explain the legal character of events in the international arena is no longer capable of dealing with the realities of a new world order.

There is a theoretical need to separate the legal and political processes in the international realm. The existing confusion is apparent in the idea that the United Nations Security Council is the proper forum in which to deal with the legal aspects of matters like secession. This is little more than an assertion of the political primacy in the international arena however. The Security Council has few, if any, of the properties of a court or tribunal and is not in a position to rule on matters of law. Nor is it in a position to rule on the legality of its own actions.

The rather *ad hoc* actions of the Council are motivated by the political interests of the member states, as they should be, rather than by established legal principles. It has no real obligation to justify its actions, respect precedent or even maintain the consistency of its rulings. This would arguably interfere with its function, which is to provide a forum for the expression of the political will of the most powerful states.

The courts are consultative bodies. The judicial process is a reflective process, which provides us with a set of reasons why a court is compelled, in some rigorous sense, to reach a certain conclusion. Judicial proceedings are primarily justificatory. The actions of a court, with all its imperfections, proceeds on the basis of principle rather than the wishes of the parties. The political process tends to subordinate general rules to the facts of specific cases. The law subordinates the facts to rules.

The differences between the legal and political processes are ultimately a professional and a psychological matter. The training and status of judicial actors, along with the accoutrements of office, puts judges in a more neutral position than political actors. There are many policies with respect to the appointment and establishment of the judiciary that may effect the matter one way or the other. The political process is partial, by its nature, and does not lend itself to an impartial scrutiny of questions like secession.

It is the development of an international criminal law that seems most likely to change our understanding of the international law and erode the principle of political primacy. This is because the criminal law is the most deeply moral of all legal jurisdictions and is inherently compulsory. The authority of criminal courts ultimately comes from moral principles rather than political consensus.[4] This is evident in the development of the English criminal law, which was developed by the judiciary. Like the criminal law, the law of human rights derives from a moral order that takes precedence over agreement.

Any court that decides a question like secession needs some form of inherent jurisdiction, which gives it the capacity to act independently of any political actors. This is a moral independence, which provides a separate source of legitimacy than political authority. It rests on rational inference and a consensus in principles and values. The judicial task is more aligned with the Aristotelian virtue of prudence, and *phronesis*, than with ethical decision making. It is concerned with process, and the parameters in which power can be legitimately exercised, rather than with the moral or political rectitude of individual decisions.

The limits on such a process must be acknowledged. The development of a legal right of secession in the international sphere would not take the matter out of the political realm. It would merely introduce a legal remedy and provide the means of exercising the political right of self-determination in situations where a state oppresses a minority. The matter is more complicated than a remedial theory or a theory based on self-determination might suggest, since a minority may possess a political right of secession outside of any legal rights. This may still require the intervention of an impartial legal body, on issues such as the terms of a plebiscite or the division of the national debt.

Further Inquiry

The discussion in the present book is a precursor. We need a more extensive discussion of the limits of legitimacy and the question of what makes a state illegitimate. It is necessary to develop specific criteria to determine at what point a state no longer possesses a valid claim to moral, political or legal authority. It is not entirely clear that the contemporary world wishes to develop legal institutions that can deal with such issues, but the future is relatively clear. There is already an ongoing attempt to create 'a global ethic' based on the major religious traditions, and comparable work needs to be done in the legal arena. The principles employed by institutions with international jurisdiction must respect the moral, legal and political values of a transnational, inter-state community of peoples. Perhaps it is important to recognize that domestic courts have begun work on such a body of principle, in recognizing the universal character of the rights of the person.

If there is to be a new International Court of Justice, with an independent and inherent jurisdiction, it is important to determine which principles of interpretation would govern the exercise of its powers. The first and most important of these principles is probably a principle of narrow interpretation, under which a world court would only exercise its jurisdiction in circumstances where a fair hearing and the necessary relief are not available in other forums. There is an appellate character to the role of such a court that needs consideration. It is important to integrate domestic systems into a global system, without depriving state courts of their jurisdiction over most of the issues that make their way into the courts.

All this raises practical legal problems. One example is that disputes concerning secession arise between states and ethnic or religious groups within the state, which have no status in international law. This needs attention. The argument that states are the only legitimate actors in the international arena is no longer compelling. There is also the vexing question of the sanctions that should be available, if a state steps outside the legitimate parameters of its authority.

As a final matter, it is important to consider the political issues that lie behind these questions. The borders between individual states are dissolving and it is unclear whether states will ultimately survive in their present form. The future of the European Parliament will inevitably diminish the authority of national governments and it is impossible to predict the manner in which the state system will survive the economic integration that is taking place in the world. In these circumstances, it is important to examine the institution of the state itself, and forms of government more generally.

There is no doubt that states have enjoyed a privileged place in history and political science. They have shown remarkable resilience in the flux of time. It is by no means clear, however, that states are metaphysically necessary. This does not affect the position I have set out. Whatever means of political association we adopt, the issues that arise in the context of secession will be there, in one form or another. The essential argument of the present book is that there are legal means for resolving such conflicts, which avoid the terror and bloodshed of civil strife. Those means must be developed and pursued.

Notes

1 Camilleri, 'Rethinking sovereignty in a shrinking, fragmented world', p. 38. See, for example, Michael Barnett, 'Sovereignty, nationalism and regional order in the Arab states system', in Biersteker and Weber, *State Sovereignty*, pp. 148–89, at p. 176, along with the sources listed in ibid., at note 117.

2 The international scrutiny of individual states has also increased. The reports of bodies like the Committee on Economic, Social and Cultural Rights and the International Labour Organization are invasive.

3 Bayefsky, 'Cultural sovereignty', p. 57. At p. 48f, Bayefsky discusses the passage of a General Assembly Resolution 45/163, 18 December 1990, which addresses the subject of United Nations action 'in the human rights field through the promotion of international co-operation and the strict observance of the principle of non-intervention'.

4 The criminal jurisdiction comes into play in the case of secession, since the rights of an oppressed minority can often be traced to crimes against humanity and other illegal acts by state authorities.

Select Bibliography

Academic and Philosophical Sources

'A survey of human-rights law: the world is watching' (1998), *The Economist*, 5 December, 1–16.

Applbaum, Arthur Isak (1992), 'Democratic legitimacy and official discretion', *Philosophy and Public Affairs*, **21** (3), 240–74.

Aquinas, Thomas (1920, 1948), *Summa Theologica*, complete English edition in five volumes, trans. by the Fathers of the English Dominican Province, Westminster, MD: Christian Classics.

Armour, Leslie (1976), 'Law and revolution', *Philosophical Context*, **5**, 79–88.

Barkin, J. Samuel (1998), 'The evolution of the constitution of sovereignty and the emergence of human rights norms', *Millenium: Journal of International Studies*, **27** (2), 229–52.

Barnes, Rudolph C. (1996), *Military Legitimacy: Might and Right in the New Millenium*, London and Portland, OR: Frank Cass.

Barry, Brian (1995), *Justice as Impartiality: A Treatise on Social Justice*, vol. II, Oxford: Clarendon Press.

Barry, Norman (1989), 'The state and legitimacy', in Phillips Griffiths, A. (ed.), *Key Themes in Philosophy*, Royal Institute of Philosophy Lecture Series: 24, supplement to *Philosophy*, 1988, Cambridge: Cambridge University Press, pp. 191–206.

Bauhn, Per (1995), *Nationalism and Morality*, Lund: Lund University Press.

Bayefsky, Anne F. (1996), 'Cultural Sovereignty, relativism, and international human rights: new excuses for old strategies', *Ratio Juris*, **9**, 42–59.

Beetham, David (1991), *The Legitimation of Power*, Atlantic Highlands, NJ: Humanities Press.

Beran, Harry (1983), 'What is the basis of political authority?', *The Monist*, **66** (4), 487–99.

Beran, Harry (1987), *The Consent Theory of Political Obligation*. London: Croom Helm.

Biersteker, Thomas J. and Cynthia Weber (eds) (1996), *State Sovereignty as Social Construct*, Cambridge: Cambridge University Press.

Biersteker, Thomas J. and Cynthia Weber (1996), 'The social construction of state sovereignty', in Biersteker, T.J. and Weber, C. (eds), *State Sovereignty as Social Construct*, Cambridge: Cambridge University Press, pp. 1–21.

Blahuta, Jason (2001), 'How useful is the analogy of divorce in theorizing about secession?', *Dialogue*, **40** (2), 241–54.

Brighouse, Harry (1998), 'Against nationalism', in Courture, J., Nielsen, K. and Seymour, M. (eds), *Rethinking Nationalism*, Calgary: University of Calgary Press, pp. 365–405.

Buchanan, Allen (1991), *Secession: The Morality of Political Divorce from Fort Sumter to Lithuania and Québec*, Boulder, CO: Westview Press.

Buchanan, Allen (1997), 'Theories of secession', *Philosophy and Public Affairs*, **26** (1), 31–61.

Buchanan, Allen (1999), 'Recognitional legitimacy', *Philosophy and Public Affairs*, **28** (1), 46–78.

Buchanan, Allen (2003), *Justice, Legitimacy, and Self-Determination – Moral Foundations for International Law*, Oxford: Oxford University Press.

Buchheit, Lee C. (1978), *Secession: The Legitimacy of Self-Determination*, New Haven, CT: Yale University Press.

Camilleri, Joseph A. (1990), 'Rethinking sovereignty in a shrinking, fragmented world', in Walker, R.B.J. and Mendlovitz, Saul H. (eds), *Contending Sovereignties: Redefining Political Community*, Boulder, CO: Lynne Rienner, pp. 13–44.

Campbell, Tom (1990), 'Obligation: social, political and legal', in Harris, P. (ed.), *On Political Obligation*, London: Routledge, pp. 120–50.

Carr, Craig L. (1983), 'The problem of political authority', *The Monist*, **66** (4), 472–86.

Cassese, Antonio (1995), *Self-Determination of Peoples: A Legal Reappraisal*, Cambridge: Cambridge University Press.

Castellino, Joshua (2000), *International Law and Self-Determination: The Interplay of the Politics of Territorial Possession with Formulations of the Post-Colonial 'National' Identity*, The Hague: Martinus Nijhoff.

Cohen, Joshua (1986), 'Structure, choice and legitimacy: Locke's theory of the state', *Philosophy and Public Affairs*, **15** (4), 301–24.

Connolly, William (ed.) (1984), *Legitimacy and the State*, with an introduction by Connolly entitled 'Legitimacy and modernity' at pp. 1–19, Oxford: Basil Blackwell.

Connolly, William (1984), 'The dilemma of legitimacy', in Connolly, W. (ed.), *Legitimacy and the State*, Oxford: Basil Blackwell, pp. 222–49.

Corlett, J. Angelo (1992), 'The right to civil disobedience and the right to secede', *The Southern Journal of Philosophy*, **30** (1), 19–28.

Copp, David (1998), 'International law and morality in the theory of secession', *The Journal of Ethics*, **2** (3), 219–45

Cotta, Sergio (1986), 'Legitimacy: a mirage?', *Diogenes*, **134**, 96–105.

Crenshaw, Martha (ed.) (1983), *Terrorism, Legitimacy, and Power: The Consequences of Political Violence*, with an introduction by Crenshaw entitled 'Reflections on the effects of terrorism' at pp. 1–37, Middletown, CT: Wesleyan University Press.

Cristi, Renato (1998), *Carl Schmitt and Authoritarian Liberalism: Strong State, Free Economy*, Cardiff: University of Wales Press.

Dewey, John (1939), 'The individual in the new society', in Ratner, Joseph (ed.), *Intelligence in the Modern World: John Dewey's Philosophy*, with an introduction by Ratner, Modern Library, New York: Random House, pp. 405–33.

Dewey, John (1939), 'Nationalism and internationalism', in Ratner, Joseph (ed.), *Intelligence in the Modern World*, New York: Random House, pp. 467–98.

Dewey, John (1939), 'International law and the security of nations', in Ratner, Joseph (ed.), *Intelligence in the Modern World*, New York: Random House, pp. 499–604, with a lengthy note by the editor.

Dodson, Kevin E. (1997), 'Autonomy and authority in Kant's *Rechtslehre*', *Political Theory*, **25** (1), 93–111.

Doyle, John P. (1997), 'Vitoria on choosing to replace a king', in White, Kevin (ed.), *Hispanic Philosophy in the Age of Discovery*, vol. 29 of Dougherty, Jude P. (gen. ed.), Studies in Philosophy and the History of Philosophy, Washington, DC: Catholic University of America Press, pp. 45–58.

Dworkin, Ronald (1977), *Taking Rights Seriously*, London: Duckworth.

Dworkin, Ronald (1978), 'Liberalism', in Hampshire, Stuart (ed.), *Public and Private Morality*, Cambridge: Cambridge University Press, pp. 113–43.

Dworkin, Ronald (1996), *Law's Empire*, Cambridge, MA: Harvard University Press.

Dyzenhaus, David (1994), 'The legitimacy of law: a response to critics', *Ratio Juris*, **7**, 80–94.

Ewin, R.E. (1994), 'Peoples and secession', *Journal of Applied Philosophy*, **11**, 225–31.

Festenstein, Matthew (1997), *Pragmatism and Political Theory: From Dewey to Rorty*, Chicago: University of Chicago Press.

Finnis, John (1998), *Aquinas: Moral, Political and Legal Theory*, Founders of Modern Political and Social Thought. Oxford: Oxford University Press.

Fishkin, James S. (1979), *Tyranny and Legitimacy: A Critique of Political Theories*, Baltimore, MD, and London: Johns Hopkins University Press.

Frankel Paul, Ellen (1983), 'On three "inherent" powers of government', *The Monist*, **66** (4), 529–44.

Friedman, Lawrence M. (1994), 'Is there a modern legal culture?', *Ratio Juris*, **7**, 117–31.

'The future of humanitarian intervention' (2001), special issue of *American Diplomacy*, July, website http://www.unc.edu/depts/diplomat/archives_roll/2001_07-09/hum_intervention/hum, accessed: 10 September 2003.

Gierke, Otto (1934), *Natural Law and the Theory of Society: 1500–1800*, 2 vols, trans. by Ernest Barker, vol. I contains an introduction by Barker at pp. ix–xci, vol. I also contains two appendices, one consisting of a lecture on 'The ideas of natural law and humanity' by Ernst Troeltsch and one consisting of a brief account of 'Gierke's conception of law', apparently by Gierke himself, Cambridge: Cambridge University Press.

Gilbert, Paul (1990), 'Community and civil strife', *Journal of Applied Philosophy*, **7** (1), 3–14.

Glendon, Mary Ann (1991), *Rights Talk: The Impoverishment of Political Discourse*, New York: Free Press.

Green, Leslie (1990), 'Consent and community', in Harris, P. (ed.), *On Political Obligation*, London: Routledge, pp. 89–119.

Habermas, Jürgen (1994), 'Human rights and popular sovereignty: the Liberal and Republican versions', *Ratio Juris*, **7**, 1–13.

Hannum, Hurst (1990), *Autonomy, Sovereignty, and Self-Determination: The Accommodation of Conflicting Rights*, Philadelphia, PA: University of Pennsylvania Press.

Harris, Paul (1990), 'The moral obligation to obey the law', in Harris, P. (ed.) *On Political Obligation*, London: Routledge, pp. 151–83.

Hart, H.L.A. (1961), *The Concept of Law*, Oxford: Clarendon Press.

Hobbes, Thomas (1991), *Leviathan*, ed. with an introduction by Richard Tuck, Cambridge: Cambridge University Press.

Hodson, John D. (1983), *The Ethics of Legal Coercion*, Dordrecht and Boston, MA: D. Reidel.

Horowitz, Donald L. (1998), 'Self-determination: politics, philosophy, and law', in Moore, M. (ed.), *National Self-Determination and Secession*, Oxford: Oxford University Press, pp. 181–214.

'human rights'. *Encyclopaedia Britannica Online*, website http://www.britannica.com/, accessed 20 June 1999.

Hume, David (1882), 'Of the origin of government', in vol. 3 of Green, Thomas Hill and Grose, Thomas Hodge (eds), *David Hume: The Philosophical Works*, London; repr. 1964 Aalen: Scientia Verlag, pp. 113–77.

Hume, David (1882), 'Of the original contract', in vol. 3 of Green, Thomas Hill and Grose, Thomas Hodge (eds), *David Hume: The Philosophical Works*, London; repr. 1964 Aalen: Scientia Verlag, pp. 443–60.

Kittrie, Nicholas N. (1995), *The War Against Authority: From the Crisis of Legitimacy to a New Social Contract*, Baltimore, MD: Johns Hopkins University Press.

Kretzmann, Norman (1988), 'Lex iniusta non est lex', *American Journal of Jurisprudence*, **33**, 99–122.

Kymlicka, Will (1995), *Multicultural Citizenship: A Liberal Theory of Minority Rights*, Oxford: Oxford University Press.

Lipset, Seymour Martin (1984), 'Social conflict, legitimacy and democracy', in Connolly, William (ed.), *Legitimacy and the State*, Oxford: Basil Blackwell, pp. 88–103; an excerpt from Seymour Martin Lipset (1981), *Political Man: The Social Bases of Politics*, Baltimore, MD: Johns Hopkins University Press.

Locke, John (1960), 'The Second Treatise of Government: An Essay Concerning the True Original, Extent, and End of Civil Government', in

Laslett, Peter (ed.), *Two Treatises of Government: A Critical Edition with an Introduction and Apparatus Criticus*, Cambridge: Cambridge University Press.

Machan, Tibor R. (1983), 'Individualism and the problem of political authority', *The Monist*, **66**, (4), 500–516.

MacIntyre, Alasdair (1984), *After Virtue: A Study in Moral Theory*, 2nd edn, Notre Dame, IN: University of Notre Dame Press.

Margalit, Avashai and Joseph Raz (1990), 'National self-determination', *Journal of Philosophy*, **87**, 439–61.

Marston, Jerrilyn Greene (1987), *King and Congress: The Transfer of Political Legitimacy, 1774–1776*, Princeton, NJ: Princeton University Press.

Martin, Rex (1990), 'The character of political allegiance in a system of rights', in Harris, P. (ed.), *On Political Obligation*, London: Routledge, pp. 184–217.

McKim, Robert and Jeff McMahan (eds) (1997), *The Morality of Nationalism*, Oxford: Oxford University Press.

Miller, David (1995), *On Nationality*, Oxford: Clarendon Press.

Miller, David (1998), 'Secession and the principle of nationality', in Moore, Margaret (ed.), *National Self-Determination and Secession*, Oxford: Oxford University Press, pp. 62–78.

Moellendorf, Darrel (1996–97), 'Liberalism, nationalism, and the right to secede', *The Philosophical Forum*, **27** (1–2), Fall–Winter, 87–99.

Moore, Margaret (1996), 'On reasonableness', *Journal of Applied Philosophy*, **13** (2), 167–78.

Moore, Margaret (1998), 'The limits of liberal nationalism', paper presented to the Canadian Political Science Association Meetings, University of Ottawa, June.

Moore, Margaret (2001), *The Ethics of Nationalism*, Oxford: Oxford University Press.

Nagel, Thomas (1987), 'Moral conflict and political legitimacy', *Philosophy and Public Affairs*, **16** (3), 215–40.

Navaratna-Bandara, Abeysinghe M. (1995), *The Management of Ethnic Secessionist Conflict: The Big Neighbour Syndrome*, Aldershot: Dartmouth.

Nielsen, Kai (1990), 'State authority and legitimation', in Harris, P. (ed.), *On Political Obligation*, London: Routledge, pp. 218–251.

Nielsen, Kai (1993), 'Secession: the case of Québec', *Journal of Applied Philosophy*, **10**, 29–43.

Noreña, Carlos G. (1997), 'Francisco Suárez on democracy and international law', in White, Kevin (ed.), *Hispanic Philosophy in the Age of Discovery*, vol. 29 of Jude P. Dougherty (gen. ed.), Studies in Philosophy and the History of Philosophy, Washington DC: Catholic University of America Press, pp. 257–74.

Norman, Wayne (n.d.), 'Domesticating secession', MS, a draft of 'The ethics of secession and the regulation of secessionist politics', 31 pp.

Norman, Wayne (1998), 'The ethics of secession as the regulation of secessionist politics', in Moore, Margaret (ed.), *National Self-Determination and Secession*, Oxford: Oxford University Press, pp. 34–61.

O'Brien, Conor Cruise (1983), 'Terrorism under democratic conditions: the case of the IRA', in Crenshaw, Martha (ed.), *Terrorism, Legitimacy, and Power: The Consequences of Political Violence*, Middletown, CT: Wesleyan University, pp. 91–104.

Oxford English Dictionary (1989).

Papanoutsos, E.P. (1973–74), 'Law and revolution', trans. and adapted by John P. Anton, *Philosophy and Phenomenological Research*, **34**, 201–8.

Pasquino, Pasquale (1988), 'Locke on king's prerogative', *Political Theory*, **7** (2), 198–208.

Paul, Jeffrey (1983), 'Substantive social contracts', *The Monist*, **66** (4), 517–28.

Philpott, Daniel (1995), 'In defence of self-determination', *Ethics*, **105**, January, 352–85.

Philpott, Daniel (1995), 'Sovereignty: an introduction and brief history', *Journal of International Affairs*, **48** (2), Winter, 353–68

Philpott, Daniel (1998), 'Self-determination in practice', in Moore, Margaret (ed.), *National Self-Determination and Secession*, Oxford: Oxford University Press, pp. 70–102.

Pogge, Thomas W. (1998), 'The bounds of nationalism', in Courture, Jocelyn, Nielsen, Kai and Seymour, Michel (eds), *Rethinking Nationalism*, Calgary: University of Calgary Press, pp. 463–504.

Ragazzi, Maurizio (1997), *The Concept of International Obligations Erga Omnes*, repr. 2000, Oxford Monographs in International Law; Oxford: Oxford University Press.

Random House Dictionary of the English Language (1987).

Riley, Patrick (1982), *Will and Political Legitimacy: A Critical Exposition of Social Contract Theory in Hobbes, Locke, Rousseau, Kant, and Hegel*, Cambridge, MA: Harvard University Press.

Scharr, John H. (1984), 'Legitimacy in the modern state', in Connolly, William (ed.), *Legitimacy and the State*, Oxford: Basil Blackwell, pp. 104–33; excerpts from 'Legitimacy in the modern state', in Philip Green and Sanford Levinson (eds) (1969), *Power and Community: Dissenting Essays in Political Science*, New York: Random House.

Shue, Henry (1997), 'Eroding sovereignty: the advance of principle', in McKim, Robert and McMahan, Jeff (eds), *The Morality of Nationalism*, Oxford: Oxford University Press, pp. 340–59.

Sidgwick, Henry (1919), *The Elements of Politics*, 4th edn, London: Macmillan; repr. 1969, New York, Kraus.

Simon, Robert L. (1983), 'Justice and the authority of states', *The Monist*, **66** (4), 557–72.

Smith, S.A. de (1968), 'Constitutional lawyers in revolutionary situations', *Western Ontario Law Review*, **7**, 93–110.

Starovoitova, Galina (1996), 'Sovereignty after empire: self-determination movements in the former Soviet Union', report of the United States Institute of Peace, June, available at: http://www.usip.org/pubs/peaceworks/pwks19/intro19.html, accessed 27 May 2003.

Taylor, Charles (1985), *Philosophy and the Human Sciences*, vol. 2 of Philosophical Papers, Cambridge: Cambridge University Press.

Taylor, Charles (1995), 'Cross-purposes: the Liberal-Communitarian debate', in Taylor, Charles, *Philosophical Arguments*, Cambridge, MA: Harvard University Press, pp. 181–203.

Taylor, Richard (1983), 'The basis of political authority', *The Monist*, **66** (4), 457–71.

Tesón, Fernando R. (1988), *Humanitarian Intervention: An Inquiry into Law and Morality*, Dobbs Ferry, NY: Transnational.

'The evolution of modern western legal systems: socialist law systems', *Encyclopedia Britannica Online* website at http://www.eb.com:180/cgi-bin/g?DocF'macro/5003/71/60.html, accessed 1 October 1998.

United Nations website at http://www.un.org/, accessed 29 October 2003.

Vattel, Emerich de (1883), *The Law of Nations or Principles of the Law of Nature Applied to the Conduct and Affairs of Nations and Sovereigns*, trans. Joseph Chitty, with notes and references by Edward D. Ingraham, Philadelphia.

Wade, H.W.R. (1955), 'The basis of legal sovereignty', [**1995**] *Cambridge Law Journal*, 172–97.

Waldron, Jeremy (1995), 'Minority cultures and the cosmopolitan alternative', in Kymlicka, Will (ed.), *The Rights of Minority Cultures*, Oxford: Oxford University Press, pp. 93–119.

Weber, Max (1984), 'Legitimacy, politics and the state', in Connolly, William (ed.), *Legitimacy and the State*, Oxford: Basil Blackwell; selections from Hans Gerth and C.W. Mills (eds) (1958), *From Max Weber: Essays in Sociology*, New York: Oxford University Press.

Webster's, *Merriam-Webster Online*, website at http://www.m-w.com/dictionary.htm, accessed 12 October 2003.

Weinstock, Daniel M. (1999), 'National partiality: confronting the intuitions', *The Monist*, **82** (3), 516–41.

Wellman, Christopher H. (1995), 'A defence of secession and political self-determination', *Philosophy and Public Affairs*, **24** (2), 142–71.

Wellman, Christopher H. (1996), 'Liberalism, samaritanism, and political legitimacy', *Philosophy and Public Affairs*, **25** (3), 211–37.

West, Jason (2000), 'Impartiality and conceptions of the good: Brian Barry or Alisdair Macintyre?', *The Philosophical Forum*, **31** (1) Spring, 29–45.

Young, Iris Marion (1990), 'Five faces of oppression' in Young, Iris Marion, *Justice and the Politics of Difference*, Princeton, NJ: Princeton University Press, pp. 39–65.

Legal Sources

Conventions and Statutes

Canadian Charter of Rights and Freedoms. Constitution Act, 1982.

Declaration on Principles of International Law Concerning Friendly Relations and Co-operation among States in Accordance with the Charter of the U.N. Approved by GA Res. 2625 (XXV), 24 October 1970. Website of the General Assembly, http://www.un.org/documents/resga.htm, accessed 12 October 2003.

International Covenant on Civil and Political Rights. Adopted and opened for signature, ratification and accession by GA Res. 2200A (XXI), 16 December 1966. Website for the United Nations High Commission for Human Rights, http://www.unhchr.ch/html/intlinst.htm, accessed 12 October 2003.

International Covenant on Economic, Social and Cultural Rights. Adopted and opened for signature, ratification and accession by GA Res. 2200A (XXI), 16 December 1966. Website for the United Nations High Commission for Human Rights, http://www.unhchr.ch/html/intlinst.htm, accessed 12 October 2003.

Cases

Attorney-General of Canada v. *Lavell* (1973), [1974] S.C.R. 1349.

Harris v. *Minister of the Interior* (2) S.A. 428 (1952).

Legality of Use of Force (*Yugoslavia* v. *Belgium et al.*) (2 June 1999) General List No. 105. Website of the International Court of Justice, application to institute proceedings and request for provisional measures, http://www.icj-cij.org/icjwww/idocket/iybe/iybeframe.htm, accessed 12 October 2003.

Minister of the Interior v. *Harris* (4) S.A. 760 (1952).

Planned Parenthood of Southeastern Pennsylvania v. *Casey*, 505 U.S. 833 (1992). Website http://supct.law.cornell.edu/supct/html/91-744.ZS.html, accessed 12 October 2003.

Prosecutor v. *Duško Tadić* [1995] ICTY Yearbook 54 (App. Chamber).

Re Eve [1986] 2 S.C.R. 388.

Reference re Secession of Québec [1998] 2 S.C.R. 217.

Texas v. *White*, 74 U.S. 227 (1869).

University of California Regents v. *Bakke*, 438 U.S. 265 (1978).

Winnipeg Child and Family Services v. *G(DF)*, (1997) 3 S.C.R. 925, 152 D.L.R. (4th) 193 (S.C.C.).

Texts and Lexicons

Hogg, Peter W. (1992), 'Secession' in Hogg. P.W., *Constitutional Law of Canada*, 3rd edn, loose-leaf edn, Scarborough: Carswell, pp. 5-30–5-37.

Kokott, Juliane (1998), *The Burden of Proof in Comparative and International Human Rights Law: Civil and Common Law Approaches with Special Reference to the American and German Legal Systems*, The Hague: Kluwer Law International.

Stroud's Judicial Dictionary of Words and Phrases (1986) 5th edn, by John S. James, London: Sweet & Maxwell.

Words and Phrases, 1658 to Date: All Judicial Constructions and Definitions of Words and Phrases by the State and Federal Courts From the Earliest Times, Alphabetically Arranged and Indexed (1940, 1972; with updates to 1993), St. Paul, MN: West.

Words & Phrases: Judicially Defined in Canadian Courts and Tribunals (1993), Scarborough: Carswell.

Other Sources

European Court of Human Rights website. 'Organisation and working of the court.' http://www.dhcour.coe.fr/eng/organisation.html, accessed October 1998; with a link to the *Convention for the Protection of Human Rights and Fundamental Freedoms* (Rome, 1950).

ICTY (International Tribunal for the Prosecution of Persons Responsible for Serious Violations of International Humanitarian Law Committed in the Territory of the Former Yugoslavia since 1991) Yearbook 1995. United Nations.

Index